SOCIAL EUROPE

Longman Sociology Series

Series Editor:
ROBERT BURGESS, University of Warwick

Editorial Advisors:
JOE BAILEY, Kingston University
JOAN CHANDLER, Plymouth University .
CHRIS RHODES, London Guildhall University

Published Titles:
Social Europe, 2nd Edition
Joe Bailey (ed.)

Disability and Society
Len Barton (ed.)

Frontiers of Identity
Robin Cohen

Women and Career
Julia Evetts

Poverty and Wealth
John Scott

Shaping Women's Work
Juliet Webster

Forthcoming Titles:
Gender, Pain and Emotion
Gillian Bendelow

Patterns of Social Inequality
Huw Beynon (ed.)

A Question of Knowledge
Richenda Power

LONGMAN SOCIOLOGY SERIES

Social Europe

edited by Joe Bailey

2nd edition

LONGMAN
London and New York

Addison Wesley Longman Limited,
Edinburgh Gate, Harlow,
Essex CM20 2JE, England
and Associated Companies throughout the world.

*Published in the United States of America
by Addison Wesley Longman Inc., New York*

First published 1992
Fourth Impression 1997
Second Edition 1998

ISBN 0582 31609 X PPR

British Library Cataloguing-in-Publication Data

A catalogue record for this book is
available from the British Library

Library of Congress Cataloging-in-Publication Data

A catalogue record for this book is
available from the Library of Congress.

Set by 35 in 10/11.5pt Times
Produced through Longman Malaysia,LSP

CONTENTS

LIST OF FIGURES AND TABLES

SERIES EDITOR'S PREFACE

The Longman Sociology Series consists of books written specifically for first and second year undergraduate students. Each title covers one key area of sociology and aims to complement other materials.

The series is forward looking and attempts to reflect topics that will be included in syllabuses for sociology and social policy. It provides a range of volumes that bring together conceptual and empirical material. In addition, volumes in the series also examine key controversies and debates, drawing on commentaries using conceptual and empirical material from a range of authors.

Each volume in the series, whether authored or edited, covers an area that would be commonly found in sociology and social policy syllabuses. The focus of each volume is on theoretically informed empirical work with policy relatedness.

The volumes are intended for an international audience and therefore comparative material is introduced, where appropriate, in a form that is suitable for first and second year students.

This is the second edition of *Social Europe*, which brings together a distinguished group of contributors who focus on the ways in which sociologists can contribute to the analysis of European affairs. Whilst most of the authors have maintained the basis of their original contributions this edition has been fully revised and brought up to date to reflect the changes that have happened in European societies since the book was originally published in 1992. The first edition was widely used by students and researchers and was very well received. I am sure that the second edition deserves to be used on a range of courses on issues of current significance in Europe.

January 1998
Robert G. Burgess
University of Warwick

This book is about modern western European societies. It is concerned both with the individual national societies that go to make up western Europe and with the potential unity of these societies.

The audience for this book will already be concerned with sociology. Readers will already be sensitised to the importance of understanding 'how these things are done elsewhere' – that is, to the significance of a comparative understanding of social phenomena. But the 'elsewhere' in question has rarely been so explicitly European and 'these things' rarely so clearly about changing social structures and responding institutions. These are not academic and rarefied views of social processes but are the very basis of everyday policy and practice. They concern the familiar organisations in which we work and live. This book of specially commissioned essays by British sociologists can be seen as contributing to a sociology of, for and in Europe. It does not attempt to be comprehensive; for instance, there is no explicit treatment of poverty or of culture. But it does try to lay out some of the most basic conditions and consequences of major social changes taking place now across Europe. These are the currency of any debate about Europe as a society and as a sociological entity. In this sense it is intended as a basic guide to the significance of the sociological data now available to us. These chapters contain materials helping to construct a comparative understanding of modern Europe beyond the oversimplifications we see in the flood of 'Euro-journalism' and the campaigning of self-interested politicians.

The book is by British sociologists, which may seem somewhat insular given the overall theme. This exclusivity is only for the subsidiary purpose of showing how pertinent and useful some of the material produced by sociologists in this country is to an analysis of Europe. Social scientists in general have a higher status in other European countries than in Britain. Yet the quality and relevance of contemporary sociological work, as illustrated here, shows how counter-productive this short-sightedness has been and will continue to be. Insularity and ignorance of other societies are deeply laid in British intellectual life, and sociology, as a foundation discipline of any social understanding, has suffered because of this. These essays provide an example of the value of British sociology in a Britain which must increase its depth of understanding of its place in a changing

Europe: an understanding which is accelerating in its rise up the political and popular agenda.

This book will be useful in a number of ways: as a resource for students now taking European studies courses; as a set of data and ideas which will help student projects take on issues conventionally addressed, but with a comparative European slant which is currently hard to find systematised; as focused information for those who sense that the social issues and problems they are familiar with in Britain need a wider European context for a real understanding; and finally as an aid to demystifying the welter of simplistic generalisations of social pundits on social affairs.

PREFACE TO THE SECOND EDITION

This is the second edition of *Social Europe*. Each contributor has revised and brought up to date the data in their chapter, updated references and, where appropriate, remarked on changes in relevance and significance. Most of the authors have maintained the basis of their original analyses, incorporating information available since 1992 where necessary and helpful. The coverage and penetration of the 1992 analyses is continued and the robustness and pertinence of the descriptions and conclusions remain. One of the intentions of the original book was to show to students the value and interest of empirical work by British sociologists and how the making of sociological sense depends on the provision of reliable empirical information. This aim is maintained in the current volume and has no less importance as the increasingly turbulent political and journalistic debates about the meaning of Europe become ever more sociologically 'informed'. Reliable information and the sociological imagination which can see its significance are still at a premium and the analyses of European social structures and institutions presented in *Social Europe* are as important for sociology students now as they have ever been.

ACKNOWLEDGEMENTS

We are grateful to the following for permission to reproduce copyright material:

Eurostat for Table 2.2 from *Rapid Reports: Population and Social Conditions*, Figure 4.1 and Table 6.1 from *Demographic Statistics* (1990); Gower Publishing Company for Table 2.5 from *British Social Attitudes* by R. Jowell, S. Witherspoon and L. Brooks (1989); Macmillan Press Ltd for Tables 11.1 and 11.3 from *Contrasting Values in Western Europe* by S. Harding *et al* (1986); Sage Publications Ltd for Table 2.1.

LIST OF CONTRIBUTORS

Joe Bailey is Professor of Sociology and Head of the School of Social Science at Kingston University. He has taught courses on the sociology of Europe for nearly two decades. He is the author of *Ideas and Intervention* (Routledge 1980) and *Pessimism* (Routledge 1988). His research interests are in the relation between sociological thought and views of the future and he is currently researching the connection between public and private views of progress and decline.

Stan Clark is a Senior Fellow in the Department of Sociology, Social Policy and Social Work Studies at the University of Liverpool and was formerly a Lecturer in the Department. In the past he conducted research into the employment training of young people in Britain, Germany and Poland. Currently, he is working in the area of Victorian studies.

Lynne Chisholm moved from a Chair in Education at the University of Marburg, Germany, to work in the Reflection Group Secretariat at Directorate-General XXII (Education, Training, Youth) of the European Commission. She is a widely published specialist in education, training and youth transitions in European research and policy context, with particular interest in gender-related questions. She is Board Vice-Chairman of ISA RC34 (Sociology of Youth) with responsibility for the Europe region, and is a founding member of CYRCE (Circle for Youth Research Cooperation in Europe), based in Berlin. Recent publication activities include co-editing and contributing to *Growing up in Europe* (Walter de Gruyter 1995), *The Puzzle of Integration* (Walter de Gruyter 1995) and *Youth, Citizenship and Social Change* (Avebury 1997).

Grace Davie is a Senior Lecturer in Sociology at the University of Exeter and specialises in the sociology of religion; from 1994–98 she was the General Secretary of the International Society for the Sociology of Religion. She has a particular interest in patterns of religion outside the formal churches and in the significance of the religious factor in the building of modern Europe. She is the author of *Religion in Britain since 1945* (Blackwell 1994) and numerous articles on the religious situation of modern Europe. She is currently preparing a book on religion in Europe for Oxford University Press.

Howard Davis is Professor of Social Theory and Institutions in the School of Sociology and Social Policy, University of Wales, Bangor. His publications on class and comparative social structure include *Beyond Class Images* (Croom Helm 1979), with R. Scase, *Western Capitalism and State Socialism* (Blackwell 1985) and, with C. Rootes, *A New Europe? Social and Political Transformation* (UCL 1994). Other publications include research on media and the cultures of broadcasting in Western and Eastern Europe, some in collaboration with the Glasgow Media Group. He is currently working on a book on media sociology.

Angela Glasner is Regional Consultant for the East and West Midlands with the Higher Education Funding Council for England (HEFCE). She was Head of the School of Social Sciences at Oxford Brookes University before joining HEFCE as an Associate Director in the Quality Assessment Division in 1995. Her current research interests and recent publications focus on the quality enhancement of the teaching and learning process in higher education.

Christel Lane is Lecturer in Sociology in the Faculty of Social and Political Sciences, University of Cambridge, and a Fellow of St John's College. She has published widely in the fields of comparative political economy/economic sociology of European countries. Her most recent book is *Industry and Society in Europe* (Edward Elgar 1995).

Michael Levi is Professor of Criminology at the University of Wales, Cardiff. He has published several books on fraud and on the control of organised crime, as well as on other aspects of policing and violent crime. His specialist interests include violent crime and substance abuse and he has carried out research on a variety of aspects of white-collar crime and organised crime. He has also conducted research into jury decision-making. In 1997 he was appointed as scientific expert on organised crime to the Council of Europe and he is a member of the Data Protection Registrar's Advisory Group.

Mike Maguire is Professor of Criminology and Criminal Justice at Cardiff University of Wales. He has conducted research and published in a variety of fields, including policing, prisons, parole, victims, burglary, street crime and criminal statistics. He is co-editor of the influential *Oxford Handbook of Criminology* (Oxford University Press 1994, 1997). He is also a former member of the Parole Board of England and Wales. He has a particular interest in proactive crime investigation, having undertaken a major study of its organisation and effectiveness, and having written on aspects of its regulation in both national and cross-border contexts.

Ian Procter is Senior Lecturer in Sociology at the University of Warwick and Chair of Department (1997–2000). His research interests include the life course, especially the interface of family and work in life transitions. He is currently working on a book with M. Padfield, *Young Adult Women*, to be published by Cassell in 1998.

John Rex is a Research Professor at the Centre for Research in Ethnic Relations, University of Warwick. He was a member of UNESCO International Experts Committee on Racism and Race Prejudice, 1967, and was President of the International Sociological Association's Research Committee on Racial and Ethnic Minorities 1974–82. He has written many books, including *Ethnic Mobilisation in a Multi-Cultural Europe* (1994) and *Ethnic Minorities and the Modern Nation State* (1996).

John Simons is a sociologist specialising in the sociology of family building, and has worked on the development of theory and methods of enquiry in this field. He is Managing Editor of the journal *Population Studies*, and an Honorary Research Fellow at the Centre for Population Studies at the London School of Hygiene and Tropical Medicine. He is currently engaged in policy-oriented research on adult relationships, is Head of Research at One plus One, an agency specialising in marriage and partnership research, and a Trustee of the London Marriage Guidance Council.

Bridget Towers is Senior Lecturer in Sociology at Kingston University where she teaches health and social policy. She is also Director of the MA pathway in Health Management. Her research interests and publications are in the field of international public care and the health/social care interface. She is currently working on the decline of the 'convalescent' sector of health service provision.

CHAPTER 1

Social Europe: unity and diversity – an introduction

JOE BAILEY

Is Europe a society? Europe is a geographical unit with, increasingly, its own political and economic institutions. But Europe is not just the official 'European Union' or any particular political and administrative alliance. Within the obvious geographical limits, it is defined by our purposes. Specialist legal definitions and everyday, commonsense meanings are plainly different. It is what some writers would call a 'discourse object' – something which is contested by interested parties all the time.

Europe is a major object of popular concern – both of anxiety and enthusiasm – in our everyday lives. It is the focus of enormous media coverage, of constitutional discussions, of political warnings, of ideological encouragement, of cultural fears. It is plainly the object of sociological investigation (and this is certainly one sense of the word 'society') in social surveys and research reports. But is it a social, as distinct from a political or economic, unit? Is it experiencing the same forces of social change, similar social structures, institutions and organisations? In a 'globalising' world (Albrow 1997) is it an economic and cultural 'space' to be compared with other large blocs in the contemporary world (Therborn 1995)?

Is Europe *becoming* a society? The current concern about Europe and our place within it may be an important marker of a profound social change taking place. The priority given to the political and economic dimensions of the European community – especially with the bulldozing pressure of EMU (European Monetary Union) as the focus for all current political energy – should not deter us from examining the sociological significance of what is now happening. We should try to locate these dramatic shifts of social organisation in Europe within our understanding of social change generally within the world.

Sociology has been concerned with social change above all else. It came into existence as a discipline to make sense of the dramatic social changes taking place in Europe in the eighteenth and nineteenth centuries. Sociology's current relevance and importance is that it tries to understand the very profound shifts now taking place in social arrangements. It is somewhat odd, then, that it has neglected Europe as a focus for these concerns. Disappointingly little has been written, in English, by sociologists specifically about Europe as a unit over the last 30 years (for example, Archer 1978; Archer and Giner 1971 for earlier approaches and Therborn 1995; Edye and Lintner 1996; Spybey (ed.) 1997 for recent attempts to fill the gap). Since the Second World War, at least, the significant comparator for British sociologists has been the United States, rather than Europe. The definition of Britain as part of Europe, at least in formal, legal terms, over this same period has pushed other social sciences – especially economics and political science – into an eager attention to Europe as a major focus for their work. The collapse of communism in central and eastern Europe forced these same social scientists to concentrate on what Europe might mean in territorial and legal terms and on 'another' Europe.

The need of the British to use the United States as their reference point is still there, of course: the power of the English-language community as a social entity *per se* should not be underestimated and is unlikely to decline. Europe, however, (whatever geographical limit is chosen) is now a rival for attention – but apparently abidingly less so for sociologists than other social scientists. Why? I will provide some reasons later in this introduction.

This book displays the very high quality and useful work that British sociologists are now doing on Europe. As the debate about how European countries are to be united shifts from the preoccupations about markets (that is, a debate dominated by economics) to arguments about intergovernmental relations and forms of federalism (a debate about politics) and then back to a concern with labour markets, a common currency and banks (economics again), the social and sociological structures which underpin economics and politics are becoming an obvious, attention-demanding issue. Politicians and the general public can see that both incompatibilities and connections between national organisations depend on the 'fit', or the lack of it, between social structures and institutions in different European countries. This book shows how specifically sociological comparison is essential if we are to make sense of the social changes experienced in all European societies as they come to grips with the idea that they are irreversibly connected with one another. All the work done by political scientists, economists, historians and social geographers depends on assumptions about how social institutions and organisations work and how people continue to behave predictably (or not) within them; in other words, upon a sociology. This should not need saying, it is so obvious, but, plainly, it does as the lack of reference to sociological work by other social scientists attests.

Sociology and Europe

What do we mean when we speak of Europe? How is the object 'Europe' constructed in various 'discourses'? For some time now Europe as an economic entity and as a market has seemed dominant, with Europe defined as a set of political problems increasing in urgency but, essentially, revolving around supervening economic concerns. The social is seen as somehow attached and residual (Teague 1989). In fact the social – 'the social area' or 'social dimension' in old EC – and now EU-speak – (Commission of the European Community 1988) – has been remarkably restricted. Initially this was to matters contained in the European Social Charter (1981) (health and safety, equal opportunities and training all treated as work-related issues). More recently the (so far more rhetorical than real) attempts to erect a 'social model' or a concern with 'social quality' (see Beck, van der Maesen and Walker (eds) 1997, for example) are still in the smothering shadow of an economistic perspective.

This is certainly not a mistaken view of the social but it is a narrow official understanding of it. It is a consequence of the dominance in political debate of economic issues following the priority given to economic integration as the foundation of a genuine European community. The political and military dimensions of unity follow close behind the economic. Issues of cultural and historical difference are treated as separate and parallel matters, but again with little reference made, beyond the journalistic, to their sociological formation. The sociological nature of the different societies in Europe and the possibility of a European society itself is marginalised in all these debates.

This is another way of saying that a sociology of (or for) Europe still has a very low salience in the current political discussions, which are likely to have profound effects on all our lives. The hierarchy of these discussions – economic-political-journalistic-cultural-sociological in sequence – is understandable. The dominance of markets and elections as the shapers of discourse and policy is undeniable. But all these issues are also sociological. It is impossible to talk of matters like the deregulation of a single European currency, a common labour market policy, federalism, common military organisation and the significance of nationalisms without a sociological understanding of the formation and organisation of the societies which will face changes in all these areas. It is not that there is a shortage of data or thought. Whole sections of the quality press are devoted to Europe: publications are increasing rapidly in economics, political science and general cultural commentary. If anything, there is an overload of attention to Europe; but there is a distinct lack of fundamental understanding of Europe as a society – actual or becoming.

Political issues are made: they are not self-evident. Information and argument are deliberately selected by those engaged in publicising an issue in the public arena. In the (re)construction of the meaning of Europe sociology, as a primary form of both description and analysis, must have a much more prominent part. If this contribution is not explicitly demanded by the movers and shakers of European social change, the demand for it will break through by force of events. The sheer instability of our social institutions, as many of the chapters in this book show, will require a sociological understanding of them as unforeseen problems if we do not now begin to consider them as issues which can be influenced, shaped and, indeed, coped with.

Social change and comparison

The current time is extremely significant. The sense that our societies are going through changes which are rapid, unpredicted, unsettling and potentially both dangerous and, perhaps, benevolent is almost palpable. We are all made aware of dramatic *events* happening – understandings and accords, treaties and agreements, new laws, even, only a short time ago, physical constructions like the Channel tunnel. The understanding of social change is the analysis of the social *processes* behind these events and which gives them significance. We are unavoidably interested in the future (Bailey 1988, Ch. 6) even if it appears to us just as a series of events. Our current uneasiness about what might or could happen in Europe (and indeed in the interconnected, 'globalised' world as a whole) is informed by 'patterns' of social change. These patterns, attempts to see order within apparent confusion, are what many sociologists have been busy trying to delineate since the subject was formalised. Such patterns are essential to our sense that the world is comprehensible and not formless or arbitrary.

Western Europe has been seen as a set of advanced industrial societies which were the first industrialisers and modernisers (Giddens 1981a). Eighteenth- and nineteenth-century Europe gave birth to both industrial society and to the discipline of sociology which self-consciously examined it. Little wonder that Europe has been the testbed of theories of social change – change seen as inevitable evolutionary 'progress' with some societies in the vanguard; change seen as the diffusion of culture or technology via military conquest or trade; change seen as repetitive cycles or as journeys to an inevitable Utopia or disaster (Therborn 1995 provides the most extensive and gripping account of such narratives). A whole range of theories (or perhaps 'patterns' would be better) have been used to account for the apparent similarities in direction taken by different nation states and, by extension, to explain their variations (Kumar 1978).

The most influential of the modern theories have stressed technological determinism in one way or another. Theories of 'convergence' stated that there was a logic of industrialism which forced political and cultural practices into line with it and which could not be stopped. Values, culture, political organisation and daily behaviour itself tended to develop, albeit by different routes, to the same final social formation required by industrial production (Dunning and Hopper 1966). Theories of 'post-industrialism' (Bell 1973) attempted to describe industrial societies as inevitably shifting to knowledge-based, service economies having solved the problems of production which inspired industrialism. In both cases the machine, whether the steam engine or the micro-processor, was privileged in understanding the source and sequence of change. Technology was seen as the prime mover of societies.

These were patterns which were useful as illuminating devices but which provoked considerable debate about their methodological adequacy and logical basis. They were without doubt creators of a sense of order within historical confusion, of a sequence of events elevated into a process which could be seen to operate across what is now western Europe and beyond. An understanding of social change is almost a psychological requirement. These two approaches with their strong message of social progress and optimism functioned to allow us to deal with the future of our societies as not only connected by trade and treaty but as, essentially, playing out together a benign logic of social development, dependent on a shared technology.

The utility of these particular patterns has now declined. It is hard now to point to a theory of social change which commands majority support in our culture as a whole, let alone among professional sociologists. The retreat from grandiose prescriptions about the future has led to a more cautious approach to long-term change (though see Albrow 1997 as an interesting exception). The chapters in this book display a careful attempt to map sequence and direction in social changes taking place but do not attempt grand theories of social change itself. Several show that technology is by no means a clear magnet for change and is an unreliable basis for understanding its patterns. Towers' chapter on health and illness discusses the very uncertain effects of development in medical technology on health policy and the conflicts over its place in health improvement. Lane's discussion of 'industrial orders' demonstrates the dominance of institutional and political features in shaping the use of manufacturing technology in industrial competition between societies. Glasner shows that the new technology has not remedied persistent gender imbalances between men's and women's work.

The need to understand social change as a holistic pattern, however, is still there, but, as Archer commented some years ago, the best starting point is an historical examination of patternings rather than the dogmatic imposition of abstract theoretical models (Archer 1978). One of the most impressive current attempts to analyse the developmental trends and institutional features of modern industrial societies has been that in one section of the work of Anthony Giddens (1981b, 1985). For Giddens 'modernity', a new social order, emerged in Europe, characterised by four institutional dimensions: capitalism, industrialism, surveillance (the state control of information and monitoring) and military power. These dimensions are basic and irreducible to one another; that is, they are the fundamental social formations which we need to describe in order to understand how a particular society developed and to compare this development with other societies. They are a vocabulary for understanding social change and a description of the 'building blocks'.

They are not an abstract theoretical model but rather a distillation and generalisation of actual historical patternings.

What is significant about Giddens' work – and there are other similar attempts, for instance, by Lash and Urry (1987) – is that it is a quintessentially sociological approach to understanding the similarities and differences between societies. It is directed not at the superficial appearance of economic and political behaviour, at the fluctuating and the transitory, at events, but tries to lay out the very basic forms of social organisation through which change or stability in different societies occurs. It is the language of the patterning of history. This is a significant part of sociology's job.

Similarities and differences

The intention of this book is to flesh out the significance of these categories, or similar ones, and to contribute to the empirical understanding of European social structure now against this categorical background. The chapters here describe and analyse particular social changes, not social change itself. Sociology makes sense of the world by linking levels of description and analysis in this way, and perhaps more coherently than any other social science.

If we wish genuinely to compare how, say, social control is accomplished, as Levi and Maguire do, or religious belief and belonging are still significant, as Davie does, in the countries of western Europe, we will arrive at a description of likenesses and differences. If we wish to go further and make sense of these similarities and divergences, we will need an account of the basic social formations which we can observe varying or converging and into which health and social control fit. This is what a comparative sociology of social change can do. It provides a template to make events and information understandable when seen together. The cost of not doing this is that we retreat into a naïve evolutionism whereby societies are treated as more or less advanced along some preordained path of development which is, somehow, naturally 'given' and visible through the data themselves. Recent writers on social change have proposed exactly such a forshortened and self-serving account of change in eastern Europe (Fukuyama 1990), describing the 'end of history' and certainly the foreclosing of intelligent politics. There are plainly homogenising tendencies at work in Europe, such as the centralisation of economic policy-making or the 'harmonisation' of legislation in the EU, and in the world as a whole, such as the 'globalisation' or 'planetisation' of the capitalist economy (Crompton, Hantrais and Walters 1990). But a comparative sociology of Europe displays the resistance of national differences to this process. It locates these variable resistances within social forms which can be readily understood in the way that, for instance, Giddens suggests. What we see in the descriptions of Europe in this book are the coexistence of pressures for both uniformity and difference, convergence and divergence, continuities and ruptures, connection and separation. This sounds rather rhetorical but it is, as the chapters show, real. The power of cultural and historical experience to resist new demands for control coming from 'outside' and the attempts by international agencies to overcome these resistances is the story of the European Union. National identities expressed in culture, language and ideology, seen through the prism of 'historical' memory and articulated through political organisations are powerful and, in eastern Europe, perhaps sometimes dominant. The pressures for interlinkage, commonality and even community between sovereign countries are extremely strong now in western Europe. The pressure for separation and the pressure for joining together meet in different geopolitical contexts. In western Europe national identity is resistant but not dominant and is probably declining. Here the running is made by the demand to unify. In the East the demand to separate has had priority but this is, perhaps, now beginning to change. In a Europe which will unite East and West it is unclear whether these opposed pressures will take the form simply of a dilemma (opposing demands to be absorbed by social institutions) or more seriously of a contradiction (a tendency to destroy the preconditions on which unity depends) (Offe 1975).

Without doubt, making sense of the differences between countries and what they simultaneously share as advanced industrial societies is the most difficult and most important task of any social science with Europe as its focus. There remains a considerable problem for sociologists in clarifying how significant apparent differences really are. Are they different configurations of the same dimensions, as some writers have suggested is the case, with apparently different national values (Harding, Phillips, with Fogarty 1986)? Davis' chapter on social stratification describes the variable effects on social class of different combinations of the same two structuring dimensions of the market and the welfare state.

Is it possible to consider divergence within uniformity? These are analytical issues which can only make sense if informed by careful comparative analyses of relevant data, and this latter task is what the writers in this volume have attempted.

So this collection should be seen as fitting into a more extensive task which remains to be addressed. This first part is the bringing together of sociologically informed comparisons of the performance of particular social organisations in the face of clear changes in the underlying social structure. As Lynne Chisholm says at the beginning of her chapter on education and training, we can see coherence 'if we regard European societies as responding to sets of common problems with a range of different solutions, which themselves are structured by divergent forms of social and cultural organisation and relationships'. The next step will be to construct a general pattern.

Lest this sound too high-faluting it is important to stress the basic practicality of the descriptions in this book. They perform a number of very useful and pertinent services. First, they not only show *autres pays, autres moeurs* but also clarify Britain's own position and condition compared with those of its neighbours. Too often we are vague about how, say, education or industrial relations are actually conducted in Europe and we believe the facile generalisations of our politicians, or, more usually, their lack of any systematic reference to fellow Europeans' experience for fear of inspiring a sense of relative deprivation in their audience. Selective ignorance of this kind is exceptionally valuable at this juncture though increasingly hard to maintain (see Spybey (ed.) 1997 Chs. 11 and 13). Here Chisholm and Procter, for example, have laid out in a conceptually clear way up-to-date European maps of these institutions.

Second, the chapters provide information to allow us to see newly shared problems; Levi and Maguire set out the new problems of crime control as physical borders become less significant; Rex does the same sort of thing for immigration. The major social problems emerging because of the extension of European social identity have been 'peripheralisation', 'marginalisation' and 'dualisation' (Vadamme 1985) and now 'social exclusion' and the meaning of a 'citizens' Europe' (Comité des Sages 1996). Significant variations in unemployment, citizenship rights, poverty and homelessness across the European continent are seen as leading to 'social dumping' (Betters 1989). In turn, this will inspire social policy on a European scale hitherto only hinted at (though see Hantrais 1995 for its limited nature so far). These chapters provide some of the sociological basis for understanding the emerging policy debate.

Third, the overall effect of the book is to counterpoint the previous concentration on the United States characteristic and traditional in British sociology. This has been declining a little in recent years as other parts of the world in the global 'triad', especially Japan, have claimed our attention. But the bulk of comparative material used is still about America, and over the last decade it is North American experience that has had the most influence on Britain's national policy formation – ironically, during the period of the greatest expansion in Europeanisation elsewhere in the continent. A parody of Britain's recent stance on European economic and political union might be that British politicians have championed deregulation and neo-liberalism over the *dirigisme*, social co-operation and consensus more common among our fellow Europeans and that our mentor in these views has been the United States. Clear descriptions of the variety of west European experience are plainly relevant and timely.

Organisation of the book

The first section of the book is concerned with some of the basic social structures which are the foundations of advanced industrial societies.

Demography, social stratification, industry, gender and race are significant formative dimensions of social change. Social structures are enduring, deeply laid social formations with a wide geographical reach. The social structures chosen in Part One are profound bases of European social order and social change. The fertility and age structure of the population, the ethnic and gender formations of that population, the patterning of inequality through the market and the state and the control and performance of industry are all quite fundamental to our understanding of any modern society. These are the structuring forces at work now, however we wish to label them. Naturally they do not exhaust our categories of social structures, and issues of state formation (for example, Davis and Scase 1985) and the role of civil society (Cohen and Arato 1994) both merit further analysis for sociologists of contemporary Europe. All the chapters deal with shifts and resistances in the operation of these structures and the potential meshing or friction as the separate national societies interact within a wider Europe.

Part Two is concerned with the social institutions through which these structures operate as ongoing sets of social practices. Six categories of social institutions are described and analysed here: those dealing with education and training, trade unions, crime and policing, health, religion and leisure. Social institutions are standardised, rule-bound organisations affecting large numbers of people. This distinction between the levels of structures and institutions is intended to be of heuristic use; that is, as a useful aid to analysis in approaching social changes. The idea that structures give rise to institutions which in turn exist as organisations is simply a mapping device which allows us to approach the wide variety of social practices and behaviours in Europe and to begin the task of comparison.

The aim of the selection of institutions in Part Two, as in Part One, is not to provide an exhaustive overview but to display some of the most obvious (and interesting) social organisations in our lives in a European context. It could obviously be extended.

Themes and continuities

It is important to understand the common threads running through the various chapters. The authors addressing their own specialisms from within the data available to them display issues which are the significant substantive topics for future analysis. They also exemplify some common methodological and theoretical matters and shared issues of values.

Common substantive issues

The most overwhelming obvious common preoccupation under this heading is the relationship between the diversity of national and regional experience and the pressure for uniformity which was mentioned earlier.

Every contributor sets their work within this context because it unavoidably shapes the very appearance of all social changes. Thus in Simons' chapter on demography the shared forces of fertility and mortality decline meet different policy responses. In Lane's chapter on industry the deep roots of the distinctively different industrial structures in France, Germany and Britain resist the common pressures of international competition. In Rex's chapter the common issue of the relation between immigrant communities and their 'host' states is met in dramatically diverse ways depending on the historical and political character of different societies. And so on. Every chapter addresses this issue of the widespread sharedness of social forces and the enduring distinctiveness of national responses.

An attached common issue is the power of the restructuring forces and the impossibility of separate societies avoiding them. The changes in market and welfare-state activity, described by Davis, and which have forced a massive change in social-class structure in western European societies are deeply laid. The shift to primary health care and the rising official level of health goals in the context of the need to ration resources is faced in all European societies, east and west, as Towers describes. The 'embeddedness' of national legal and political systems plainly resists this homogenising pressure, and successfully, as many authors show. Can this level of diversity and cultural distinctiveness continue? The inheritance of the past is massively resistant, but is it determinant? Procter, in his chapter on trade unions, points out that historical distinctiveness may, in fact, be renewed through the interaction of transforming forces from the wider world and strong national traditions.

A third common thread is the existence of 'groupings' of societies within Europe. It is possible to see historical 'blocs', as Davis describes the predominantly or officially Catholic and Protestant countries or those with other shared religious traditions. This idea of common cultural backgrounds is reinforced by Clark's chapter on the distinctive experiences of leisure in festivals and alcohol use still responding to the enduring Catholic/Protestant and urban/rural divides. But other groupings are also significant. The relatively rich countries of Germany and Denmark compare revealingly with the poor countries in the EC of Portugal, Spain and Ireland in the distribution of welfare. This has effects on social class formation and experience, as Davis shows. Legal traditions and policy priorities divide societies in respect of their criminal justice policies, and this could isolate some societies, as Levi and Maguire show. The point here is that it is possible to see Europe not as a collection of disparate societies but as groups of states with important shared features which will become very important, enabling or resisting potentials in the face of demands to unify or harmonise.

A fourth shared feature is the issue of what we might call 'mediation'. In the face of powerful external forces – for instance, for 'harmonisation' – adoption, adaptation and transformation, as Clark calls them, may be both the strategies and outcomes of countries' responses. That is, that national institutions and practices convert these pressures into forms which can be absorbed. Chisholm, in her discussion of education and training, shows how the classifying and preparing functions of educational institutions intervene differently in different societies in the transitions of youth into employed adults. National policy is made in a context of existing organisations and practices which interpret and bend outside demands. There are national characteristics in the definition of illness and treatment, as Towers remarks, which will condition what might otherwise be taken as perfectly unequivocal demands for 'health'. Her inclusion of the thirty-eight targets of the European Region of the World Health Organisation is an example of a pan-European agreement which will function only in a locally adapted way.

A final shared feature is the address to the role of the official Europeanising organisations, such as the EU, and the future. Sociologists are engaged in speculating about the likelihood of particular formally legislated standards becoming adopted in practice. Glasner provides a particularly convincing example of strong EU demands being made about the treatment of women in all institutions of society, demands backed up by a variety of vigorous national women's movements. But in practice this legislation is very slow indeed to have substantial practical effects. Levi and Maguire focus on cross-Europe policing and criminal justice policies as trans-European crime grows more obvious and serious. Both they and Rex note that one of the more vigorous (rather sinisterly) cooperative attempts to legislate change across Europe is concerned with border control and its implications for the regulation of immigration as well as illicit goods.

Prediction is not the function of this book. But all the contributors are concerned with the directions of social changes in their areas. Sociologists necessarily deal with the future in a conditional way by laying out the trajectories of change, the conditions and consequences of particular shifts and, most important of all, the data which help us to guard against the ignorant optimism or doom-saying which characterises so much popular discussion of the future of Europe.

Common issues of theory and method

This book is concerned with description and analysis, and this raises issues of both data and of analytical tools and terms. All the chapters are descriptive and use data on a European scale. There are significant problems in the collection of regular, reliable and comparable data which make sociological comparison very difficult compared with, for instance, the description of economic performance, as Davis notes. Continuous and detailed monitoring is difficult with, at best, usually two or three societies being reliably comparable. Many of the chapters focus on a limited set of societies and aim for a deeper penetration of issues on a limited scale. So Lane focuses on Germany, France and Britain in the discussion of industry; Procter on Germany, Italy and France in describing trade unions. Elsewhere Eurostat and other data collections allow some broad-brush comparisons between EC countries, as in the case of Davis' report on social stratification or Rex's on race and ethnicity. The most extensive data – for instance, that used in Simons' chapter on demography – does allow reliable and ambitious generalisations to be made. But overall the limitations of the data are the most serious difficulty for sociologists working on Europe.

Sociology is an empirical discipline. The purpose of this book is to make sociological sense of the information. Other kinds of information than reliable time series of aggregate behaviour are highly relevant, and the sections by Davis and Clark make use of qualitative as well as quantitative information. But comparative research is hampered by the current paucity of hard data. What is presented here will be a useful data guide for students to use and extend where possible.

All the chapters are also analytical. Some emphasise analysis like Chisholm's account of education and training, which is a sophisticated account of the changing and problematic *functions* of these institutions. Davis also is concerned with conceptualising social mobility and social 'closure', among other issues, as outcomes of the operation of various levels of institution from the state and the market to the experience of the local workplace. Some chapters, by contrast, are extensive and detailed descriptions first, followed by analytical speculation, such as Simons' on the reasons for fertility changes and Procter's on the likely variability of trade-union response to market liberalisation. Yet other sections make clear that just how the relevant topic is to be defined, and hence just what are relevant data is itself an analytical issue which must be engaged immediately, testing out the available information against concept formation. Davis on religion and Towers on health both do this. Indeed, the whole volume is predicated on some sort of interplay between conceptual speculation and the revelations of data. As I said at the beginning of this introduction, the very nature of 'Europe' is a contested matter: the contest is as much conceptual as factual.

The tools of analysis of sociology are essentially terms which make sense of general patterns of data which would otherwise remain opaque. They are ideas or concepts which clarify the emergence of a pattern from a mass of apparently unconnected facts. The terms used by the contributors are conventional within the discipline of sociology: they are the terms used to describe the various parts of social structures, organisations and behaviours.

It is important to note the variety of what the separate authors have done. Within the remit of a 'social Europe' the contributors illustrate a range of approaches characteristic of British empirical sociology.

Further, no limiting geographical definition of Europe has been imposed beyond an intention to concentrate on 'western' Europe, though several chapters – for instance, those on education and training and on health – show how useful it is to see the hitherto communist societies in east and central Europe as both comparable and connected to EU and Nordic states. A flexible (and thus again contested) geographical definition of Europe is a feature of all social science work which is aiming to come to grips with it as a social entity. Accepting official definitions of its unity can be useful for a particular purpose. But the nature of Europe is in the process of being decided as we write.

A systematic survey which asks the same questions of the same set of societies is certainly sociologically valid and is occasionally done (for example, Harding, Phillips, with Fogarty 1986), but depends on the sociological imagination being first applied to the issues – which is what is done here. These chapters are part of the effort to draft the pertinent questions to ask for the next stage of sociological enquiry.

Finally what all these chapters share is a respect for the diversity of values and practices which they describe and analyse. There is sometimes a nearly hidden sub-text in the official creation of a 'new' Europe that pluralism and the tolerance and even celebration of variety in social life is unworthy. This book illustrates the fascinating variation of social arrangements on which the social science disciplines are predicated.

References

Albrow, M. (1997) *The Global Age*, Oxford: Polity Press.

Archer, M. S. (1978) 'The theoretical and the comparative analysis of social structure', in S. Giner and M. S. Archer (eds) *Contemporary Europe: Social Structures and Cultural Patterns*, London: Routledge & Kegan Paul.

Archer, M. S. and Giner, S. (eds) (1971) *Contemporary Europe: Class, Status and Power*, London: Routledge & Kegan Paul.

Bailey, J. (1988) *Pessimism*, London: Routledge.

Beck, W., van der Maesen, L. and Walker, A. (eds) (1997) *The Social Quality of Europe*, The Hague: Kluwer.

Bell, D. (1973) *The Coming of Post-Industrial Society*, New York: Basic Books.

Betters, L. (ed.) (1989) *The Future of European Social Policy*, Deventer (Netherlands): Kluwer.

Cohen, J. and Arato, J. (1994) *Civil Society and Political Theory*, Cambridge Mass.: MIT Press.

Comité des Sages (1996) *For a Europe of Civic and Social Rights*, Brussels: European Commission Directorate-V.

Commission of the European Community (1988) *Social Europe: the Social Dimension of the Internal Market*, Luxembourg: Directorate General for Employment, Social Affairs and Education.

Crompton, R., Hantrais, L. and Walters, P. (1990) 'Gender relations and employment' *British Journal of Sociology*, 41(3): 329–49 (issue on 'Britain in Europe').

Davis, H. and Scase, R. (1985) *Western Capitalism and State Socialism*, Oxford: Basil Blackwell.

Dunning, E. and Hopper, E. (1966) 'Industrialization and the problem of convergence: a critical note', *Sociological Review* 14(2): 163–86.

Edye, D. and Lintner, V. (1996) *Contemporary Europe*, New Jersey: Prentice Hall.

European Social Charter (1981) Council of Europe Directorate of Press and Information, Strasbourg.

Fukuyama, F. (1990) 'Are we at the end of history?' *Fortune*, 15 Jan. 1990.

Giddens, A. (1981a) *The Class Structure of the Advanced Societies*, London: Hutchinson.

Giddens, A. (1981b) *A Contemporary Critique of Historical Materialism*, London: Macmillan.

Giddens, A. (1985) *The Nation State and Violence*, Cambridge: Polity Press.

Giner, S. and Archer, M. S. (1978) *Contemporary Europe: Social Structures and Cultural Patterns*, London: Routledge & Kegan Paul.

Hantrais, L. (1995) *Social Policy in the European Union*, Basingstoke: Macmillan.

Harding, S., Phillips, D. with Fogarty, M. (1986) *Contrasting Values in Western Europe*, London: Macmillan.

Kumar, K. (1978) *Prophecy and Progress: the Sociology of Industrial and Post-industrial Society*, Harmondsworth: Penguin.

Lash, S. and Urry, J. (1987) *The End of Organised Capitalism*, Cambridge: Polity Press.

Offe, C. (1975) 'Legitimacy versus efficiency', in L. Lindberg, R. Alford, C. Crouch and C. Offe (eds) *Stress and Contradiction in Modern Capitalism*, Lexington, Ma: D.C. Heath.

Spybey, T. (ed.) (1997) *Britain in Europe: An Introduction to Sociology*, London: Routledge.

Teague, P. (1989) *The European Community: the Social Dimension*, London: Kogan Page.

Therborn, G. (1995) *European Modernity and Beyond: the Trajectory of European Societies 1945–2000*, London: Sage.

Vandamme, J. (ed.) (1985) *New Dimensions in European Social Policy*, London: Croom Helm.

PART ONE

Changing Social Structures

CHAPTER 2

Social stratification in Europe

HOWARD H. DAVIS

The division of societies into social strata defined by differences of
wealth, income, power and prestige is one of the most complex and
fascinating problems of social and political analysis. Structured social
inequalities are the key to answering the fundamental question: what
kind of society is this and how is it changing? From a European perspective, the question concerns both the differences between countries
and the structural features which they have in common. Are some more
equal than others? Do they share similar characteristics because they
have market economies? Do differences arise when they pursue alternative social policies? This chapter addresses these topics through a broadly
comparative approach, beginning with a discussion of some of the concepts which are necessary for the analysis of social stratification. It then
considers the patterns in a range of European countries using available
economic and social data to show how these patterns are changing. Finally,
the chapter considers some interpretations of major social divisions.

'Stratification' is a metaphorical term which refers to the hierarchical
ordering of social relationships. It implies that social similarities and
differences are systematic, not random, and that members of each social
stratum have important characteristics in common such as occupation,
income, life chances and culture. These social characteristics may be
reflected in a sense of common identity, but this is not always the case.
In European sociology (though not, significantly, in its North American
counterpart) the usual way to describe large-scale social groupings has
been through the vocabulary of 'class' and class analysis. This is because
the most influential theories – namely, those of Karl Marx and Max
Weber – emphasised the economic foundations of social stratification
and the essential connection between industrial capitalism and social
order since the Industrial Revolution. Marx's theory of class conflict
was based on the assumption that the nineteenth-century owners and
controllers of capital were segregated from the rest of the population,
who lacked property and depended on selling their labour for an income.
This fundamental difference was reflected in a class structure sharply
divided between the bourgeoisie and proletariat, whose divergent interests created a high propensity for conflict. Although Marx's expectation
that these conflicts would intensify and lead to proletarian revolution

have seemed less and less relevant in western Europe as economic growth has continued and as political systems have matured, this has not diminished the value of certain aspects of his theory. The key assumption that organisation for capital accumulation through industrial market production shapes the social structure of modern societies is still applicable and useful in explaining the social condition, consciousness and culture of different groups. However, Marxist theories have rightly been criticised for overestimating material conditions, the system of property relations and the division of labour, and for underestimating the importance of social boundaries which derive from other characteristics such as ethnic origin, religion and gender. Any contemporary study of stratification has to take account of these other lines of cleavage which do not always have their origins in the economic circumstances of a particular group. Nationalism, ethnic conflicts and new social movements seem to have replaced class antagonism and workers' struggles at the centre of the political stage, creating a need for more complex models of social stratification. Some of these issues are treated at greater length elsewhere in this volume (see Chapters 6 and 8).

While Marxist and Weberian approaches to stratification identified the working class as a key actor in the shaping of industrial societies, and both were concerned with the socialist project for the transformation of society, Weber was also concerned with the social distinctions arising from status or prestige. Although he assumed that class relations were fundamental in industrial societies and that they were the main determinant of life chances through inequalities of access to the market, he also acknowledged that some distinctions arise because certain groups can impose values through religion, education, ideology, or customs which may exclude other groups or maintain a monopoly on social opportunities. In the twentieth century, the state has become the main alternative source of social structuration in European societies because of its powers to regulate and modify the market. The extent to which the formal equality of participants in the labour market or the equality of rights of citizens may be subverted by the status order or the mechanisms of the welfare state is particularly important for stratification analysis today, as the economic class system of the industrial societies is becoming more diffuse and differentiated.

Armed with a concept of stratification which includes economic, social and cultural aspects, it is necessary to specify the measures of social difference which will allow us to define the various social strata. First, however, it would be quite wrong to assume that boundary lines can be drawn like those on a map. On the one hand, the class boundaries of modern societies are highly permeable and allow for significant amounts of mobility between social groups. On the other, it is not possible to allocate all individuals to a particular class or status group because individuals are agents who actively combine characteristics like ethnicity or occupation or political allegiances in different degrees, which may 'contradict' the facts of their background. What the analysis of stratification involves is the identification of the shared economic and social circumstances which become a basis for action by groups. Not all class situations lead to collective action but they do have a tendency to generate *similar* reactions, even though it is possible for individuals to pursue their interests in widely different ways. The complex nature of stratification therefore creates the need for a number of measures which will allow social divisions to be compared from different angles. None of the measures suggested here is designed solely for the purpose of comparing stratification systems, and most data are collected for other purposes.[1] However, for general comparison they have to serve.

Three types of indicator are commonly used, which reflect the economic, social and cultural aspects of social differentiation. The first set of measures relates to market conditions and includes ownership and non-ownership of property and other forms of wealth, occupation or position in relation to the labour market including those who are not in employment, and income. The second type of indicator is related to consumption, and includes housing tenure and other forms of private and collective consumption such as education, health and the means of private consumption. The third set of measures tries to identify the variations in culture and consciousness through opinion and attitude surveys and establish the similarities and differences between strata in their subjective aspect.

The distribution of income, wealth and poverty

The way in which economic resources are allocated throughout society in the form of wealth and income is a basic indicator of the extent of social as well as economic inequality. A person's income, whether from earnings or from their ownership of capital, is almost invariably reflected in their social position, lifestyle, status and even state of health. Income is therefore a useful starting point for comparison between countries because it is easy to measure in principle, and is one of the forms of economic data which are collected continuously in the European countries. However, income is a continuous variable and it does not describe patterns of stratification as such, only the general range of income inequalities. It is in fact derived from several different sources, which can have important implications for social stratification. The first source of income is wages, salaries and earnings from self-employment. Working for an employer and working on one's own account represent two distinct types of employment relationship which may be reflected in social conditions, opportunities and consciousness. The issue of whether the 'petty bourgeoisie' (the stratum of small business owners and self-employed) has greater affinity with the bourgeoisie or the working class from which it springs has been a perennial issue in stratification analysis.

Income may also derive from ownership of assets such as property, land or shares. The rents, dividends and interest which accrue to the owners of these assets vary enormously between large-scale institutions and small private investors. Again, the distribution of these forms of wealth and income has profound implications for social and political analysis. Did the privatisation programme of the Thatcher government create a new kind of mass participation in the system of wealth creation, or did the increase in small-scale share ownership merely disguise a shift in economic power from state monopolies to private monopolies?

The third form of income, known as transfer income, is state pensions and state benefits of various kinds. This accounts for a large and rising proportion of total income because of the changing age profile of the European population (an increasing proportion above retirement age) and continuing poverty, unemployment and the need for social security and income support. The proportion of income accounted for by these transfer payments is a useful indicator of the boundaries between certain social strata.

Studies spanning several decades have shown that there is a very skewed pattern of income distribution in the European countries, which, for most of the postwar period, has been moving slowly towards more equality. However, the late 1970s saw a reversal in this trend in the United Kingdom and probably in many other European countries as a result of economic recession and the rightward shift in economic policy. In order to make comparisons across time and between countries, the total income at a particular time is divided up into the 'shares' which various sections of the population receive. Thus, in the 1960s, the share of the top 20 per cent was 44.2 per cent of total income in the United Kingdom, 52.9 per cent in West Germany and 53.7 per cent in France. The proportion in Sweden was 44.0 per cent (Atkinson 1983: 26). A decade later, the same differences could be found between these countries, but at somewhat lower levels. It appears then that Britain occupied an intermediate position in terms of income inequality. It still has a lower degree of inequality than France but a greater degree of inequality than Sweden. This is illustrated by the measure known as the Gini Coefficient, which summarises the overall distribution of income and wealth in a society by calculating a value between 0 (which represents complete equality) and 1 (which represents total concentration). This is a simple, rather crude index but it has been used as a guide by many authors, including Lane and Ersson (1987). Their analysis is based on four separate sources of data on the distribution of household and individual income, and it leads them to the estimates and ranking shown in Table 2.1.

These results for the early 1970s have a similar pattern of variation to those mentioned above, with the expected decline from the 1950s and 1960s. In general terms, the countries of southern Europe have the most pronounced inequalities and the Scandinavian countries have the most even distribution. An interesting feature is that the larger countries

Table 2.1 **Income inequality in European countries**

	Gini index	*Rank order*
Austria	0.369	8
Belgium	0.340	4
Denmark	0.380	9
FR Germany	0.383	10
France	0.417	13
Greece	0.460	14
Ireland	0.361	7
Italy	0.398	11
Netherlands	0.354	5
Norway	0.307	2
Spain	0.355	6
Sweden	0.302	1
Switzerland	0.401	12
UK	0.318	3

Source: From J-E. Lane and S. O. Ersson (1987: 83)

with similar levels of economic development – namely, France, Germany and the United Kingdom – vary quite significantly. France has one of the highest levels of inequality and the United Kingdom one of the lowest; West Germany occupies an intermediate position.

According to these general comparisions, the postwar trend has therefore been in the direction of more equality, but a closer inspection of the effects of taxation and welfare shows that the benefits of redistribution have not been evenly spread throughout society. The Royal Commission on the Distribution of Income and Wealth examined this issue closely in the United Kingdom and found that, although the wealth of the top 1 per cent was much reduced by the 1970s, much of the redistribution occurred within the top 10 per cent. The intermediate groups have received a larger share of the redistribution than the poorest, whose position, according to a comparative study by Lawson and George (1980), improved only very slightly or not at all in the period up to 1980. In 1985 the top 1 per cent still owned 20 per cent of net personal wealth and the top 10 per cent more than half. The overall effect of economic growth on social inequality is, to use a familiar illustration, like the effect of a marching column: the column advances and the last rank (or most of it, at least) eventually passes the point which was reached by the vanguard some time before. The distance between the front and the rear does not change as the column moves forward. Although the rich have stayed rich or become richer, the position of the poor remains relatively unchanged. However they are defined, the poor continue to make up a large proportion of the European population, largely because of low incomes and unemployment. The 'poverty line' according to

*Table 2.2   **Poverty in the EC, 1985, defined as households or persons
receiving 50 per cent or less of the respective national average***

	% households	% persons
Belgium	6.3	7.1
Denmark	8.0	7.9
FR Germany	10.3	10.5
Greece	20.5	21.5
Spain	20.3	20.9
France	18.0	19.1
Ireland	18.5	18.4
Italy	12.0	14.1
Netherlands	6.9	9.6
Portugal	31.4	32.4
UK	14.1	14.6
EUR 12	14.1	15.5

Source: Eurostat 1990; figures for Luxembourg unavailable

an EC definition, is an income half or less than half of the country's
national average income per person. The countries which have levels of
poverty above 15 per cent of the population include Portugal, Greece,
Spain and Ireland, which are on the periphery of Europe and less developed. The lowest levels of poverty (below 10 per cent) are in Belgium,
Denmark and The Netherlands. Italy and the United Kingdom are near
average in the intermediate category. The United Kingdom has been
moving in the direction of the 'peripheral' countries with a high level
of poverty (18 per cent in 1990) through a combination of economic
recession and rigid government policies on transfer payments.

Consumption

The rise of the welfare state in the European countries in the postwar
decades brought about a large-scale shift from private to collective forms
of provision in housing, education, wealth and other key aspects of consumption. The scale of social expenditure is represented by Table 2.3,
which shows significant increases for each country over two decades,
notwithstanding variations in GDP growth rates and national policies to
expand or curb social expenditure.

   Although the growth in state expenditure has been universal, the
effects of this on stratification have been more complex. Esping-Andersen
(1990) has described the varieties of 'welfare capitalism' which affect
the stratification system in different ways, and not always with egalitarian
results. He concludes that 'the welfare system is not just a mechanism
that intervenes in, and possibly corrects, the structure of inequality; it
is, in its own right, a system of stratification' (p. 23).

Table 2.3 **Total social protection expenditure as a percentage of GDP**

	1970	*1980*	*1990*
Belgium	17.7	28.0	26.9
Denmark	19.6	28.7	29.8
FR Germany*	21.5	28.6	26.9
France	19.2	25.5	27.7
Ireland	13.2	20.6	19.4
Italy	17.4	19.8	23.6
Netherlands	20.8	30.4	32.2
UK	15.9	21.6	22.7

* The 1990 data include the new German Länder

Source: Compiled using Social Indicators for the European Community: selected series, Eurostat (1984); Eurostat Review 1977–86, table 3.5 (1988); Eurostat Yearbook 1996

The first variety of welfare system is 'social democratic' and the most egalitarian because it embodies the principle of universal rights and universal solidarity. In this type, all are dependent, all can benefit and all have the obligation to contribute to the system of insurance. Such a system encourages a high level of participation in the labour market by both women and men and minimises the number of people dependent on transfer payments. It requires a high degree of political consensus and commitment to an egalitarian social philosophy.

The second type is 'corporatist', and is associated with those countries which have a strong state tradition and a history of granting privileged status and welfare provision to civil servants. In this case, welfare is not designed to make provision on the basis of universal criteria of need or to redistribute income but to maintain status differentials. Benefits and provisions vary for different social strata and serve to reinforce the social hierarchy. The social rights of each stratum are embedded in the conservative and usually religious traditions associated with corporatism.

The third variety is the 'liberal welfare state' which intervenes in the market as little as possible and gives low levels of benefit which are subject to strict entitlement rules. At the same time, it has mechanisms to encourage the market through subsidies for private medical schemes, housing and pensions. The political context for this is liberal individualism with a strong emphasis on the work ethic. The effect on stratification is to emphasise class dualism: the main recipients of welfare are the working class and the poor, while the middle class benefits from the system of subsidies to the private sector.

In practice, as Esping-Andersen is quick to point out, these varieties of welfare capitalism do not correspond perfectly with individual countries. Each country has elements of each type, although one may predominate. To see how they compare, Esping-Andersen made a detailed

Table 2.4   **Rank order of welfare states: combined score based on pensions, sickness and unemployment benefits, 1980**

United States	13.8
Ireland	23.3
United Kingdom	23.4
Italy	24.1
France	27.5
Germany	27.7
Finland	29.2
Switzerland	29.8
Austria	31.1
Belgium	32.4
Netherlands	32.4
Denmark	38.1
Norway	38.3
Sweden	39.1

Source: Table 2.2 in Esping-Andersen (1990), de-commodification score based on SSIB data files

study of pensions, sickness benefits and unemployment insurance, and derived a composite score based on the strictness of the rules which govern people's access to benefits, the levels of benefits relative to normal earnings, and rights to protection against the risks of unemployment, disability, sickness and old age. He calls this the 'de-commodification score' to indicate the degree of dependency on the market, a low score being typical of market-orientated countries and a high score being typical of countries with well-developed systems of social rights. The results are summarised in Table 2.4.

The pattern of variation illustrates the effect of the three welfare-state regimes. The lowest scores (which include the United States for comparison) relate to the countries which have a strong liberal market tradition. They include the United Kingdom because, in spite of the influence of the Labour Party immediately after the war, the social democratic tendency was not maintained. Although the welfare state initially encouraged access to social consumption on the basis of need, this has been significantly eroded by the growth of private provision. The Anglo-Saxon countries are therefore closest to the 'liberal' welfare-state regime. The countries with intermediate scores include France, Germany, Italy and Switzerland, where the traditions of conservative corporatism and Christian democracy are relatively strong. Finally, the highest scores are found among the Scandinavian countries, and in Belgium and The Netherlands.

This analysis of welfare-state regimes therefore complements the analysis of inequalities of wealth and income, and helps to explain the relationship between the inequality-generating mechanisms of the market and the mechanisms of the welfare state which may either reinforce or counteract these mechanisms according to the priorities of social policy. It is important to note that the consequences for stratification are not directly related to the scale of social expenditure. Similar overall levels can accentuate or reduce the social cleavage between the working class and the middle class, between those groups which are most dependent on direct state support and those which benefit from subsidies to private consumption.

Arguments about the relationship between the welfare state and stratification have traditionally taken the line that economic growth and changing patterns of welfare and consumption have weakened the importance of class. It is said that this can be seen in the reduced significance of class voting, class awareness and industrial conflict. It is certainly true that industrial and occupational changes have enlarged the middle class at the expense of the working class, but the link between position in the labour market and consumption position is nevertheless very close. Neither 'affluence' nor 'welfare' have replaced the significance of class structure. They have contributed to it in new and distinctive ways.

Stratification and social consciousness

The extent and nature of awareness of social differences by the members of a population is an important question with political as well as cultural implications. The evidence for consciousness of social structure and social inequality reveals some interesting facts. First, at the most general level, the range of social inequality in European societies can be compared with the attitudes in that society to issues of social justice and the need for social change. One source of data is the Eurobarometer series of surveys carried out by the EC, which show that there are significant variations in public attitudes measured by simple questions on social organisation and the need for reform. Such data need to be handled with some scepticism because apparently similar questions may acquire different meanings as the culture and context changes. However, while there is a large majority in all the countries of the EC in agreement with the need for reform rather than revolution, there is also some suggestion that attitudes are most polarised in the countries where the range of social inequality is greatest.

More precise investigations of attitudes to inequality and welfare have been carried out in several European countries through the International Social Survey Programme (Jowell, Witherspoon and Brook 1989). Using data from Austria, Italy, The Netherlands, West Germany and the United Kingdom, they show how far attitudes to inequality are class-based. There is a positive relationship between attitudes and social class but this is combined with a high level of general agreement across

Table 2.5   **State welfare and class solidarity in four European countries**

	Britain	West Germany	Austria	Italy
% favouring . . .				
. . . more spending on health care:				
Poorest quartile	90	54	73	82
Wealthiest quartile	84	33	59	78
. . . more spending on pensions:				
Poorest quartile	87	51	61	79
Wealthiest quartile	63	32	50	75
. . . more spending on unemployment benefits:				
Poorest quartile	59	41	27	63
Wealthiest quartile	25	19	13	52
Government should reduce income differences between those with high and low incomes:				
Poorest quartile	58	63	70	79
Wealthiest quartile	37	52	62	64

Source: International Social Survey Programme, reported by P. Taylor-Gooby in Jowell, Witherspoon and Brook (1989: 49–51)

nations and between classes. This is illustrated in Table 2.5, which uses income levels defined as the top and bottom quarters of the population as an alternative to class proper.

The results show that the wealthy in Britain have less enthusiasm for redistribution than the wealthy in the other countries but that there is a broad consensus among both poor and wealthy in all the countries for improved levels of spending on health care. This corresponds with the expectation that a country with a 'liberal' welfare regime will express the divergence of interests between the middle classes and the poor (see Esping-Andersen 1990: 30–1; Halsey 1988: 29–33). However, these surveys show that cross-national variations are not particularly marked except in the valuation of inequality as an obstacle to advancement, or as the stimulus to personal gain. From this kind of evidence it is difficult to sustain the once-popular argument that Britain is a particularly class-conscious or class-ridden society compared with others in Europe.

Comparative studies of values show only small variations along class lines except with respect to values connected with work and occupation. The European Values Project, for example, found no great disparity between European value systems and encountered most variation in terms of moral, personal and religious values which cut across rather than conformed to the main cleavages of the stratification system (Harding and Phillips, with Fogarty 1986: 217–18). This apparent lack of any strong connection between the objective features of stratification (income, occupation, access to welfare) and subjective attitudes to society has attracted the attention of researchers in a number of European countries. The core issue is that pronounced social inequalities are not necessarily associated with strong awareness of them or with political opposition to them as might be anticipated. In fact, where a correlation exists, it may be, as Lane and Ersson found, that the more even the income distribution between various strata the higher the class consciousness and the degree of unionisation (1987: 85–6). They interpret this by saying that equalisation of income is a product of a high level of class consciousness but, as they acknowledge, this fails to account for the origins of class consciousness in the first place. In a detailed comparison of class radicalism in France and Britain, Gallie (1983) looked for the causes in terms of income level, the technological character of the work setting, and the ideological influence of the trade unions. He found that none of these was the key to explaining the higher levels of radicalism in France, and showed that it was work grievances and the direct experience of more managerial control – more authoritarian in France than Britain – which provided the answer. In countries where the system of industrial relations is more institutionalised, the subjective response to inequalities of income and power may be more accepting or fatalistic. This and other empirical studies show that day-to-day experiences of social inequality are too complex and varied to allow for simple predictions of collective behaviour on the basis of positions in the stratification system. Everyday experience in the 'workplace' (which may be the home as well as the office or factory) is where the objective and subjective aspects of social stratification combine and interact. This is why occupational categories are most commonly used to describe the system of stratification. They are one of the best indicators available of position within the productive system and the social and political characteristics which are likely to be associated with typical positions.

We can now integrate the analysis of the market situation of each stratum (defined by the source and amount of wealth and income) with their social situation (defined by their occupation or position within the division of labour and system of authority relations). These are connected in turn with differences of status and lifestyle. A composite classification which is relevant to most European societies will include the following categories:[2]

1 a capitalist class, comprising business proprietors, and owners of large-scale shareholdings, land and property
2 a service class, comprising two strata: directors, managers and higher-grade professional employees; and lower-grade professionals, managers and technical workers
3 a working class, comprising two strata: clerical, secretarial and routine non-manual workers; and skilled manual workers

4 a lower working class: comprising semi- and unskilled manual workers and those who regularly depend on state benefits because of low wages or unemployment.

The 'capitalist class' is the smallest but the most powerful of the categories. In modern industrial societies this stratum, which includes members of the economic, political and cultural élites, forms about 1 per cent of the total population. Although much of their wealth and power is hidden from general view, their importance is not diminished by their lack of conspicuous consumption. The character of this stratum varies between countries according to their patterns of history and social development. In Britain, the term 'establishment' is often used to describe the typical relationships and patterns of influence which operate within the ruling group. The oldest of the industrial societies, Britain has long since combined the features of the old aristocracy with the capitalist class to form a relatively cohesive ruling group defined by its control over the industrial firms and banks which dominate the economy, its monopoly of social privilege, and its capacity to steer the political system. Although it is no longer entirely based on leading families, there are closely interlocking social networks which are reinforced from one generation to the next by the exclusive mechanisms of private education. It has a cohesive culture which is based on a shared conception of the 'nation' and the identification of the national interest with its own interests. It exercises its power in subtle ways, as Coates says, protecting itself through 'its own exclusivity, low public profile, and astute public orchestration of the pre-capitalist institutions of monarchy and aristocracy' (in Bottomore and Brym 1989: 43).

The character of the capitalist class in France derives from the structure of capital and the distinctive role of the state in promoting a technocracy in public administration. The relatively late arrival of industrialisation in France meant that even as late as the 1970s, half of the 200 largest companies were still family-controlled. Marceau (1989) has described how the restructuring of capital in the subsequent decades brought about a convergence between owners and controllers of capital so that, through family ties, similarities of education, and parallel career paths in public administration or industry, the distinction between ownership and control has become relatively unimportant. The *grandes écoles*, the élite institutions of higher education, are the proving grounds for talent and sustain a modern form of legitimacy for the ruling class, namely 'technocracy', which is sufficiently broad to include the exercise of power through both private and public institutions. The Paris-based élitist technocracy of France complements the inegalitarian social system and has at least as much social and political homogeneity as its parallel stratum in Britain. It retains its legitimacy not through the acceptance of tradition but because the mechanisms of exclusion are ostensibly designed to create professional rulers rather than privilege for its own sake.

In contrast to both Britain and France, which have distinctive capitalist classes, Germany has no easily identifiable ruling group. There are several reasons for this, including the discontinuities resulting from the Second World War, the enhanced opportunities for mobility into the economic élite during the postwar boom period, and the attempt systematically to integrate all social strata into the social market economy. This does not mean that there is no capitalist class in Germany, only that it has greater fluidity and less social and political cohesion than in Britain and France. As Ardagh observes, its prosperity and lack of inherited privilege makes the stratification of German society more like that of the United States than any other country in Europe (1988: 146).

This comparison between the capitalist classes in three European countries illustrates the fact that countries with a broadly similar range of social inequality may exhibit varying degrees of permeability across their social boundaries. In an extreme case, a highly unequal and élitist social system could nevertheless be called 'open' if it encouraged a high rate of social mobility. In contrast, a relatively egalitarian society could be called 'closed' if it had powerful exclusionary mechanisms to discourage movement between strata. Studies of social mobility have to contend with some of the most intractable problems of international data comparison, and it is impossible to do justice to this question here.

However, it is possible to draw two general conclusions – which are presented in a useful summary by Heath (1981: 193–223). First, the overall or mass-mobility rate depends on the changing pattern of occupations. If, for example, the number of non-manual jobs increases at the expense of manual jobs, this will be reflected in the mobility rates within and between generations for the two strata. Countries which have experienced recent rapid industrialisation tend to have high structural mobility rates, and it is usual to find conspicuous inequality linked with rising egalitarian expectations. On the other hand, in the mature industrial societies, where occupational shifts are more moderate, mobility of this type will necessarily be limited. Second, social and cultural factors can make a difference. Heath's comparison shows that, after allowing for the pattern and rate of change in the occupational structure, European societies can be grouped in two ways: according to their relative maturity (the 'newer' societies are more open than the 'old'); and according to their political experience (countries with long periods of socialist government are more open than those with a history of mainly conservative or right-wing governments). Thus Sweden is most open, Britain is in an intermediate category, and France, Germany, Italy and Spain are more closed. Careful analysis permits a distinction to be made between structures of inequality and their relative openness, which can vary independently, but the results in practice show that there is usually a close connection between equality and openness in social structures. As Heath points out, this should not come as a surprise, because national characteristics do not vary randomly, 'they come as more or less firmly tied bundles whose individual components cannot easily be pulled apart or altered at will', even by governments (1981: 223). The system of social stratification and the policies of government are inextricably linked.

The most striking development in the stratification system in recent decades has been the growth of the professional and managerial strata and the corresponding decrease in manual occupations in manufacturing industry. The rise of what is often called the 'service class', with a vast array of new occupations, creates problems of definition as well as difficulties in interpreting its political significance. It is not simply a question of the expansion of the 'middle classes' or white-collar employment generally, although on average nearly two-thirds of all workers in western European economies are in service occupations (that is, not in agricultural or industrial occupations). It concerns the emergence of a new and powerful stratum within the broad category of services with its own distinctive economic position and social identity. According to Goldthorpe's definition, the service class includes professionals, administrators and managers whose positions involve the application of specialised knowledge within the framework of bureaucratic organisations, whether public or private (Goldthorpe 1982). The increasing scale, complexity and rationalisation of the capitalist productive system has created the need for this stratum to control and coordinate the functions of capital on behalf of the capitalist class. It typically accounts for between 10 and 25 per cent of all employees. Their distinctiveness comes from a strong market situation owing to their professional expertise, combined with a work situation which allows a high degree of autonomy and discretion.

Previous arguments about the service class (for example, Dahrendorf 1963) were naturally concerned with its political orientation, yet they found it difficult to reach a conclusion. The service relationship to capital implied that their chief loyalty would be to the ruling group but the influence of advanced education, the experience of mobility and the ideology of rationality and progress appeared to give the service class a certain independence from the conservative culture and politics of the superordinate stratum. More recent evidence of service-class formation in three European countries (Erikson, Goldthorpe and Portocarero 1979) points to other reasons for divided loyalties. The very rapid growth of the service class has encouraged recruitment from a wide range of social strata, including the working class. Their closeness to working-class origins and social heterogeneity suggests that a new class identity has not had sufficient time to develop. The 'demographic' and 'sociocultural' identity of the stratum has so far been inhibited (Goldthorpe 1982: 174–5). This tends to be confirmed by studies carried out in individual countries. In France, for example, Boltanski (1987) made a study of *cadres* but found it impossible to identify precise boundaries or collective action based on common attributes and shared interests. What is likely, as the service class matures, is that it will find a place which is more than simply an appendage of the capitalist class but one which is unlikely to bring it into conflict with the class above. As the process of economic and political integration in Europe develops, the role of the service class will be enhanced through its characteristics of expertise, mobility and relative lack of commitment to traditional or national culture.

The fate of the working class across Europe has provoked writers in many countries to pronounce on its demise, its transformation or even its reincarnation. The universal and incontrovertible facts are these: that the mass-employment manufacturing industries which were the backbone of working-class communities and labour organisations have either been eliminated through global competition or altered out of recognition by the application of new technologies; that there has been a numerical decline in the main categories of working-class occupations; and trade unions have suffered a significant decline in membership. This has radically altered the framework for the interpretation for the sociology of this stratum. In the 1950s and 1960s the participation of workers in the new prosperity seemed to be a part of the process of integration of the formerly dichotomous and conflictual class structure. For more than a decade, research focused on the evidence for '*embourgeoisement*' and indicators of change or decline in the patterns of industrial and class conflict (Goldthorpe *et al.* 1969). Today, the themes of fragmentation and even destruction of the working class are ascendant, as economic recession, technological change and the collapse of socialism in eastern Europe have created a radically different set of conditions.

The changing industrial structure has undermined the once fundamental boundaries between skilled and semi-skilled workers and the status distinction between 'white-collar' and 'blue-collar' work. Each stratum had its own typical patterns defined by the type of income and employment contract (wages or salaries), the type of skill (manual or non-manual), and working conditions (the shop floor or office). These all contributed to distinctions in the pattern of consumption, housing, lifestyle and culture. Today, the internal divisions of the working class relate to the new features of the capitalist production system which responded to the competitive pressures of the 1970s and the 1980s by 'shaking out' large numbers of workers from the key industrial sectors. Production has been reorganised into 'core' and 'peripheral' activities in order to achieve maximum flexibility at minimum cost. Instead of a division between types of work and occupation, this creates a new division between workers with strong contractual and social ties to their employer and workers with relatively loose ties. The core consists of qualified workers on permanent contracts, with higher levels of earnings and commitment to the organisation. Skilled workers who have survived the recession have seen their earnings increase in real terms. Under 'flexible specialisation', as it is often called, the much larger group of peripheral workers has less security and is more likely to be self-employed or on temporary or part-time contracts. One of the advantages for the employer is that job demarcations are removed and working practices are made more flexible. The position of the employee is likely to deteriorate into one of low security, low wages and low opportunity.

There is no sharp boundary between relatively disadvantaged workers and the unemployed. There is a case for describing the latter (and the poor generally) as an 'underclass' because they are not fully integrated into the class structure (Dahrendorf 1987). The case against describing them in this way is that the condition of unemployment is, for the majority who escape long-term unemployment, intermittent, and there is constant movement up and down the lower ranks of the working class. The fact that poverty may be a result of low wages, stage in the lifecycle or single-parent status as well as unemployment suggests that the new poor are part of a working class which has become increasingly fragmented. Dependency on income from employment may be exchanged for dependency on the state, but this does not always involve a radical transition in income or status.

The impact of recession and economic change in Europe in the 1980s led to a number of studies of the relationship between formal employment and informal economic activity, whether of the self-service variety (for example, self-build or do-it-yourself) or work in the semi-legal or black economy (see Pahl 1989). Pahl and other researchers had expected to find an increase in self-provisioning and informal economic activity to cope with growing insecurity at the margins of the labour market. This was only partly confirmed. The evidence shows that unemployed people are the least likely to be engaged in informal work, and low-wage households have few of the resources needed to make the most of opportunities for such work. The effect is to polarise households into 'work-rich' and 'work-poor': that is, households which have multiple earners and which can use their own labour, skills and tools to improve their position, and households which are denied these opportunities because of age, disability or because they only have a single earner.

The detailed study of social stratification in European societies has usually been carried out in the context of single societies. Some studies compare two, or not usually more than three, countries. There are certainly no equivalent social data to match the continuous and detailed monitoring of economic performance throughout Europe. This makes it difficult to draw general conclusions. However, there is a family resemblance between the systems of social stratification in the European countries because they have in common the same, and increasingly internationalised, capitalist production and market system. They also have in common the features of state welfare. These two aspects of contemporary society create the framework for social differentiation. We have seen that within this framework there is considerable room for variation both in the objective features which divide the strata and in the subjective responses and collective action which they may inspire. In thinking about comparative stratification it is prudent to bear in mind the following advice from a discussion of the do's and don't's of class analysis (Giddens 1982: 164–6).

The first rule is not to extrapolate from short-term trends. Each decade of the postwar period has brought its own style of sociological analysis and interpretation: from the promise of 'classlessness' in the years of the economic miracle to the resurgence of class and class conflict in the 1970s, and the 'recomposition of class' in the 1980s. Too much emphasis on the short term leads to perceptions of change which overlook the continuities of social structure and exaggerate the speed of current developments.

The second rule is not to generalise from a single society. The United States can hardly be used today, as it was in the past, as the prototype of industrialism, and as a symbol of the European future, because Japan and the European societies themselves show the possibility of viable alternative paths of development. Perhaps the contemporary illusion for Europeans is the idea of an integrated 'European society' to which all the individual countries will converge. Whether this is seen in a positive or a negative light, the evidence does not support the idea that national societies will be rapidly subsumed into a common type.

The third rule is to accept the contingent character of social change, not to assume that there is a single force or tendency causing societies to develop along a predetermined path. The interaction between the class dynamic of the economic system and the citizenship dynamic of the state welfare system best illustrates this point in the European societies. The interplay of similar structures and processes can lead to a variety of outcomes.

Finally, there is an increasingly important rule, which is to recognise the international context of social change and to use comparative evidence as far as possible. Social analysis has been no less insular and national in its concern than most other aspects of society. The dearth of good comparative social data is an obstacle which will have to be removed if we are to gain a better understanding of the divisions and conflicts within social Europe.

Notes

1 In fact, there are very few measures, whether economic, social or cultural, which are completely standardised between the European countries. Measures of income, employment, occupation, consumption and so on are constructs which vary according to the conditions of each country and are collected by organisations at the national level. For a discussion of some of the problems involved in comparing labour market data from many countries, see Bean (1989) or Hakim (1991).

2 This is applicable to the capitalist societies of western Europe, not to state socialism in eastern Europe, where the boundaries of stratification were defined

by the party-state system and not by the market. Recent changes in these countries are likely to bring about some convergence towards the western types of stratification. For a discussion of the contrasts between the capitalist and state socialist forms of stratification, see Davis and Scase (1985).

References

Ardagh, J. (1988) *Germany and the Germans*, Harmondsworth: Penguin Books.

Atkinson, A. B. (1983) *The Economics of Inequality*, 2nd edn, Oxford: Oxford University Press.

Bean, R. (ed.) (1989) *International Labour Statistics: a Handbook, Guide and Recent Trends*, London: Routledge.

Boltanski, L. (1987) *The Making of a Class: Cadres in French Society*, Cambridge: Cambridge University Press.

Bottomore, T. and Brym, R. J. (eds) (1989) *The Capitalist Class: an International Study*, Brighton: Harvester Wheatsheaf.

Dahrendorf, R. (1963) 'Recent changes in the class structure of European societies', in S. Graubard (ed.) *A New Europe?*, Boston: Beacon Press.

Dahrendorf, R. (1987) 'The erosion of citizenship', *New Statesman*, 12 June, pp. 12–15.

Davis, H. and Scase, R. (1985) *Western Capitalism and State Socialism*, Oxford: Basil Blackwell.

Erikson, R., Goldthorpe, J. H. and Portocarero, L. (1979) 'Intergenerational class mobility in three western European societies', *British Journal of Sociology*, 30(4): 415–41.

Esping-Andersen, G. (1990) *The Three Worlds of Welfare Capitalism*, Cambridge: Polity Press.

Gallie, D. (1983) *Social Inequality in France and Britain*, Cambridge: Cambridge University Press.

Giddens, A. (1982) *Profiles and Critiques in Social Theory*, London: Macmillan.

Goldthorpe, J. H. (1982) 'On the service class, its formation and future', in A. Giddens, and G. Mackenzie (eds) *Social Class and the Division of Labour*, Cambridge: Cambridge University Press.

Goldthorpe, J. H., Lockwood, D., Bechhofer, F. and Platt, J. (1969) *The Affluent Worker in the Class Structure*, Cambridge: Cambridge University Press.

Hakim, C. (1991) 'Cross-national comparative research on the European Community: the EC Labour Force Surverys', *Work, Employment and Society*, 5(1).

Halsey, A. H. (1988) *British Social Trends since 1900*, London: Macmillan.

Harding, S. and Phillips D. with M. Fogarty (1986) *Contrasting Values in Western Europe*, London: Macmillan.

Heath, A. (1981) *Social Mobility*, London: Fontana.

Jowell, R., Witherspoon, S. and Brook, L. (1989) *British Social Attitudes: Special International Report*, London: Gower.

Lane, J-E. and Ersson, S. O. (1987) *Politics and Society in Western Europe*, London: Sage.

Lawson, R. and George, V. (1980) 'An assessment', in V. George and R. Lawson (eds) *Poverty and Inequality in Common Market Countries*, London: Routledge & Kegan Paul.

Marceau, J. (1989) *A Family Business? The Making of an International Business Elite*, Cambridge: Cambridge University Press.

Pahl, R. E. (1989) 'From "informal economy" to "forms of work": cross-national patterns and trends', in R. Scase (ed.) *Industrial Societies: Crisis and Division in Western Capitalism and State Socialism*, London: Unwin Hyman.

CHAPTER 3

Industrial structure and performance: common challenges – diverse experiences

CHRISTEL LANE

The advent of the Single European Market (SEM) has focused our attention on Europe as a new industrial unit which will also bring in its train trends towards common social and political patterns of organisation. It is intended that this larger entity will combine the industrial strengths of the various member states and cancel out their individual weaknesses. It is thus designed to create the industrial competitiveness *vis-à-vis* American and Asian rivals which at present eludes individual economies. But at the present time, economic and social unity is still a remote goal, and diversity between member states is more striking than homogeneity.

This enduring diversity of industrial structure and organisation is seen as having been shaped by the social and political institutional framework of each society, giving rise to industrial orders. The moulding of national industrial orders has occurred throughout the period of modern industrial development, but the distinctive cast of each order was forged at the very beginning of the industrialisation process. An examination of the industrial structure and organisation of the three largest member states – Germany, France and the United Kingdom – will serve to illustrate the existing diversity and focus attention on the different ways in which common challenges are being faced. Such challenges emanate both from the changing world economic framework, particularly from shifts in markets for industrial products and the accompanying intensification of competition, and from the acceleration of technological change.

Industrial development and structure

In all three countries, the pace and the nature of industrial development was determined by the way the necessary capital was provided and by the origins and industrial orientations of the early entrepreneurs. Britain's industrialisation started almost a century before that of its continental rivals. The early stage of development was dominated by the large merchant entrepreneurs (Fox 1985) and entailed the parallel weakening of artisan craft producers. This ensured the early dominance of a merchant ethos over a productivist one. All through the nineteenth century, the connections between industry and the banking sector remained underdeveloped and held back the emergence of large firms. The first impulses towards the industrial concentration at the turn of the last century resulted in only very partial large-firm development in the more traditional industrial sectors.

The creation of a significant sector of large, publicly quoted companies came only at the end of the 1920s and embraced also the then more modern industries, such as chemicals, electrical engineering and vehicle building. The new ease of raising capital on the stock market led to a rapid expansion of the corporate sector and the simultaneous shrinkage of the small and medium-sized enterprise (SME) sector, giving Britain a somewhat unbalanced industrial structure. Also notable in the British case is the early emergence of multinational companies (MNCs), taking advantage of the easy access to foreign markets, created by Britain's imperial status. This was, however, paralleled by the early entry into Britain of American MNCs, particularly in the more modern industrial sectors.

Since the early 1970s, there has occurred a halt in this trend towards industrial concentration, and the 1980s and 1990s have witnessed a significant revival of the SME sector. But even today, Britain's industrial structure remains the most polarised, with a highly concentrated large-firm sector, on the one side, and a relatively large proportion of very small enterprises, on the other.

In Germany, large and giant firms evolved during the first decades of its industrialisation period: that is, in the decades around the turn of the nineteenth century. The fast pace of industrialisation meant that merchant capital was never accumulated in sufficient quantity to finance expansion, and capital was instead made available by the large universal banks, also created during the early industrialisation period (Kocka 1975). Large firms have decisively shaped industrial organisation and structure ever since. But the SME craft sector of the economy, due to early state protection and promotion of the craft form of production, survived the onslaught of the industrial giants relatively well (Streeck 1986). This has meant that, in Germany, large industrial firms have always existed side by side with smaller family-owned and managed craft enterprises and that interaction between, and reciprocal influence of, the two has been common. This long coexistence explains why the craft ethos – namely, a production orientation and an emphasis on skill and product quality – has remained much more prominent in Germany than in the other two European countries (Piore and Sabel 1984).

At the end of the Second World War tough anti-trust laws, introduced by the Americans, led to some industrial deconcentration, but merger activities during the 1960s and 1970s restored the old pattern of concentration and industrial structure. The SME sector, after some decline in the postwar period, has nevertheless remained a vigorous and important part of German industry (Doran 1984). Despite this early evolution of industrial giants, MNCs were slow to develop in post-1945 Germany, and internationalisation was attained through the cultivation of a strong export orientation. Since the mid-1980s, however, outflows of foreign direct investment have increased dramatically, but Germany's stock of FDI remains lower than that of the UK.

France's pattern of industrial development has differed significantly from that of both of its European rivals. Although industrialisation started in the second half of the nineteenth century, development occurred unevenly and haltingly. Notwithstanding the creation of a few large firms in the more modern sectors, France remained essentially a country of petty entrepreneurs until the 1950s. Family-owned SMEs, dedicated more to the preservation of family patrimony and control than to a quest for expansion, gave their indelible stamp to French industrial culture and structure (Landes 1969; Trebilcock 1981). Although pockets of artisanal producers have remained in some sectors of industry the craft culture and its organisational forms had essentially been destroyed in the wake of the French Revolution, through politically motivated legislative intervention by the state (Schriewer 1986). Explanations for French relative economic backwardness range from the downward pull of a large agricultural subsistence sector, coupled with slow population growth and fragmented home markets, to the shortage of capital for industrial expansion, resulting from the underdevelopment of both bank lending and of a stock market.

A significant corporate industrial sector came into existence only from the late 1950s onwards, particularly during the 1960s and early 1970s. Industrial concentration ensued under pressure and guidance from a modernist state, concerned to equip French industry with large firms, sufficiently strong to compete on increasingly more open and expanding world markets. Extensive state control of the financial system made it possible to channel the necessary expansion capital into targeted industrial sectors and firms. The group structure of the French economy, whereby several large firms are combined in the form of a financial holding company to pool resources, dating from the early period of industrialisation (Scott 1985: 133), became perpetuated also at this modern stage. Further concentration occurred during the early 1980s when nationalisation was accompanied by the injection of new capital and further merger activities. The slow evolution of large corporations also meant that MNCs developed late in France and never acquired the significance that they possess in the British context.

Thus, from the 1960s onwards, a few large industrial groups came to dominate the French economy and to pose a severe threat to the many SMEs, nurtured in a less competitive industrial environment. The late emergence of the corporate sector meant that interaction with the SME sector never became very close and that, instead, two disparate industrial sectors came to exist side by side. This dualism has been further

Table 3.1   **Employment and turnover by size of enterprise in 1992 (in %)**

Very small enterprises (0–9 employees)		
	Share of employment	Share of turnover
Germany	24	17
France	29	20
UK	27	21

Small enterprises (10–49 employees)		
	Share of employment	Share of turnover
Germany	18	18
France	19	21
UK	12	17

Medium-sized enterprises (50–249 employees)		
	Share of employment	Share of turnover
Germany	18	26
France	14	19
UK	19	21

Large enterprises (>250 employees)		
	Share of employment	Share of turnover
Germany	40	39
France	38	40
UK	42	41

Source: Eurostat (1996a: 364)

accentuated by the heavy involvement of the state in the expansion and shaping of the corporate sector, and the continuation of family domination in the SME sector. From the 1980s onwards, however, more state support was extended also to the latter sector which, as in Britain and Germany, experienced a period of revival (Vickery 1986) and many SMEs became closely integrated into the large industrial groups, losing their independence in the process (Dubois and Linhart 1994).

Table 3.1 provides figures for the early 1990s, affording a comparative perspective on industrial structure in Europe. These figures show that the industrial structure of the three countries is now similar. The overall proportion of employment in SMEs in 1992 was 59.9 per cent in Germany, 63.4 per cent in France and 57.7 per cent in the UK, and corresponding figures for turnover were 61, 60 and 60 per cent respectively. These averaged-out figures hide one important difference: France and

Table 3.2 **Decline in manufacturing employment between 1974 and 1994 (%)**

France	UK	Germany
−9.3	−16.6	−10.2

Source: OECD (1996: 43)

the UK still have a significantly larger share of employment and turnover in very small and small enterprises (0–49 empls.) than Germany where the large medium-sized enterprises (250–500 empls.) – the *Mittelstand* – remain a dominant category (Eurostat 1996a: 364, 366; Quack and Hildebrandt 1994: 15–16).

The remaining differences in the degree of concentration are well illustrated by the following focus on the industrial giants: of the 100 largest firms (in terms of turnover) in Europe in 1988, twenty-eight were British (including the two Anglo-Dutch firms), twenty-four German and seventeen French. Of the twenty largest, four were British (two Anglo-Dutch), seven German and four French (*L'Expansion*, Dec. 1989/ Jan. 1990: 149). These figures show Britain leading in the number of large firms, Germany in the number of giants and France coming third and joint second respectively. They also make clear that the large firms of all three countries are important players on world markets. All these statistics on industrial structure in terms of firm size show that differences in historical development have given way to more convergent trends during the last few decades. But such purely quantitative indicators of growing similarity still hide important enduring divergences in more qualitative aspects of manufacturing industry. These will receive consideration in the following profile of contemporary industry in our three European countries.

Industrial organisation and performance in the 1990s

There are significant differences in the importance of manufacturing industry both among the three societies and within each over time. All three have experienced a significant decline of manufacturing industry during the 1970s and 1980s, with Britain being by far the most seriously affected. Germany was the least affected of the three until reunification in 1992 (see Table 3.2 on changing employment figures). This decline has been due to world recession but also signals a loss of competitiveness in both traditional industries and the more advanced industries, *vis-à-vis* the newly industrialising countries of South East Asia and *vis-à-vis* Japan, respectively. The 1980s and 1990s have thus been a period

Table 3.3   **Share in EU external trade as a
proportion of trade by all member states, 1995**

Germany	29.3
France	15.0
UK	12.8

Source: Eurostat (1996b: 19)

of industrial decline and of sustained attempts to halt or reverse that decline through the adoption of a new manufacturing policy, moving away from the mass production of standardised goods.

By 1994, employment in industry (including construction) had reached the following level: in France and Britain, 19 and 18 per cent of all civilians employed were in industrial employment, whereas in Germany the proportion was a significantly higher 25.6 per cent (OECD 1996: 3). The differential performance of the three manufacturing sectors is indicated by the following comparative figures on export and trade balance.

The share in extra-EU trade by the three countries in 1995 is shown in Table 3.3, and this is matched by a positive trade balance of 26.7 and 15.4 billion ECU for Germany and France respectively and a negative balance of −20.1 billion ECU for the UK (Eurostat 1996a: 19). This difference between the three countries is more marked when we consider only the trade balance in manufactured goods. For 1994, the relevant figures were 78.8, 9.0 and −14.6 thousand million ECU for Germany, France and Britain respectively (Eurostat 1996b: 292).

These general quantitative indicators need to be supplemented by data showing how the various strengths and weaknesses are constituted. Germany's relative industrial strength lies in the following facts: it has achieved an international position in a very broad range of industries and, in each of these, can rely on a large cluster of mutually reinforcing industrial segments (Porter 1990). Successful industrial segments include mechanical and electrical engineering, chemicals and pharmaceuticals, cars, printing and precision optics. Firms tend to concentrate on technologically sophisticated goods, often produced in short runs or to special order. They draw on a deep knowledge base, as well as on a large pool of highly skilled labour. The productivist ethos and the cooperation between craft and industrial producers outlined earlier contribute strongly to the attainment of these goals.

The German drive for excellence in engineering design has also had a retarding influence. Germany lacks competitive advantage in semiconductors/computers and most goods heavily reliant on electronics. But German firms have been adept at incorporating electronic components into a wide range of products. In the more traditional and crisis-ridden industries, extensive restructuring and modernisation has taken place and most have managed to return to a satisfactory competitive position (Katzenstein 1989, various chapters).

The French economy displays a more uneven development and less balanced industrial composition. Thus, we find some sophisticated high-tech sectors, such as weapons technology, the nuclear industry and electronic communication, existing side by side with industries like textiles and mechanical engineering where technological sophistication and skill intensity have remained low. French strengths in high-tech sectors lie in sophisticated technological design and less in efficient production organisation. With the dramatic reduction of state support for these industries since the mid-1980s, however, it is less certain that they will remain internationally competitive in the second half of the 1990s (Wright 1995). France also retains a strong position in traditional industries, such as food, drink and beauty products. The restructuring of crisis industries started later than in the other two societies and has not yet been completed.

Britain has continued to lose ground in all the modern industries and cannot boast of across-the-board strength in any one of the core industries, although pockets of excellence remain in such industries as pharmaceuticals (Porter 1990). Competitive strength is now found only in traditional industries, such as food (biscuits and confectionery), drink and tobacco. Generally too many enterprises have retreated from competitive markets for technologically sophisticated goods and have instead concentrated on low-skill and low-value goods (Williams, Williams and Haslam 1990). The restructuring of the crisis industries appears to have succeeded only in the steel industry. Despite extensive improvements in areas like labour relations and work practices, core weaknesses remain, and the transition to a new manufacturing policy has only been imperfectly accomplished (Lane 1989: Ch. 7).

Aspects of industrial order

It is assumed that the social institutional framework in which industry is embedded has a strong influence on its organisation. Interaction between production organisation and its social-institutional environment is referred to as industrial order (Herrigel 1989). A focus on industrial order examines the support systems available to industry and analyses both their degree of availability and the nature of their impact. Of the different social and political institutions with an impact on industrial organisation, four will be singled out for discussion: the state; the financial system; the educational system; and the support structures resulting from industry's self-organisation, such as trade associations and chambers of various kinds. Space available dictates that only outline features of the three industrial orders can be indicated.

The state–industry relationship is shaped both by the political philosophy guiding intervention and by the structure of the state, most notably by whether a country has a highly centralised or a more decentralised political structure. In France, there is a long tradition of a highly directive state and of a marked concentration of power at the centre. During the early decades of the postwar period, this *dirigiste* and highly centralised stance on the part of the state was well suited to a far-reaching modernisation of industry, targeting particularly large firms in the most advanced industrial sectors. The preferred instruments of intervention have been indicative planning, nationalisation and extensive state control over credit allocation. Such policy has, at the same time, often bypassed the large family-owned sector of SMEs, particularly in the more traditional industries, and has indirectly undermined their viability. The centralisation of economic decision-making and resource allocation made it difficult for SMEs to get access to state-sponsored support structures. Since the second half of the 1980s, faith in the effectiveness of *dirigisme* has greatly declined and the market has received greater emphasis. By comparative standards, however, the French state remains both directive and centralised (Cerny 1989) and its influence persists through the system of *pantouflage*: widespread mid-career change by high state officials into top management positions in industry (Bauer 1988). Even many privatised companies were kept under state influence both through the state appointment of top managers and the allocation of shares (ibid). This has had multiple consequences, such as exceptionally high élite cohesion, a hierarchical business structure and bureaucratic management style. The overall effect is that in the French industrial order, state-sponsored support structures have a strong weight and weaken self-organisation. But a high degree of state regulation of industry does not necessarily equal high effectiveness, and state penetration of the SME sector is much weaker than in the large-firm sector.

The German pattern of state-industry relations is very different from the French. The philosophy of the social market economy emphasises competition in the free market and eschews detailed state intervention in industry, except in its acknowledgement of responsibility for the social costs to labour resulting from economic restructuring. At the same time, the central state provides a uniform and strong regulatory framework in such spheres as industrial relations and training, and thus contributes to relatively homogeneous forms of industrial organisation, both across industries/regions and size categories of firms. The federal political structure grants local states (the *Länder*) significant economic resources and competencies and thus ensures that state-sponsored support structures are relatively well-attuned to local needs and to the requirements of SMEs which operate more strongly at this lower level. Thus, the German state has considerable involvement in industry, but the strong degree of self-organisation established by industry ensures that this involvement does not turn into direction and interference. Since the mid-1990s, however, market liberalism has also become more influential in Germany.

In Britain, yet a different pattern of state–industry relations prevails. The philosophy of *laissez-faire*, dominant during most of the postwar period but compromised in times of pressing economic crisis, has made for a patchy and ineffective industrial policy. State reluctance to intervene is paralleled by industry's insistence on a hands-off relationship. Comprehensive regulatory frameworks on aspects of industrial organisation were never developed, and variation between regions, industries and types of firms has remained pronounced. This is particularly notable in the fields of industrial relations and training. The dominance of market criteria, together with a relatively centralised political structure, has meant that, for a long time, state help for the sector of SMEs was underdeveloped and failed to check the decline of this sector. Although the last two decades have seen a reversal of this policy of neglect, there still remain many problems in the targeting of aid to the small-firm sector (Bannock and Albach 1991). In the British context, neither large firms nor SMEs can rely on consistent and dense state-sponsored support systems.

The manner in which industrial enterprises raise their capital and the way their relation to the financial system is structured constitute a second important dimension of industrial order – an excellent discussion of bank-industry relations is provided by Vittas (1986). British firms mostly raise capital by issuing shares on the stock market, and the stock exchange forms the centre of the British financial system. The banking system, divided between investment and clearing banks, is highly centralised, and bank lending – where it occurs – has never led to close bank–industry relations. Thus British relations between the financial system and industrial firms are purely market relationships. They impose both constraints of high, short-term financial returns on industrial management and obviate the performance of support-and-control functions on the part of the financial institutions. The absence of the latter has been particularly detrimental to the development of smaller firms. The pressure for quick financial returns is widely held to have shaped managerial investment behaviour in a negative fashion. It is connected with insufficient investment in both skill development and technological innovation. Last, the relative case of mergers and takeovers, facilitated by the British financial system, militates against the development of strong medium-sized firms; and hence of a balanced industrial structure.

The French financial system has undergone significant changes during the 1980s. Until the mid-1980s, it had the following characteristics: credit-based financing, centred on intermediary financial institutions; strong state influence over the conditions of lending, and a weakly developed stock market. Although such a system has made it possible for state-directed industrial restructuring and modernisation to take place, it has also, until recently, made it difficult for smaller firms to get access to credit. The political decentralisation of the 1980s has, however, brought industrial funding closer to the SMEs. The relations between financial institutions and enterprises have tended to be purely functional and did not extend into the areas of consultancy and control. From the mid-1980s onwards, several significant changes were implemented which served to reduce state dependence of large enterprises. Some of the large French banks have begun to copy the German model and have started to acquire substantial industrial portfolios (*The Economist*, 4 August 1990: 67–8); the volume of state-administered credit dramatically declined; and the stock market grew greatly in importance (Cerny 1989; Boucek 1993).

The German financial system is mainly credit-based, and the cost of credit is determined purely by the market. The stock market remains underdeveloped. The large universal banks form the centre of this system, and their relations with industry are regarded as close. Long-term relationships are built up between a given firm and its house bank, and lending is normally accompanied by supportive supervision and informed consultancy. Banks own substantial amounts of industrial equity and also act as proxies for smaller investors. They are represented on the boards of most large companies, and the latter do, in turn, have seats on the banks' boards. Groups of banks sometimes form 'crisis cartels' to assist in the restructuring of traditional industries, such as steel, and of ailing giants, such as the electro-technical firm AEG in the 1980s. Since the mid-1980s, however, dependence on bank credit by large companies is said to have declined slightly, and complaints about bank incompetence have become more frequent (Lane 1995: 52–8). In addition to the 'Big Three' there are countless regional and local banks which cater very satisfactorily to the needs of SMEs.

These long-established close ties between German industry and banking have left a strong imprint on industrial culture. They have contributed to the maintenance of long-term investment horizons and, coupled with the engineering orientation of German industry, have resulted in steady technological updating and the parallel development of the necessary skill resources. The active industrial involvement of banks has facilitated the formation of a self-regulating industrial community which justifies the non-interventionist stance of the state, discussed above.

Industry depends not only on the easy availability of capital but also on an ample supply of suitably educated and trained human resources. Hence the educational system forms another crucial component of industrial order. For reasons of space, consideration of the university-educated minority will be omitted, although it is important both for the areas of management and of R&D. Instead, the focus will be on the vocational training of the majority of the labour force. The issues at stake are both the levels of education and training by a given population and its content which, in turn, depends on the closeness of ties between industry and institutions of education and training.

A highly trained labour force equips industry not only with the necessary technical skills but also has a decisive impact on attitudes and orientations which shape industrial organisation and culture (for details, see Lane 1989: Chs 2–4). Among the many areas affected are length of hierarchy and ease of vertical and horizontal communication, attitudes towards, and capabilities in, the field of technological innovation, adaptability to change, as well as the balance between extrinsic and intrinsic employee motivation and the resulting standards in the quality of products and services.

Germany's strong craft tradition is manifested in a highly developed system of vocational education and training (VET), and the social prestige of that system rivals that of general education. The highly standardised dual system (that is, both college- and industry-based) provides courses for manual and non-manual occupations from the apprenticeship level upwards to that of master craftsman. It thus offers career ladders as well as ensuring the homogeneity of standards at various levels. The strong role taken by industry in determining the content and supervising the implementation of training ensures that the practical component remains prominent. The involvement of the Chambers of Craft and Industry in monitoring the system keeps craft standards diffused throughout industry. State involvement means both a financial contribution (one-third of the costs) towards the more theoretical college-based part of VET and the maintenance of the general regulatory framework, while union participation ensures some input also from labour. The high participation rate – around 65 per cent of those eligible have at least a Skilled Worker Certificate – has decisively shaped all aspects of industrial organisation.

The features of continuity, homogeneity and achievement of high and widely diffused standards, characteristic of the German system of VET, are all sadly lacking in the British system. VET was developed relatively late in a 'feast or famine' fashion and has never achieved the same importance and social recognition as general education. There exists a confusing variety of training and validating bodies and a wasteful overlap between them, and continuity between the various levels of VET is not ensured. The weaknesses of the British system are now widely recognised, and there have been periodic attempts to restructure it during the last fifteen years. The initiative for remodelling the system has come from the state, but the latest stage in this process – the formation of Training and Enterprise Councils (TECs) – signals the realisation that schemes will only succeed with the active participation of employers.

The two main components of the system of VET are the traditional apprenticeship and the various new training schemes. The latter, introduced and organised in different forms during the 1980s, have expanded at the expense of the former. The new schemes have overcome some of the rigidities of the union-administered apprenticeships and have reached a larger proportion of young workers, but they have not yet managed to reach the same high levels of training standards. Although progress has been made in the standardisation of training levels to be reached, standards remain low by comparison with Germany, and the gap between the two countries in skill resources available to industry remains wide.

In France, VET was first systematically promoted in the late 1950s although, until recently, it stayed at a low level both in terms of social

Table 3.4   **Numbers qualifying in engineering and technology, 1985 (per 100 000)**

	Britain	France	Germany
Doctorates	1.2	.5	1.6
Masters and enhanced degrees	4.0	11.0	7.0
Bachelor degrees	25.0	27.0	34.0
Technicians	51.0	63.0	72.0
Craftsmen	62.0	167.0	197.0

Source: National Institute of Economic and Social Research, quoted by
The Economist, 13 January 1990. Extract from table

prestige and in the degree of currency it achieved. During the 1980s, big efforts have been made to extend both the reach of VET, and to raise levels of skill at intermediate and advanced levels. The main part of VET is provided in the state-administered and financed educational system, while a compulsory levy on industry ensures that employers provide further training for their employees. The relative availability of skilled employees at various hierarchical levels in the three societies is indicated by Table 3.4. It shows that France has advanced much further than Britain in catching up with Germany.

A last feature of industrial orders in Europe to be discussed is the degree of self-organisation of enterprises in industry-wide and/or regional associations of a formal and informal kind. Such permanent and temporary producer associations can facilitate cooperation, regulate competition and undertake representation *vis-à-vis* political authorities and labour organisations, such as the ones discussed above. They ensure that supplies of capital, skills and knowledge are of the right kind or quantity and that they are made available on advantageous terms and are targeted in an appropriate manner. Such intermediary organisations are particularly vital for SMEs.

The prevalence of intermediary organisations in our three societies will be densest where, as in Germany, the craft form of production has endured but may also be sustained by family and neighbourhood networks, as in France. In the British case, where neither craft-based nor family/neighbourhood-based organisation has been preserved, intermediary organisations have remained weak and fragmented. This may be illustrated by looking at the role of chambers in the three societies. In Germany, Chambers of Craft and Industry are statutory bodies with compulsory membership contributions. They not only provide the usual range of business services but also perform a central role in the provision of a skilled labour force and the maintenance of skill standards. In France, Chambers can also rely on a compulsory levy to finance a range of business services, but the lack of involvement in the field of training deprives them of the key position they occupy in German industry. The

British Chambers of Commerce, relying on voluntary membership, have insufficient financial and organisational resources to have a strong impact in any area of business organisation (Bennett 1996).

The picture is similar when we turn to industry-based trade organisations. Whereas in Britain the majority of associations tend to be weak and fragmented and thus unable to regulate sectoral competition or provide the more costly services, such as the provision of scientific knowledge by research institutes, in Germany the opposite is the case (Bennett 1996; Lane and Bachmann 1997). The lack of influence of British associations over their members makes them unfit to assume the role of interlocutors between government and firms. In the German context, in contrast, trade associations perform the functions of 'private government', regulating their members on behalf and in lieu of the state and thus shield them from direct political intervention. In France, where state intervention is more accepted, the role of intermediary trade organisations is consequently much weaker. The state is most likely to deal directly with large firms. SMEs have traditionally been out of the state's reach and have thus often formed their own, more informal self-help groups. Such networks of mutual assistance are said to have increased notably during the 1980s (Amadieu 1990).

Conclusions

This review of the industrial structure and organisation in three large European societies has outlined a picture of enduring diversity. This diversity is not simply one of structure and performance which can be altered by the adoption of appropriate policy measures. It has deep roots in the social-institutional framework of each society and is mainly the result of complex historical processes. This is not to say that national moulds have been cast for ever and that industrial change is impossible. Indeed, the German pattern of industrial organisation owes some of its features to fundamental social and political changes, initiated – partly on the instigation of the Allied victors – only in the postwar period. Similarly, France has fundamentally adapted its pattern of industrial organisation during the last thirty years and has slowly moved closer to that of its German neighbour. But convergence towards a single pattern of industrial organisation in the wake of European integration is not likely to occur in the near future.

References

Amadieu, J-F. (1990) 'France', in W. Sengenberger, G. Loveman and M. Piore (eds) *The Re-emergence of Small Enterprises*, Geneva: International Institute for Labour Studies.

Bannock, G. and Albach, H. (1991) *Small Business Policy in Europe*, Report for the Anglo-German Foundation of London: AGF.

Bauer, M. (1988) 'The politics of state-directed privatisation: the case of France 1986–88', *West European Politics*, II(4): 49–60.

Bennett, R. J. (1996) 'The logic of local business associations: an analysis of voluntary Chambers of Commerce', *Journal of Public Policy*, 15(3): 251–78.

Boucek, T. (1993) 'Developments in post-war French political economy: the continuing decline of *dirigisme*?', in J. Sheldrake and P. Webb (eds) *State and Market: Aspects of Modern European Development*, Aldershot: Dartmouth Press.

Boyer, R. (1986) *La Flexibilité du Travail en Europe*, Paris: La Découverte.

Cerny, P. G. (1989) 'From *dirigisme* to deregulation? The case of financial markets', in P. Godt (ed.) *Policy-Making in France*, London: Pinter.

Doran, A. (1984) *Craft Enterprises in Britain and Germany*, A study for the Anglo-German Foundation by the Economists Advisory Group, London: AGF.

Dubois, P. and Linhart, P. (1994) 'Industrial networks and corporate cultures: the French case', in C. Mako and P. Novoszath (eds) *Convergence versus Divergence: the Case of the Corporate Culture*, Budapest: Institute for Social Conflict Research, Hungarian Academy of Sciences and Communication and Consultation.

Eurostat (1996a) *Eurostat Yearbook 1996: a Statistical View on Europe 1985–1995*, Office for Official Publications of the European Community: Luxembourg.

Eurostat (1996b) *External and Intra-European Union Trade. Monthly Statistics, 12*, Office for Official Publications of the European Community: Luxembourg.

Fox, A. (1985) *History and Heritage: the Social Origins of the British Industrial Relations System*, London: Allen & Unwin.

Herrigel, G. (1989) 'Industrial order and the politics of industrial change: mechanical engineering', in P. Katzenstein (ed.) *Industry and Politics in West Germany: Towards the Third Republic*, Ithica, NY: Cornell University Press.

Katzenstein, P. (ed.) (1989) *Industry and Politics in West Germany: Towards the Third Republic*, Ithaca, NY: Cornell University Press.

Kocka, J. (1975) *Unternehmer in der Deutschen Industrialisierung*, Goettingen: Vandenhoek & Ruprecht.

Landes, D. (1969) *The Unbound Prometheus: Technological Change and Industrial Development*, Cambridge: Cambridge University Press.

Lane, C. (1989) *Management and Labour in Europe*, Aldershot: Edward Elgar.

Lane, C. (1995) *Industry and Society in Europe. Stability and Change in Britain, Germany and France*, Aldershot: Edward Elgar.

Lane, C. and Bachmann, R. (1997) 'Cooperation in inter-firm relations in Britain and Germany: the role of social institutions', *British Journal of Sociology*, 48(2): 226–54.

OECD (1996) *Historical Statistics 1960–1994*, Paris: OECD.

Piore, M. and Sabel, C. (1984) *The Second Industrial Divide*, New York: Basic Books.

Porter, M. (1990) *The Competitive Advantage of Nations*, London: Macmillan.

Quack, S. and Hildebrandt, S. (1994) 'Hausbank or fournisseur? Bank services for small and medium-sized enterprises in Germany and France'. Paper presented at the ESF-EMOT Workshop on 'Financial Services', Paris, 30 Sept.–1 Oct.

Schriewer, J. (1986) 'Intermediäre Instanzen, Sellbstverwaltung und berufliche Ausbildungsstrukturen im historischen Vergleich', *Zeitschrift für Pädagogik*, 32: 69–90.

Scott, J. (1985) *Corporations, Classes and Capitalism*, 2nd edn, London: Hutchinson.

Streeck, W. (1986) *The Territorial Organisation of the Continental Powers and the Logics of Associative Action: the Case of Artisanal Interest Organisations in West Germany*, Research Unit on the Labour Market and Employment, Berlin: Wissenschaftszentrum.

Trebilcock, C. (1981) *The Industrialization of the Continental Powers, 1780–1914*, London and New York: Longman.

Vickery, L. (1986) 'France', in P. Burns and J. Dewhurst (eds) *Small Business in Europe*, London: Macmillan.

Vittas, D. (1986) 'Bankers' relations with industry: an international survey', *National Westminster Bank Quarterly Review*, Feb.

Williams, K., Williams, J. and Haslam, C. (1990) 'The hollowing out of British manufacturing and its implications for policy', *Economy and Society*, 19: 456–90.

Wright, V. (1995) 'The state and major enterprises in Western Europe: enduring complexities', in J. Heyward (ed.) *Industrial Enterprise and European Integration*, Oxford: Oxford University Press.

CHAPTER 4

Population trends

JOHN SIMONS

One feature of Europe's population in the late twentieth century dominates all the others: its reluctance to reproduce itself. A 1989 United Nations review commented 'Europe is literally melting away like snow in the sun' (United Nations 1989: 8). Taking a similar view when he was France's Prime Minister, Jacques Chirac, said 'In demographic terms, Europe is vanishing. Twenty or so years from now, our countries will be empty, and no matter what our technological strength, we shall be incapable of putting it to use' (quoted in the Paris daily, *Libération* in October 1984, in an interview from which excerpts are printed in *Population and Development Review*, 11(1): 163).

The faltering of reproduction, and the consequent ageing of the population, will be the main theme of this chapter. It starts with a review of the main features of Europe's demography. This is followed by a section on interpretations of the fertility decline as the principal cause of population ageing. The final sections deal with the social consequences of population ageing and its policy implications.

Main demographic features

Growth

Europe's population of around 700 million is still growing, but slowly. Its share of world population is falling, steadily. In Table 4.1 the trend in the population of Europe since 1950 is contrasted with figures for the world as a whole, for developed countries, and for developing countries. Europe's share of world population falls from 22 per cent in 1950 to an estimated 10 per cent in 2010. Population barely increased in Europe in the early 1990s, and is expected to start declining early in the next century.

Mortality

Because population growth depends on the excess of births over deaths (ignoring the effects of migration), population decline can occur if

Table 4.1 Population trends in Europe and the world, 1950–2010: population (millions), Europe's share (%) of world population (in parentheses), and growth rate (%) (UN medium variant projections)

	Population				Growth rate			
	1950	1995	2000	2010	1950–55	1980–85	1990–95	2005–10
Europe	549 (21.8)	727 (12.6)	730 (11.8)	729 (10.4)	1.0	0.4	0.2	0.0
Eastern	221	309	307	304	1.4	0.6	−0.1	−0.1
Northern	78	94	95	96	0.4	0.2	0.3	0.2
Southern	109	144	145	145	0.8	0.4	0.1	−0.1
Western	141	181	183	184	0.7	0.1	0.6	0.0
Developed countries	809	1167	1186	1213	1.2	0.6	0.4	0.21
Developing countries	1711	4550	4973	5819	2.1	2.1	1.9	1.52
World	2520	5716	6158	7032	1.80	1.7	1.6	1.3

Source: United Nations (1995: 213, 214)

mortality is high enough. In the event, the substantial decline in mortality during this century has considerably reduced the level of fertility required for population replacement (Sardon 1990: 17).

A commonly used measure of a country's mortality is life expectancy at birth, which is a summary measure of mortality across all ages in a population. Life expectancy at birth is independent of the age structure of a population, and can therefore be used to compare one population with another. (Differences in age structure, such as large differences in the proportion of the elderly, can yield large differences in crude death rates even between populations with the same expectation of life at birth.) Another important measure of mortality is a country's infant mortality rate, which is usually measured as the number of deaths of children under 1 year of age per thousand live births. Shown in Table 4.2 are trends and projections for both life expectancy at birth and infant mortality rates for Europe and for regions of Europe separately. Also shown are trends for developed and developing country groups, and for the world as a whole.

For Europe as a whole, life expectancy at birth reached 68 years for males and nearly 76 years for females in the early 1980s, and is expected to reach 71 years for males and nearly 79 years for females in the first decade of the next century. Eastern Europe has lagged behind the rest of Europe in extending the life span (Meslé 1996). Until recent years, the sex differential in mortality had widened over several decades. The differential now seems to have stabilised, though it is still widening in some countries. The relative advantage of women has been attributed to various factors: greater congenital robustness, behavioural factors (such as less consumption of alcohol) and less exposure to hazardous environments.

The increase in life expectancies means that higher proportions of the population are to be found in older age groups. For Europe as a whole, the percentage of the population aged 60 years or more rose from 12 per cent in 1950 to 17 per cent in 1985, and is projected to rise to 20 per cent by the end of the century.

The increase in life expectancy is largely attributable to the decline in mortality associated with cardiovascular disease, especially coronary diseases. However, these remain the main cause of death among men over the ages of 35 or 40, followed by cancer in the age group above 40. On the other hand, cancer is the main cause of death among women between the ages of 25 and 60, and circulatory disease after the age of 60 (United Nations 1989: 101).

Over the past three decades, infant mortality in Europe has declined substantially, from 72 per thousand live births in the early 1950s to 12 in the early 1990s. Infant mortality still accounts for high proportions of total mortality in the developing countries, but a negligible amount in the developed countries.

Defining its strategy for the achievement of 'Health for all by the year 2000', the European Region of the World Health Organisation

Table 4.2 Life expectancy at birth (years), males and females, and infant mortality rate (infant deaths per thousand live births), Europe and the world, 1950–2010 (UN medium variant projections from 1995)

| | Life expectancy | | | | | | | | Infant mortality rate | | | |
| | 1950–55 | | 1980–85 | | 1995–2000 | | 2000–10 | | 1950–55 | 1980–85 | 1995–2000 | 2000–10 |
	M	F	M	F	M	F	M	F				
Europe	63.4	68.5	67.8	75.7	69.3	77.3	71.0	78.5	72	18	12	10
Eastern	61.8	68.4	64.1	73.6	63.7	74.1	66.1	75.5	91	23	17	14
Northern	66.8	71.5	70.8	77.3	73.4	79.3	74.6	80.3	33	10	7	6
Southern	61.5	65.1	70.9	77.1	73.9	80.0	75.0	81.0	76	18	10	9
Western	65.1	69.9	70.7	77.7	73.9	80.4	75.0	81.3	46	10	6	6
Developed countries	63.9	69.0	69.2	76.7	71.2	78.6	72.7	79.6	59	15	9	8
Developing countries	40.2	41.8	57.3	59.8	62.4	65.3	64.6	67.8	179	88	63	53
World	45.1	47.8	59.4	63.1	63.7	67.8	65.8	70.0	156	79	57	49

Source: United Nations (1995: 458, 460, 462, 492, 494, 496, 498, 500) declared that 'The first aim of the European Strategy is to ensure equity in health between and within countries' (quoted in United Nations 1988a: 395). It seems likely that equity within countries will be harder to achieve than equity among them. Although mortality rates have declined in all social categories, the pattern of social differentials seems to have remained largely unchanged.

According to a review of recent studies in several European countries presented to a European Population Conference in 1987 (Valkonen 1987), mortality for adult men is higher among manual workers (especially unskilled manual workers) than among non-manual workers. The mortality of those with basic education only is approximately double that of university graduates. The inverse association between mortality and status still applies, almost always, when deaths are subdivided by cause. For women, differences in mortality are generally smaller than for men. This is said to be because mortality caused by some cancers (such as breast cancer and cancer of the uterus) and by accidents or violence is either positively or irregularly associated with social status.

The studies reviewed suggest that, for both men and women, social class differences in mortality had increased in the preceding ten to twenty years in some countries and remained constant in others. In the case of infant mortality there appeared to have been some improvement in the inverse association between social class and mortality. In Denmark and Sweden, socioeconomic differences in the components of infant mortality had been almost eliminated.

Although much of the research in this field has been concerned with specific risk factors, it is believed that the greater part of socioeconomic differentials in mortality is caused not by specific risk factors or inequalities in health care but by the general inequality of living conditions and related differences in lifestyle (Valkonen 1987: 245; Meslé 1996: 141).

Marriage, cohabitation, divorce

Figure 4.1 shows what happened to the marriage rate in European Community countries after the 1960s, when the proportion of people who were or had been married reached an historically unique peak in Europe. Evidently the popularity of marriage went into steep decline between the 1970s and the late 1980s. The trends for most European countries outside the EEC have been broadly similar, though the timing and magnitude of the decline have varied between regions. In most of Europe the rate has continued to decline but more slowly (Sardon 1986; Monnier 1996: 1010).

One reason for the decline in marriage rates has been an increase of two to four years in the mean age at marriage in most European countries since the 1970s. This has been related to the rise of cohabitation which has also made a direct contribution to the decline in marriage rates. The available data on cohabitation have been assembled by Kiernan (1996).

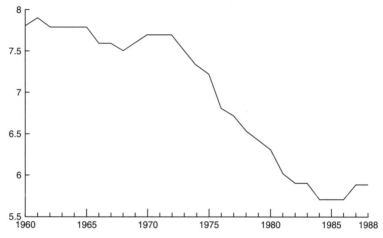

*Figure 4.1   **Marriages per thousand population, European Community, 1960–1988***

Source: Eurostat (1990: 182)

Commenting on them she says that in all countries for which a time series of data is available, it is clear that there has been a large increase in the proportions of women cohabiting. Cohabiting in the early twenties is a relatively common practice, especially in the Nordic countries with seven in ten Swedish and Danish women cohabiting at these ages. But cohabitation is much less common than marriage as a form of union at older ages (even in Sweden and Denmark) which suggests that marriage has not been rejected permanently.

A growing reluctance to get married has been accompanied by an increasing reluctance to stay married. Monnier (1996: 1026) shows for a series of years the percentage of a cohort of marriages that would end in divorce if the cohort experienced the divorce rates by duration of marriage that applied in the specified year. In 1993 this percentage, which has doubled or trebled since 1970 in a number of countries, ranged from 46 in Sweden to 7 in Italy. The figures for England and Wales and France were 45 and 35 respectively. The percentage appeared to stabilise in a number of countries during the late 1980s.

Fertility

The change that has had, and will continue to have, the greatest impact on European demography (and much else) is the decline of fertility to levels insufficient to replace populations.

A commonly used measure of current fertility is the total fertility rate (TFR), which is the average completed family size implied by the age-specific fertility rates achieved by a population in a specified year. In most European countries the rate fell from around four children per woman at the beginning of the century to a level well below that required for renewal of the population throughout the period 1925–45 (Sardon 1990: 17). After the Second World War, the TFR rose again to above the replacement level in most countries and appeared to be stabilising. In the mid-1950s there was a widespread rise, which reached a peak in 1965 in most countries.

The behaviour of the TFR over recent decades in a number of European countries is shown in Table 4.3. Also shown are projections for the period 1995 to 2010. With the mortality pattern of modern Europe, the TFR needs to be about 2.1 to ensure population replacement. The only European country shown in the table with fertility above this level in 1994 is Iceland.

Between the mid-1960s and the mid-1970s, fertility declined rapidly in north, west and central Europe. In Italy, Portugal and Spain, the decline from the mid-1960s was continuous; it was more moderate than elsewhere in Europe for the first ten years but became much steeper after 1974. Since the mid-1970s, European fertility rates have declined less rapidly in a number of countries or have stabilised. There was even a modest recovery in some.

Analyses of the demographic statistics reveal that the fertility decline has been caused largely by a decrease in third and higher-order births, together with an increase in the proportion of childless women. Changes have also occurred in the age at which women start childbearing. For European Community countries, the average age fell from 25.5 years in 1960 to 24.4 in 1970. The average has since risen in all Western countries. In a useful review of European fertility pattern and trends in the early 1990s, Coleman (1996: 28) notes the effect of the rising age of maternity in increasing the proportion of births that occur to women aged over 30. One of the most extreme cases is that of The Netherlands where age-specific fertility rates at age 20–24 almost halved between 1975 and 1991, and almost doubled at ages 30–34 and 35–39. Around the latter year, an average of 34 per cent of the total fertility rate in western European countries was contributed by women over age 30. In contrast, the percentage was generally between 10 and 20 per cent in eastern European countries.

Reporting in 1982 on an analysis of the fertility decline, Calot and Blayo (1982) offered two alternative characterisations of the phenomenon. One of these saw the decline as the first downswing of an infinite series of oscillations of fertility somewhere near the level required for population replacement. The alternative characterisation saw the decline as the resumption of the historical decline of fertility to levels well below the replacement level, after an accidental upturn that was a consequence of two world wars. In the event, total fertility rates have since been relatively stable in northern and western Europe though generally below

Table 4.3 Total fertility rate, Europe, 1970–2010 (UN medium variant projections from 1995)

	1970	1980	1990	1994	1995–2000	2000–05	2005–10
Eastern Europe							
Bulgaria	2.17	2.05	1.81	1.37	1.50	1.50	1.57
Czech Republic	1.90	2.10	1.89	1.50	1.83	1.83	1.90
Germany (East)	2.19	1.44	1.52	0.77			
Hungary	1.97	1.91	1.87	1.64	1.71	1.71	1.78
Poland	2.20	2.25	2.04	1.80	1.88	1.88	1.95
Romania	2.89	2.43	1.83	1.41	1.50	1.50	1.57
Slovakia	2.41	2.31	2.09	1.66			
Northern Europe							
Denmark	1.95	1.55	1.67	1.80	1.70	1.70	1.77
Finland	1.83	1.63	1.78	1.85	1.92	1.99	2.06
Iceland	2.79	2.48	2.31	2.21	2.23	2.23	2.16
Ireland	3.93	3.23	2.19	1.86	2.10	2.10	2.10
Norway	2.50	1.72	1.93	1.87	2.00	2.07	2.10
Sweden	1.92	1.68	2.13	1.88	2.10	2.10	2.10
UK	2.43	1.90	1.84	1.74	1.81	1.81	1.88

Southern Europe							
Albania	5.16	3.62	3.03	–	2.66	2.47	2.28
Greece	2.34	2.21	1.43	1.35	1.40	1.40	1.47
Italy	2.42	1.64	1.29	1.22	1.27	1.27	1.34
Portugal	2.83	2.19	1.47	1.44	1.55	1.55	1.62
Slovenia	2.20	1.95	1.46	1.32	1.45	1.45	1.52
Spain	2.85	2.18	1.33	1.22	1.23	1.23	1.30
Western Europe							
Austria	2.29	1.65	1.45	1.44	1.60	1.67	1.74
Belgium	2.25	1.68	1.62	1.55	1.71	1.78	1.85
France	2.47	1.95	1.78	1.65	1.74	1.74	1.81
Germany (West only 1970–1994; East and West combined 1995–2010)	1.99	1.45	1.45	1.35	1.30	1.30	1.37
Luxembourg	1.98	1.51	1.60	1.72	1.72	1.79	1.86
Netherlands	2.57	1.60	1.62	1.57	1.61	1.61	1.68
Switzerland	2.10	1.55	1.59	1.49	1.67	1.74	1.81
Developed countries*	2.36	1.91	1.83	1.70	1.71	1.71	1.78
Developing countries*	5.96	4.63	3.83	3.48	3.28	3.09	2.91
World*	4.88	3.91	3.38	3.10	2.97	2.84	2.72

* Data for 1970–94 refer to the following periods: 1965–70, 1975–80, 1985–90, 1990–95 (United Nations 1995: 324, 328)

Sources: Data for 1970–94 – Monnier (1996: 1020); data for projections – United Nations (1995: 330, 332) the level of 2.1 needed for population replacement. There have been marked declines in southern and eastern Europe.

The TFR can be a misleading index of potential family size because it is affected by shifts in the timing of births – short-term shifts and shifts caused by a systematic change in the age of women at first and subsequent births (Brass 1989: 17). For example, it has been shown that when the age at maternity was declining, the TFR misrepresented the underlying trend to an extent that was sufficient to mask the onset of the fall in completed fertility in the generations producing children during the period (Sardon 1990: 21).

One of the most striking new trends in recent years has been the increase in the proportion of births that have occurred outside marriage. The increase has been associated with the fall in marriage rates and the increases in cohabitation and divorce. In western and northern Europe in 1994, unmarried parents produced between a third and a half of all births. The proportion has been increasing sharply in eastern Europe in recent years, but remains generally low in southern europe (Monnier 1996: 1011).

Ageing

Largely as a consequence of fertility decline (which has shifted the age distribution upwards) but partly as a consequence of mortality decline (which has meant more survivors in the older age groups) the population of Europe has been ageing. This is not a new phenomenon. It started with an historical fertility transition a century ago, accelerated when fertility dropped to a low level during the Depression years of the 1930s, slowed down as a result of the baby boom after the Second World War, and finally accelerated again as a result of the fertility decline in the mid-1960s. Although the process could be reversed by an upturn in births, this would have to be a remarkable one: a speedy and sustained (and very unlikely) return to a total fertility rate well above replacement level.

One measure of ageing is change in the median age. For Europe as a whole, the median age – 29 years in 1950 – is expected to increase to 40 years by 2010. In sub-Saharan Africa by contrast, both the median age in 1950 and the projected median age in 2010 is 18 years (United Nations 1995: 468). The trends in age structure, median age and dependency ratio are shown in Table 4.4. The proportion of the population in the economically active age range is expected to increase into the century as the high-fertility generations of the 1950s and 1960s reach working age. Subsequently the proportion of dependants is expected to increase, owing largely to the effect of the low-fertility generations which arrived after the baby boom, but also to the effect of declining mortality.

*Table 4.4 Age structure (% in different age groups), median age and
dependency ratio (population aged 0–14 and 65+ as % of population aged
15–64), Europe, 1950–2010 (UN medium variant projections from 1990)*

	1950	*1980*	*1995*	*2010*
Age group				
0–4	9.2	7.2	5.7	5.6
5–14	17.0	15.0	13.5	11.2
15–24	17.3	16.2	14.1	12.4
60+	12.1	16.0	18.8	21.3
Median age	29.2	32.6	36.0	40.0
Dependency ratio				
0–14	26.2	22.2	19.2	16.8
65+	8.2	12.4	13.8	15.5
Total	34.4	34.6	33.0	32.3

Source: United Nations (1995: 492)

International migration

According to data assembled by Salt (1996), there were around 18.3
million foreign nationals legally resident in Europe (excluding eastern
Europe) around 1992. The figure indicates a 23 per cent increase between
1988 and 1992, of which 58 per cent (2 million people, excluding ethnic
Germans) occurred in Germany. For 13 countries for which data are
available throughout the period, numbers of immigrants rose by 12 per
cent per annum from 1985 to 1988, and by 18 per cent in the years
1988–92. Immigration (legal or otherwise) is likely to increase as its
advantages become apparent to growing numbers of the poor outside
Europe. In particular, rapid population growth and slow economic
development in countries to the south and east of the Mediterranean
create powerful pressures for northward emigration.

Le Bras (1991) roughly estimated the demographic impact of immigration on some European countries over the 40 years following the
Second World War. This showed that the impact on total population
growth had been considerable – 15 per cent in the Federal Repubic
of Germany and between 5 and 10 per cent in France, Belgium and
Sweden. Because they were relatively young, the immigrants had the
effect of making the host populations younger, but only by a modest
amount – 0.8 of a year in Belgium, 0.7 of a year in Sweden, and 0.4
of a year in Germany and France.

Interpreting the fertility decline

While research on the fertility behaviour of industrial society had produced a number of empirical generalisations, relating fertility to social class and other variables, there was still no well-established general theory that could be invoked to explain the fertility decline of the 1960s, or the rise of the 1950s. Inevitably the magnitude of the decline and its implications for the age structure of European populations gave a new impetus to attempts to find explanations for such phenomena.

There is a general assumption that, when deciding whether or when to produce a child, people in industrial societies typically take into account the expected effects of doing so on projected lifestyle. The effects will depend on the characteristics of the lifestyle and the costs of maintaining it, on the parents' income and other resources, and on the expected effects of a child on both costs and (if the earning capacity of a parent would be affected) income. The decision will also depend on the perceived importance of a child (or another child) itself to projected lifestyle, and therefore the extent to which people may be willing to forgo, say, career advancement, in favour of family-building. It is assumed that parents weigh the importance to themselves and to their preferred lifestyle of having a child or another child against any consequences that would be experienced as constraints on lifestyle.

High living standards and the cost of maintaining them make parenthood in the West expensive. As well as the direct costs, there are the costs, especially for women, of forgoing valued alternatives to parenthood. In these circumstances, fertility level is likely to depend on society's success in maintaining the commitment of its members to a core value system that makes family-building important to people despite its costs. According to the explanations offered by most analysts, it is precisely this battle that society has been losing.

Lesthaeghe (1983) believes the root cause is 'secular individualism'. As recent evidence of its influence, he cites the growing prevalence of cohabitation outside marriage, voluntary childlessness, nonconformist sexual conduct, abortion and euthanasia. Using multivariate analyses of regional data for three European countries he demonstrates a close relationship, lasting over a period of at least a century, between decline in marital fertility, falls in indicators (such as church attendance) of the influence of traditional religious ideas, and increases in such indicators of structural modernisation as the proportion of the population employed in industry.

Preston is another contributor to the doctrine that most of the fertility decline is explained by a loosening of normative controls. In the case of Americans, he says, they became 'more inclined to justify their behaviour in terms of its consequences for personal development, and less inclined to justify it on grounds of fulfilling or adhering to valued social roles'. As a result of publicity given to world population growth, responsible parenthood came to mean reducing family size to a level lower than it otherwise would have been. Sustained economic growth increased the expense of children and expanded opportunities in ways that made people increasingly restive 'under the yoke of responsible parenthood and monogamous marriage'. In short, when normative controls became inconvenient, they were abandoned (Preston 1986).

Davis (1986) suggests that there is an incompatibility, or tension, between the family on the one hand and the industrial economy on the other. The normative controls required for the maintenance of family life break down, he says, when people live in large cities, strive for social mobility, work in an impersonal environment, receive income as individuals rather than as family members, and acquire formal education in schools beyond parental control. Under these conditions, family norms are violated with impunity, and conformity is labelled 'old-fashioned' or 'conservative'. It is these characteristics of modernity that encourage trends towards later marriage, reproduction outside marriage, high divorce rates and the extensive participation of women in the labour force. According to Davis, these four trends go far towards explaining the below-replacement fertility of industrial nations.

A number of authors refer to evidence collected by surveys of beliefs and values to support the notion of a shift to nonconformist behaviour. A useful source of comparative data on the subject is a set of national surveys of cultural values conducted in European countries in 1981 and again in 1990. They were conducted under the sponsorship of a charitable foundation, the European Value Systems Study Group. In each country the respondents were a nationally representative sample of some 1200 adults aged 18 and over.

Several of the questions asked in the survey were capable of revealing something about the extent and character of commitment to the family. For example, respondents were asked whether they thought it was the parents' duty to do their best for their children, even at the expense of their own well-being. Presumably a positive answer would be one indicator of the endorsement of norms that stressed commitment to the family, while a negative answer would suggest more pragmatic ideas. In 1981 for the twelve countries, the national percentage responding positively was highly correlated (a rank order correlation of 0.9) with the total fertility rate. A positive response was given by two-thirds or more of respondents in the age range 18–44 years in five of the twelve European countries for which data were available. In contrast, less than 50 per cent responded positively in the three countries with the lowest fertility: The Netherlands, Denmark, and the Federal Republic of Germany. The fact that the survey was repeated in 1990 makes it possible to investigate the extent to which observed shifts in fertility during the 1980s were associated with changes in family-related values. Shown in Table 4.5 are the aggregate responses (means or percentages) for three age groups in each of six countries to questions asked in both survey years. In three

Table 4.5 Change in attitudes towards partnership and parenthood 1981–1990 in six European countries where fertility changed

		Denmark 81	Denmark 90	Sweden 81	Sweden 90	USA 81	USA 90	Italy 81	Italy 90	Spain 81	Spain 90	Ireland 81	Ireland 90
Total fertility rate		1.4	1.7	1.6	2.1	1.8	2.1	1.6	1.3	2.0	1.3	3.1	2.2
Whether agree fidelity very important for a successful marriage; percent agreeing.	18–24	62	83	77	92	93	93	76	87	65	69	84	89
	25–34	68	78	79	92	93	94	72	81	71	73	89	92
	35–44	72	76	73	91	89	93	82	74	78	80	90	90
	18–44	68	79	76	92	92	94	77	80	71	74	92	90
Extent to which adultery justified; mean value on scale, range 1 (= never) to 10 (= always).	18–24	3.59	2.31	3.10	2.10	2.77	2.18	3.61	3.52	3.61	3.45	2.54	2.31
	25–34	3.39	2.60	2.49	1.74	2.50	1.89	3.57	3.76	3.10	2.95	1.91	2.10
	35–44	2.68	2.24	2.61	2.19	2.38	1.98	2.71	3.68	2.61	2.53	1.76	2.08
	18–44	3.21	2.40	2.67	2.01	2.58	1.98	3.27	3.67	3.15	2.97	2.11	2.15
Whether agree marriage is an outdated institution; percent agreeing.	18–24	30	23	21	13	14	8	27	12	40	23	19	18
	25–34	23	26	17	14	10	9	32	15	35	23	16	7
	35–44	14	19	20	17	7	6	18	17	21	15	10	11
	18–44	22	23	19	15	11	8	26	15	33	20	16	12

Whether agree parents' duty is to do their best for their children even at the expense of their own wellbeing; percent agreeing.	18–24	35	40	56	58	73	74	57	69	66	66	66	57
	25–34	41	45	63	54	69	76	54	67	65	68	73	67
	35–44	47	47	69	60	69	72	57	79	79	78	81	74
	18–44	41	44	64	57	71	74	56	72	70	71	73	67
Whether agree one must always love and respect one's parents regardless of their faults; percent agreeing.	18–24	31	42	32	48	73	72	75	77	56	74	67	68
	25–34	34	38	38	48	73	75	75	79	63	75	78	72
	35–44	43	43	52	49	70	70	79	85	71	81	83	78
	18–44	36	41	43	48	72	73	76	80	63	77	75	73
Whether agree children very important for a successful marriage; percent agreeing.	18–24	15	17	24	51	56	54	50	58	61	62	47	47
	25–34	23	35	45	60	56	66	50	54	66	69	56	64
	34–44	37	43	49	64	58	58	54	57	71	76	55	64
	18–44	26	33	42	59	57	60	51	56	65	69	52	59
Ideal family size of 3 or more, percent preferring.	18–24	27	36	31	40	40	42	28	38	55	37	80	76
	25–34	30	34	27	47	38	43	23	31	46	30	80	63
	35–44	38	39	33	42	39	37	28	34	55	40	84	74
	18–44	32	36	30	43	39	40	26	34	52	35	81	71

Source: Surveys in 1981 and 1990 conducted by the International Value Systems Study Group.

of the countries (left-hand panel) total fertility rate had increased in the 1980s, and in three (right-hand panel) it had declined. Three of the questions shown are about attitudes towards partnership and four are about attitudes to parenthood.

Responses to the questions about partnership indicate a general increase in approval of fidelity and in support for the institution of marriage – whether fertility increased or decreased in the period. There is also a general increase in support for the idea that children have an absolute duty to their parents, and for the view that children are very important for a successful marriage. Responses to the question about parents' duty to children show no consistent pattern of change. The popularity of an ideal family size of three or more children shows an increase in all the three countries which had a fertility increase, especially for the younger cohorts. Italy too shows this increase despite its fertility decline during the period. Responses to this question in Ireland and Spain show a decline in the popularity of relatively large families in all three cohorts. Taken together, the results suggest that there was a shift between 1981 and 1990 towards a preference for a more traditional family structure, and that the shift was dominated by changes in attitudes to the requirements of successful partnership.

These findings were supported by a principal components analysis, using national responses obtained from the values surveys in 15 countries (13 European countries, the United States, and Canada) in 1981 and 1990 (Simons 1995). The questions used were those shown in Table 4.5 and several others. The results suggested that the fertility increase in Northern Europe had reflected a general shift towards more uncompromising attitudes to family obligations. In southern Europe and Ireland on the other hand, the fertility decline had reflected a general shift towards conformity to utilitarian attitudes. In western Europe, where change in fertility was negligible, the usual direction of movement in attitudes was towards more stress on personal autonomy.

It was suggested earlier that, in the conditions of modern Europe, fertility level was likely to depend on society's success in maintaining the commitment of its members to values that make family-building important to people despite its costs. The analysis summarised above supports this view. Sociologists will recognise the origins of these ideas in Emile Durkheim's work on social integration (e.g. Durkheim 1988).

Details of the findings summarised above, and of the theory used to interpret them, have been reported elsewhere (Simons 1995, 1986a, 1986b, 1982). Complementary findings and further theorising, based on individual-level analyses of the Values survey and other surveys have been presented in papers by Lesthaeghe (1995) Lesthaeghe and Meekers (1986) and Lesthaeghe and Surkyn (1988).

Not surprisingly, given the expense of child-bearing in the West, it has often been suggested that the explanation of fertility decline lies in the economics of reproduction. Ermisch (1996) reviews evidence to support the view that, for European countries, the percentage of women employed is strongly correlated with the divorce rate, and that in Britain there is a strong association between the number of months spent in paid employment since becoming a mother and the monthly probability of divorce. He goes on to argue that, because lone parenting is difficult and usually associated with a low standard of living, a higher risk of divorce in society will discourage childbearing and marriage. Further, because the production and nurture of children is one of the main benefits of marriage, having fewer children and having them later in life will increase divorce rates and reduce marriage rates. In short, on this view, the interaction among women's employment, divorce and fertility acts to reinforce the fall in marriage and fertility rates and the rise in divorce and women's employment.

The cost of children is another determinant. Ermisch points out (p. 154) that, in industrialised countries, jobs have tended to require more education and training. This has led to parents investing more resources in each child, which has been another factor tending to reduce fertility. One of the important resources invested in children is parental time, especially the mother's time. The cost of this time is the earnings forgone by the mother in devoting time to childcare. In consequence, fertility would be expected (p. 156) to be inversely related to women's wages relative to men's. Ermisch refers to analyses which appear to support his view that increases in women's relative pay were primarily responsible for the decline in British fertility between 1952 and 1985 and the steep fall in fertility in Japan since the early 1970s.

Social consequences of population ageing

A society supports its elderly population from its current output and income. As shown in Table 4.4, the elderly dependency ratio (the population aged 65 and over as a percentage of the population aged 15–64) is increasing, and it will continue to do so. This implies (assuming no other relevant changes) a substantial increase in the per capita cost of supporting the elderly. Because the proportion of the elderly who reach advanced ages will also increase, there will be a real increase in the burden on health and social services.

In a review of these effects, Weaver (1986) reports that, between 1960 and 1980, social security pension payments as a percentage of gross domestic product increased sharply. They doubled in the United Kingdom, Austria and Belgium, and tripled in Switzerland, Sweden and The Netherlands. This was not due to population ageing alone, but also to the fact that provisions were made more generous. The economic events of the 1970s created serious problems for the payment systems:

reserves were wiped out in the attempt to meet escalating benefit payments in the face of an eroding tax base. In response, virtually every country increased taxes.

According to Weaver, the bulge in retirements in the next century will mean insolvency for social security systems around the world. On the other hand, population ageing also implies some savings in the costs of supporting children, because there will be fewer of them. According to some analysts, these savings may at least partly offset the rise in the costs of the elderly. And the elderly might themselves encourage this to happen. An increase in their number increases their voting strength, and this may lead to an improvement in the state's contribution to their well-being, at the expense of its contribution to schooling and other resources for children (Coale 1986).

An international symposium on population was convened by the United Nations in 1987. Its report was not pessimistic about the dependency burden. It was agreed that the share of total income going to the elderly was likely to increase, but the report argued that the absolute levels of after-tax income per worker would continue to rise as a result of increased productivity and a reduced burden of youth dependency. The funding of pensions would be a problem but not an insoluble one. The reduced burden of childcare in an ageing population could help families to pay higher contribution rates. Eliminating compulsory retirement and raising the age of pension eligibility from 60 to 65 years could substantially reduce the expenditures of pension schemes, by 50 per cent in some cases (United Nations 1988b).

Evidently, much will depend on the capacity of countries to improve the productivity of the ageing labour force. The United Nations symposium mentioned above was sanguine about the prospects of doing so. To prevent the knowledge and skills of an ageing labour force becoming obsolete, opportunity and incentives for retraining could be provided. It was suggested that population ageing might actually increase per-capita income by permitting a greater labour-force participation of women, and by increasing the per-capita availability of capital. For a useful discussion of the relationships between demographic change, economic growth and social welfare, see Ermisch and Joshi (1987).

Policy implications

Pronatalist policy

Given the adverse consequences of low fertility, it is not surprising that governments in several countries have tried to persuade their populations to produce more children. According to responses to a United Nations survey in 1986, nine European countries thought their rates of population growth were too low: Bulgaria, the German Democratic Republic,

Hungary, Romania, Greece, France, the German Federal Republic, Liechtenstein and Monaco. With the exception of the Federal Republic of Germany, all these countries had instituted policies aimed at encouraging higher fertility (United Nations 1988a: 34–5). The majority of European countries regarded their growth rate as satisfactory, but five reported having made attempts to maintain the current rates.

Those countries which considered their rates of growth too low wished them to be equal to or slightly higher than the level necessary to ensure population replacement. The measures taken to achieve this aim have ranged from child allowances to housing loans and the right to paid leave from work. Such measures are often included in family policy even in countries which do not have an explicit aim of increasing fertility. Where this is the aim, the measures taken are more likely to be tuned to specific demographic events. For example, in some countries women receive a special allowance on the birth of a third child.

It is difficult to assess the effectiveness of pronatalist policy because fertility is being affected by so many other influences at the same time. According to Klinger (1987: 420) the measures taken affect attitudes to fertility for very short periods only. Most analysts appear to believe that new or increased incentives to produce a child have at most a temporary effect on the timing of births rather than on the size of the completed family (McIntosh 1986: 323). However, some successes have been reported. Calot and Hecht (1978) estimate that approximately 10 per cent of French fertility in the late 1940s and 1950s could be attributed to the effects of family policy. Hoem (1990) attributes the relatively high fertility of Sweden to social policies that have 'consistently tried to facilitate women's entry into the labor market and their continued attachment to it at minimal cost to childbearing and childrearing'. Klinger (1987) reviews evidence of the effects of pronatalist policy in several countries. Gauthier (1996) reviews a range of evidence on the demographic effects of welfare benefits, and concludes that they are very small compared to the effects of other factors.

Demeny (1986: 354) believes that measures could be devised that would be much more effective than those that have been tried to date. One of his suggestions is to allow parents to benefit directly in old age from having raised children, by allocating part of individuals' social security contributions to their living but retired parents.

International migration

Major labour migrations to western Europe occurred during the 1960s and early 1970s, but ended in the mid-1970s when the recruitment of foreign workers ceased and strong immigration controls were imposed. Subsequently, most new arrivals were family members (especially wives and children) of immigrants who had settled permanently. It has been suggested that restrictive policies may soon need to be reversed, so that immigration could be used to compensate for fertility decline and reju-venate Europe's population. The feasibility of doing so has been the subject of recent studies.

Wattelar and Roumans (1991) estimated the migratory flows that would be required to offset population ageing. They found that a policy of using migrants to top up the population of working age, to make up for short-falls, could keep the elderly dependency ratio (which they defined as the ratio of those aged 20–64 years to those aged 65 years and over) at an acceptable level of 3 to 1. However, such a policy would require annual quotas of immigrants well above those to which countries are accustomed.

In 1985 the European Population Committee of the Council of Europe set up a special committee of demographers from eight member states to consider immigration policy and other issues arising from the differ-ences in population growth rates between Europe and the Third World.

The conclusions adopted by the Committee reject the idea that immi-gration could be even a partial remedy for Europe's population prob-lem. In fact the Committee recommended that Europe make a sustained effort to promote development in countries lying south and east of the Mediterranean, as a means of eliminating the conditions that encourage people in these countries to want to come to Europe. Another recom-mendation was that Europe respond more generously than in the past to requests for help with attempts to curb rapid population growth in these countries and in the countries of sub-Saharan Africa. The committee believed it was a delusion to suppose that immigration could com-pensate for the consequences of low fertility and thought that, instead, European countries should adopt pronatalist social policies.

Conclusion

Despite the decline in fertility, it is premature to suppose that Europe faces demographic extinction. The fact that fertility rose after the long decline that came to an end in the 1930s, and boomed between the mid-1950s and mid-1960s, indicates the regenerative capacities of European societies. It has been suggested (Simons 1986b) that these earlier up-swings were a response to familist tendencies generated by 1930s anomie and enhanced by the experience of the Second World War. It is not inconceivable that fertility could rise again in response to the experience of social malaise. The relative stability of fertility in some countries in recent years and the upswings in the Nordic countries show that con-tinuing decline is not inevitable. Nevertheless, there is no reason to expect, in the foreseeable future, an upswing in Europe's fertility substantial enough to reverse the ageing process. The ageing of their populations will pose complex problems for European society, and will make heavy demands on their resources and resourcefulness.

References

Brass, W. (1989) 'Is Britain facing the twilight of parenthood?', in H. Joshi (ed.) *The Changing Population of Britain*, Oxford: Blackwell.

Calot, G. and Blayo, C. (1982) 'Recent course of fertility in Western Europe', *Population Studies*, 36(3): 349–72.

Calot, G. and Hecht, J. (1978) 'The control of fertility trends', in *Population Decline in Europe*. New York: St Martin's Press, 178–96.

Coale, A. (1986) 'Demographic effects of below-replacement fertility and their social implications', in K. Davis, M. Bernstam and R. Ricardo-Campbell (eds) Below-replacement Fertility in Industrial Societies – Causes, Consequences, Policies, *Population and Development Review*, Supplement to Vol. 12, 1986, New York: Population Council, 203–16.

Coleman, D. (1996) 'New patterns and trends in European fertility: international and sub-national comparisons', in D. Coleman (ed.) *Europe's Population in the 1990s*, Oxford: Oxford University Press, 1–61.

Davis, K. (1986) 'Low fertility in evolutionary perspective', in K. Davis, M. Bernstam and R. Ricardo-Campbell (eds) Below-replacement Fertility in Industrial Societies – Causes, Consequences, Policies, *Population and Development Review*, Supplement to Vol. 12, 1986, New York: Population Council, 335–58.

Demeny, P. (1986) 'Pronatalist policies in low-fertility countries: patterns, performance, and prospects', in K. Davis, M. Bernstam and R. Ricardo-Campbell (eds) Below-replacement Fertility in Industrial Societies – Causes, Consequences, Policies, *Population and Development Review*, Supplement to Vol. 12, 1986, New York: Population Council, 335–58.

Durkheim, E. (1988) 'Suicide and fertility: a study of moral statistics', trans. H. Sutcliffe (1992) *European Journal of Population*, 8: 175–97.

Ermisch, J. (1996) 'The economic environment for family formation', in D. Coleman (ed.) *Europe's Population in the 1990s*, Oxford: Oxford University Press, 144–62.

Ermisch, J. and Joshi, H. (1987) 'Demographic change, economic growth and social welfare', in *Proceedings of Plenary Sessions of European Population Conference, Finland, June 11–16 1987*, Helsinki: Central Statistical Office of Finland, 329–86.

Eurostat (1990) *Demographic Statistics 1990*, Luxembourg: European Community.

Gauthier, A. (1996) 'The measured and unmeasured effects of welfare benefits on families: implications for Europe's demographic trends', in D. Coleman (ed.) *Europe's Population in the 1990s*, Oxford: Oxford University Press, 297–331.

Hoem, J. M. (1990) 'Social policy and recent fertility change in Sweden', *Population and Development Review*, 16(4): 735–48.

Kiernan, K. (1996) 'Partnership behaviour in Europe: recent trends and issues', in D. Coleman (ed.) *Europe's Population in the 1990s*, Oxford: Oxford University Press, 62–91.

Klinger, A. (1987) 'Policy response and effects', in *Proceedings of Plenary Sessions of Population Conference, Finland, June 11–16 1987*, Helsinki. Central Statistical Office of Finland, 387–432.

Le Bras, H. (1991) 'Demographic impact of post-war migration in selected OECD countries', in *Migration – the Demographic Aspects*, Paris: OECD, 15–27.

Lesthaeghe, R. (1983) 'A century of demographic and cultural change in Western Europe: an exploration of underlying dimensions', *Population and Development Review*, 9(3): 411–35.

Lesthaeghe, R. (1995) 'The second demographic transition', in K. A. Mason and A. Jensen (eds) *Gender and Family Change in Industrialized Societies*, Oxford: Clarendon Press, 17–62.

Lesthaeghe, R. and Meekers, D. (1986) 'Value changes and the dimensions of familism in the European Community', *European Journal of Population* (1986) (2): 225–68.

Lesthaeghe, R. and Surkyn, J. (1988) 'Cultural dynamics and economic theories of fertility change', *Population and Development Review*, 14(1): 1–45.

McIntosh, C. A. (1986) 'Recent pronatalist policies in Western Europe', in K. Davis, M. Bernstam and R. Ricardo-Campbell (eds) Below-replacement Fertility in Industrial Societies – Causes, Consequences, Policies, *Population and Development Review*, Supplement to Vol. 12, 1986, New York, Population Council, 318–34.

Meslé, F. (1996) 'Mortality in Eastern and Western Europe: a widening gap', in D. Coleman (ed.) *Europe's Population in the 1990s*, Oxford: Oxford University Press, 127–43.

Monnier, A. (1996) 'La Conjuncture démographique: l'Europe et les pays dévelopés d'outre-mer', *Population*, 51(4–5): 1005–30.

Preston, R. (1986) 'The decline of fertility in non-European industrialized countries', in K. Davis, M. Bernstam, R. Ricardo-Campbell (eds) Below-replacement Fertility in Industrial Societies – Causes, Consequences, Policies, *Population and Development Review*, Supplement to Vol. 12, 1986, New York: Population Council, 176–95.

Salt, J. (1966) 'Migration pressures on Western Europe', in D. Coleman (ed.) *Europe's Population in the 1990s*, Oxford: Oxford University Press, 92–126.

Sardon, J-P. (1986) 'Évolution de la nuptialité et de la divortialité en Europe depuis la fin des années 1960', *Population*, 41(3): 463–82.

Sardon, J-P. (1990) *Cohort Fertility in Member States of the Council of Europe*. Strasbourg: Council of Europe.

Simons, J. (1982) 'Reproductive behaviour as religious practice', in C. Höhn and R. MacKensen (eds) *Determinants of Fertility Trends: Theories Reexamined. Proceedings of a seminar held by the International Union for the Scientific Study of Population, Bad Homburg, April 1980*, Liège: Ordina, 131–45.

Simons, J. (1986a) 'How conservative are British attitudes to reproduction?' *Quarterly Journal of Social Affairs*, 2(1): 41–54.

Simons, J. (1986b) 'Culture, economy and reproduction in contemporary Europe', in D. Coleman and R. Schofield (eds) *The State of Population Theory*, Oxford: Blackwell, 256–78.

Simons, J. (1995) 'Fertility and values in 15 western countries during the 1980s', in Ruut de Moor (ed.) *Values in Western Societies*, Tilburg: Tilburg University Press, 251–69.

United Nations (1988a), *World Population Trends and Policies, 1987 Monitoring Report*, New York: United Nations.

United Nations (1988b) *Economic and Social Implications of Population Ageing: Proceedings of an International Symposium on Population Structure and Development, Tokyo, September 1987*, New York: United Nations.

United Nations (1989) *World Population at the Turn of the Century*, Population Studies No. 111, New York: United Nations.

United Nations (1995) *World Population Prospects: The 1994 Revision*, New York: United Nations.

Valkonen, T. (1987) 'Social inequality in the face of death', in *Proceedings of Plenary Sessions of European Population Conference, Finland, June 11–16 1987*, Helsinki: Central Statistical Office of Finland, 201–61.

Wattelar, C. and Roumans, G. (1991) 'Simulations of demographic objectives and migration', in *Migration – the Demographic Aspects*, Paris: OECD, 57–67.

Weaver, C. L. (1986) 'Social security in ageing societies', in K. Davis, M. Bernstam and R. Ricardo-Campbell (eds) Below-replacement Fertility in Industrial Societies – Causes, Consequences, Policies, *Population and Development Review*, Supplement to Vol. 12, 1986, New York: Population Council, 273–94.

CHAPTER 5

Gender and Europe: cultural and structural impediments to change

ANGELA GLASNER

Introduction

Gender continues to be a major structural dimension in European societies. European women still outnumber European men, although the gap is closing: 51.2 per cent of the population is female, a ratio that is relatively constant across the member states of the European Community, highest in Portugal where in 1993 women represented 51.8 per cent of the population and lowest in the UK where they constitute just 51.06 per cent.[1] However, while they constitute a numeric majority, and despite an abundance of national and international legislation to prevent discrimination against them, women throughout Europe remain a disadvantaged group. This chapter is about exploring and understanding these gender differences. It discusses the extent to which women across Europe share experiences, for despite different cultures and traditions, there is evidence of a widespread commonality of disadvantage in the position of women both across Europe and beyond. After briefly reviewing the role played by the European Commission in attempting to establish commonality of practice across large parts of Europe, the chapter looks at the activities of women themselves through the development of feminism during the last three decades. In evaluating the impact of European Community policy and feminism, the chapter focuses on abortion and childcare as exemplars of the constraints which impinge on women's private lives, and on employment and the world of politics, as illustrations of the public arena of women's experiences. It concludes with a brief discussion of the experience of old age among European women.

There is a long history to gender differences and an equally long history to women's attempts to address the differences. Across the Western world, although not entirely throughout Europe, women's organisations from the nineteenth century campaigned for the abolition of laws that discriminated against them and for the introduction of those which would facilitate their emancipation. By the second quarter of the twentieth century, it was largely believed that women had achieved emancipation and that equality was no longer an issue.[2] However, during the 1950s and 1960s, issues of equality slowly began to re-emerge with the recognition that despite a higher involvement in employment outside the home, and apparent equality in access to education, women were still significantly disadvantaged. The late 1960s and early 1970s saw the emergence of what has been described as the Second Wave of Feminism. This period also saw the emergence of Europe as a new economic, and subsequently political and social, force. Joni Lovenduski (1988) suggests that with the emergence of feminism in the late 1960s and early 1970s, women began to influence policy processes and outcomes again, as their predecessors had in the mid-nineteenth century during the First Wave of Feminism. For Buckley and Anderson (1988) there was a 'happy coincidence' in the establishment of the European Community and the growth of the Second Wave of Feminism,[3] and this raises the question of how far the European Community has reduced discrimination against women and increased the commonality of experience across Europe.

The role of the European Community in promoting equal opportunities

Within the Treaty of Rome, signed in 1957 and implemented with respect to France, Germany, Italy, Belgium, The Netherlands, and Luxembourg in 1967, Article 119 specifically addressed women's equal rights in employment.[4] By the early 1980s, with the full membership of 12 partner nations and following the implementation of the Social Charter in 1975, equality of opportunity had become the focus of explicit attention, and in 1982 the first Equal Opportunities Action Programme was launched. The Action Programme recognised that equal pay was only the starting point for a campaign whose ultimate aim was the realisation of full participation in society for women.[5] The programme was designed to strengthen and extend existing individual rights through legislation, but also to change habits and traditions by means of positive action. On the legal front, it required member states to take action to monitor equal opportunities implementation; provide legal redress with respect to equal treatment; review protective legislation, social security entitlement, and taxation; extend equal opportunities as embedded in Article 119 to self-employed women and those working in other protected sectors such as agriculture; and to extend parental leave entitlement and abolish discrimination against pregnant women in employment.

It was thus recognised in the first Action Programme that stereotyped attitudes to the roles and responsibilities of both women and men persisted and had been accentuated by the economic crises which had spread throughout Europe in the 1970s and 1980s, and that the question of equality could not be addressed solely through economic and labour-force directed policies. The programme therefore also sought to facilitate the development of positive action budgets for training for career enhancement, and to promote the desegregation of employment.

In assessing the success of the first programme in 1986, the Commission concluded that although progress had been made, much remained to be done. A new Action Programme[6] was designed to consolidate existing rights under Community Law,[7] to follow up and develop the action launched under the earlier initiative, to engage in a broader consciousness-raising campaign, and to develop and intensify support for specific actions, particularly in relation to women's employment. In May 1991, a third medium-term community Action Programme, this time entitled 'Equal Opportunities for Women and Men' was adopted. The new programme spanning 1991–1995 and published in *Women of Europe 34* (1991) aimed to develop new initiatives directed at women in the vocational training and employment area and to achieve a better integration and more comprehensive strategy for action across the community. It had a three-pronged focus: the implementation and development of the law; the integration of women into the labour market; and improving the state of women in society. The last of these objectives is interesting: for the first time the importance of measures to promote the participation of women in the decision-making process in economic and social life is recognised and, along with the involvement of women in media and the presentation of positive images of women, is a specific target. Given the Community's original constitution it is perhaps not surprising that in the third initiative the lack of visible progress forces attention to broader social and cultural areas of community life.

In a comprehensive review of the Community's policy on the equality of women from the Treaty of Rome to the present day, Mariagrazia Rossilli concludes that, notwithstanding the goal of a more balanced participation of women in decision-making processes at all levels of society rather than simply a concern with work-related issues, the overall legislative initiatives of the 1990s are not promising. She cites as the one exception to this the recent Directive on parental leave that must be implemented in the member states through collective agreements between the social partners. The earlier Directive on the protection of the safety and health of pregnant workers was approved in 1992 with the abstention of the British and Italian governments. Opposition by the Italians was because the standard set was lower than that provided by the national law, and indeed only the position of women in Britain and Portugal was improved by the Directive. Rossilli argues that the principal factor constraining more progressive legislation is the drive to maintain the international competitiveness of the European economy. This leads, she suggests, to a '*de facto* tendency towards harmonization in a downwards direction of national protective standards' (Rossilli 1997: 73).

The concern with equal opportunities and gender-related issues has not been unique to the European Community. Randall (1987) notes the important role played by the United Nations after the Second World War in proclaiming 1975 International Women's Year and the following ten years the Decade for Women. The ten-year World Plan which launched the decade pinpointed the three critical areas for women as achieving equality with men, integration into national economic life and development programmes, and recognition of women's contribution to world peace.[8] The end of the decade saw the publication of a document containing *Forward Looking Strategies for the Advancement of Women*. Despite the non-binding nature of the document, the decade was undoubtedly important in generating a better and more informed understanding of women's position in the world, and in raising women's consciousness and governmental awareness of women's issues, including those associated with employment, the family and sexuality.

Is there a European feminist movement?

The international equality movements which developed in the 1970s and 1980s can on the one hand be seen as an outcome of the enlightenment of the individual nation states and, perhaps, a rational response to the labour-market pressures of advanced capitalism. On the other hand, it would be absurd to ignore the impact of the feminist movement over more than 100 years in raising consciousness to women's issues across the world. The movement is most certainly not a simple phenomenon to understand, and indeed we can question the extent to which it is a single movement as such. Many writers[9] identify clear distinctions, and some would argue divisions, within feminism both nationally and internationally,[10] and it is certainly the case that, despite some areas of clear consensus over the past 100 years, feminists of the world have been concerned with different issues, have espoused different agendas and embraced different strategies.

The first wave of European feminism, which spanned the period from the mid-nineteenth to the first quarter of the twentieth century, had a varied but pervasive impact across Europe. Its legacy was not only the emancipation of women but subsequently in certain countries a series of policy changes with new measures in health, education and welfare policy in the 1940s and 1950s. It was on this stage that the second wave arose in the 1970s, a renaissance, Lovenduski (1986) suggests, that began during the 1960s in a number of countries and which was by the 1970s a truly international movement. Under the umbrella of women's liberation, a great variety of new women's organisations came into existence alongside old, more established organisations. In Britain, as indeed in Scandinavia, that old wave had never been truly extinguished but has been replaced by what Banks (1981) calls 'welfare feminism' when in addition to established feminist causes, many women were active in the peace movement and others in the birth-control movement. A variety of factors, the commemoration of 50 years of suffrage, the growth of militancy among working-class women,[11] and the rise of the student left associated with revitalised Marxist parties of the 1960s, combined with growing militancy over the persisting inequalities of pay to provide the stimulus to the British and other European Second Wave feminist movements.

In Britain, marches were held on International Women's Day in March 1971, by which time four basic demands had emerged as the central British women's liberation platform: equal pay; equal opportunities in education and work; free contraception and abortion on demand; and free 24-hour nurseries. By 1978, three further demands were added: financial and legal independence; a woman's right to determine her own sexuality; and freedom from intimidation and the use of violence or sexual coercion.[12] From these demands came a variety of activities and, Lovenduski suggests, four distinct campaigns. Childcare was the earliest but least successful of all the demands, with provision actually declining after the mid-1970s, whereas the women's aid movement, most visibly realised with the setting up by Erin Pizzey of the first refuge for battered wives in Chiswick in 1972, has been an enduring phenomenon backed by the establishment in 1975 of a national Women's Aid Federation. The third demand for abortion was launched through the establishment of the National Abortion Campaign in 1975 aimed at defending the 1967 Abortion Act. Finally, there were various women against violence campaigns, realised in the opening of the first rape crisis centre in London in 1976.

Randall (1987) suggests that by the end of the 1970s, radical feminists were in the ascendency in Britain and they had set the agenda for the movement. Indeed, by the end of the decade, the issues of rape and marital violence were popularly endorsed and reflected in numerous discussion articles in the popular press and women's magazines. It was during the 1980s, however, that two further issues came to the fore. In 1978, the Organisation of Women of African and Asian Descent was founded and increasingly throughout the 1980s Black women of Afro-Caribbean and Asian descent have challenged the introspection of the White majority of the British women's movement and their conscious and unconscious xenophobia. Second, the growth of the peace movement, centring around the Greenham Peace Campaign from 1982, has challenged the traditional concerns of radical and socialist feminism and, with the involvement of women such as Pat Arrowsmith, has provided an alternative media image of the feminist woman. In the 1980s, the growing vocalisation of gay women's and men's groups, both allied to and dissociated from the radical feminist movement, gave a higher media profile to lesbian issues and to the question of women's determination of sexuality.

Second Wave feminist movements of some kind now exist throughout Europe although, as Randall notes, political liberalism and repression have resulted in some waxing and waning in Spain and Greece. In Germany, Second Wave feminism crystallised early in the 1960s, providing some impetus for the British movement. A campaign to liberalise abortion was launched there in 1970, and by 1975 a more liberal abortion law had been enacted. Randall suggests that the German movement had a particularly significant impact on changing women's expectations which in turn led to significant modifications in the recruitment criteria and policies of the main political parties by the 1980s. The movement also had a particularly active 'wages for housework' campaign, but since the late 1970s and throughout the 1980s, Green issues – both environmental and lifestyle focused – have been an important influence in the women's movement, with the growth of the Green Party providing, according to Lovenduski, a change in the political environment which provides new opportunities for the German women's movement.

In France, as in Germany, the student uprising of 1968 provided the stimulus for women's liberation, although the Mouvement de Liberation des Femmes was not formally recognised by the media until 1970, largely because of its highly fragmented nature.[13] Abortion was an early issue for French feminists with the establishment of a specific movement in 1973 which spread rapidly and was responsible for organising illegal abortions and for aiding the liberalisation of abortion law in 1973. Rather than providing a united platform for French feminism, however, this success appears to have provided a source for division. Duchen (1986) suggests this is because abortion raised potentially contentious questions about the nature of motherhood and femininity. For Lovenduski (1986) it is the absence of any subsequent mobilising issue following abortion, and the lack of any sign of a groundswell of feminist opinion which account for the pattern of feminism in France, despite a visible, public, feminist presence as illustrated by the existence of feminist bookshops and meeting places, and a news source and information agency.

In contrast to France, Italian feminism has been vibrant and against the combined backcloth of Roman Catholicism and left-wing, Marxist politics, has achieved much. Again the student movement of the late 1960s provided an impetus for the women's movement, and two groups formed early.[14] The majority of the movement, however, has been comprised of small, informal local groups with mainly consciousness-raising goals.[15] Despite this, three issues in particular seem to have provided a uniting platform for Italian feminism: divorce; workplace status; and abortion. Lovenduski suggests that happened because the methods of consciousness-raising and the small group structure, often reflected in feminist collectives in ultra-left and trade-union organisations, served the Italian women's movement well particularly because, as feminism gained strength, political parties on the left attempted to incorporate it by paying more attention to women's issues. At the end of the abortion campaign, many writers suggest that the Italian movement changed from focusing on issues of rights to those of lifestyle.[16] The legislative focus has, however, concentrated on altering the law on rape.

Dutch, Danish and Norwegian feminism, like British feminism, have had strong links with the US movement, but their unique features are largely the product of indigenous factors. In Holland, the precursor to the new women's movement was the establishment of the Man-Vrouw-Maalschappij (the Men-Women-Society), founded by professional men and women and regarded by Lovenduski as the equivalent to the reformist National Organisation of Women in the USA. However, the movement really took off with the formation of Dolle Mina in 1970. Originally including men, Dolle Mina developed demands for sexual freedom, free abortion and contraception. However, the lack of a leadership structure and the absence of a theoretical underpinning undermined the veracity of the movement, and feminism in Holland has tended to be dispersed in a variety of women's organisations, especially in the political parties and trade unions, and in specific sectors of society such as education and the social services.

In Scandinavia, Dahlerup (1988) suggest that women's liberation movements have been strongest in Denmark and Norway. The New Feminists in Norway and the Redstockings in Denmark both began in 1970, with a focus on consciousness-raising activities and diffused, decentralised organisational structures. As in Holland, existing women's groups had remained active following the culmination of the First Wave, and had actively fought for married women's rights. This meant that the decentralised structures which have characterised the Second Wave have been able to work effectively on specific issues, and have mobilised working-class women, established women's studies courses, self-help refuges and rape-crisis support, abortion rights and women's meeting places.

Swedish feminism has had a different history to that of other European movements which Lovenduski attributes to the collectivist culture of the country and to the political context. While there have been rights groups of various kinds, there has been no Second Wave feminism as such. Most of the political parties in Sweden have strong and active women's groups and women constitute a third of parliamentarians. The country has a sex-equality policy which is often held up as an exemplar of equal opportunities provision, and the long period of uninterrupted social democratic rule facilitated the continued discussion and recognition of women's rights issues at the collective rather than the individual level.

Rather different political contexts, initially authoritarianism, and subsequently the demands of new democratic constitutions, circumscribed feminism in Spain, Portugal and Greece. Lovenduski suggests that women's emancipation in Spain and Portugal has been impeded by Catholicism, combined with the difficulties of advancing sectional women's issues in the context of extremes of poverty and low levels of industrial development. In Greece, the Democratic Women's Movement was founded in 1974 with a platform which included the promotion of equal opportunities, the liberation of women as individuals and associated legal reform. It later became concerned with the official treatment of rape victims and has always proceeded along traditional rights group lines, working to reform legislation. Following the collapse of the old politico-military regime, there was a massive increase in the number of women's organisations, but an autonomous movement is still, in many senses, in the embryonic stages.

The late 1980s and 1990s have been characterised as a period of crisis for feminism. The crisis has been seen to originate from a number of tensions and challenges: between the individualism of 'identity politics' which necessarily generates a fragmented feminist politics; with postmodernism which has as a central tenet the freeing of practice from an overarching philosophical given and the grounding of social criticism in specific locations and contexts; the incorporation of male politics within the movement; and the new right post-feminism which challenges the commonality of women's experience. Roberts (1992) describes feminism as neither dead nor dying, but – in Britain at least – in need of some intensive care. During this period, then, we have tended to see feminist perspectives informing a broader repertoire of experience and culture which has resonated well with the diversification of European Community policy. What is not yet clear is how far the feminism of the 1990s is capable of shaping and informing the European policy and practices of the next decade and century.

Feminism in Europe has thus exhibited a wide variety of forms and has a broad agenda of issues and concerns. The political context has clearly been important in determining the specific form and indeed in prescribing or proscribing feminism altogether. In Italy, Holland, Denmark and Norway, the Second Wave has been strongly influenced by left-wing politics and has been predominantly led by middle-class women. In France the movement has been largely contained within the academic community, and in Germany it has been significantly diluted by conservatism. Lovenduski suggests that in the case of Italy, Britain, Holland, Denmark and Norway, the campaigns for women's liberation have been enhanced by alliances with other groups and with traditional women's organisations. This in turn has led to more broadly based movements and to a unity of interests across class barriers. Elsewhere, she suggests, the restricted success of feminist movements can be accounted for by the fact that initiatives for much change came from other sources and in some cases, for example Sweden, actually predated the Second Wave movements. This meant that there was no uniting issue or theme to pull together the various strands of feminism. Randall similarly doubts the existence of a distinctively international or even European movement but she is more ready to assert the universality with which women's consciousness has been raised, and the importance of the international information networks which now abound.

At the policy level, however, there has been some uniformity of achievement, and the dissimilarities of the constituent European movements can be stressed at the expense of a true appraisal of these achievements. Throughout Europe enfranchised women are, in secular law, free to divorce, and abortion has been legalised in most of the European Community. In most European countries there are self-help and support organisations catering for raped and battered women, and legislation has been enacted to inhibit discrimination in education and employment. There have been common platforms; but there have also been differences.

Abortion

As we shall see, childbirth impacts significantly on women's life chances. Over the past thirty years, there has been a significant decline in the number of live births since abortion became legalised.[17] Abortion is a useful mechanism for understanding the extent of Europeanisation and the way in which women's lives have changed over the last thirty years. It illustrates well the link between the changing socio-political culture and women's liberation *and* the limitations of policy. As it clearly shows, national and supranational cultural values are pervasive forces shaping women's experiences. Joyce Outshoorn (1988) notes that western European states, with the exception of Belgium, Ireland, Portugal and Greece, reformed the law on abortion in the 1960s and 1970s, yet this does not mean that abortion is uniformly available throughout Europe, and in some parts it has been fiercely resisted. A study of abortion law reform in Western nations by Field (1979) has concluded that the major obstacle to change is the existence of a strong Roman Catholic church and a predominantly Catholic population, although even a small Catholic presence appears to exert strong pressure.

As Outshoorn notes, abortion law can take many forms, and the extent of variation in Europe in those states where abortion is legal is shown in Table 5.1 below. Outshoorn suggests that three main types of abortion law can be distinguished,[18] but as the table shows, the nature of the law does not appear to directly influence the number of abortions actually carried out. Across Europe as a proportion of live births, after an initial increase throughout the period between 1975 and 1985 when the aggregate rate rose from 21.1 per cent to 24.1 per cent, the abortion rate is generally declining. While we might have expected differences in the national patterns depending on the type of abortion available, it may be easier to understand this pattern if we consider policy implementation rather than the nature of the legislation *per se*. In Britain, for example, the availability of abortion depends greatly on the regional location, and is still influenced by medical attitudes and public expenditure. As Outshoorn notes, sometimes the intentions of the law are not strongly against a woman's right to choose, but the non-cooperation of hospitals and medical personnel and the costs of abortion itself mean that women's rights and choice are heavily curtailed. Conversely, where the law has been very restrictive, as for example in Ireland and in Italy until the late 1970s, women's access to abortion has been significantly mediated by class factors such as income and ability to travel.

Table 5.1   **Abortion in Europe 1981–1992**

Country	Number of abortions				Date of initial reform	Type of abortion law
	1981	1986	1991	1993		
Belgium	–	–	–	–	None	
Denmark	42.9	37.1	32.8	27.7	1970	On demand
France	22.4	21.4	22.5	–	1975	Term
Germany	14.0	13.8	10.8	11.1	1976	Mixed
Greece	–	–	10.8	–	1986	Term
Ireland	–	–	–	–	none	
Italy	36.1	34.0	28.4	26.9	1978	Term
Luxembourg	–	–	–	–	1979	Mixed
Netherlands	11.0	9.7	9.3	9.9*	1973	Indication
Portugal	–	–	–	–	Pending	
Spain	–	–	9.27	–	1985	Indication
UK	19.6	24.6	24.6	23.6	1967	Indication

Notes:
* data relate to 1992
Abortions are defined as a percentage of live births. Data on abortions are not available for Luxembourg. With the exception of Luxembourg where they are rising, live birth rates are declining throughout Europe.

The data for 1981 are drawn from *Women of Europe, Supplement 14*, 1984 and for 1986 from *Women of Europe, Supplement 30*, 1989. The data source for 1990–1992 is Council of Europe, *Recent Demographic Developments in Europe*, Brussels 1994. Other information is drawn from Outshoorn (1988) and supplemented by information from *Women of Europe, Supplement 27*, 1988.

That the issue of abortion is highly contested and controversial is illustrated by the way it contributed to the fall of the Dutch government in 1977, and similarly helped to bring down governments in Italy, West Germany and Belgium.[19] Curiously, and contrary to this usual pattern, abortion has been a largely non-party political issue in Britain. Since 1952, all Abortion Bills have been either Private Member's Bills or introduced under the '10 Minute Rule', and the Bill which successfully introduced abortion law reform in 1967 was introduced by a Liberal parliamentarian aided by extra reading time provided by a supportive Labour government.

Legislation alone is not sufficient to secure women's rights to self-determination in pregnancy. Two other factors are of importance: first the implementation of law, and second, throughout much of Europe, the extent to which there is organised opposition and resistance to abortion. In Britain, Steel's 1967 Act provoked the formation of the Society for the Protection of the Unborn Child (SPUC), and later LIFE, and there have been repeated attempts to introduce restrictive amendments to the law stimulated by the active campaigning of both groups. Perhaps more important in terms of women's access to abortion than reformist attempts at legislation are the policies and practices which govern its administration. Randall (1987) notes that the introduction in Britain in 1982 of new forms to certify the need for abortion, the availability of beds, and the length of waiting-lists for consultant appointments all act as effective restrictions on both the form of abortion available, and its extent.

Feminists have argued that access to abortion is a critical right because women's lives are hugely affected by the birth of their children: for radical feminists, abortion symbolises women's sexual and reproductive self-determination, and for others their rights to individual freedom of choice and effective participation in the workplace and other spheres of public life. In summarising the decade to 1988, Janine Mossuz-Lavau (1988) suggests that European women are not equally armed to exercise their rights in deciding when they want to have children, although the past ten years have been marked by what she describes as a true concern for women's rights to physical and sexual self-determination, a concern which has been linked to considerable evolution over the last three decades in the nature and form of the family.[20]

The family

There can be little doubt that social and demographic forces are bringing changes to the structure of European families and communities, and the impact of these changes is widespread: government pension and welfare schemes, health-care provision and education systems all experience consequential pressures.[21] What are these changes? How can they be understood and what consequences do they have for women's lives?[22]

A series of studies carried out by the European Community's Commission[23] since 1975 have shown some shift towards the concept of a complete equality of husbands' and wives' roles, but very little real change. While the concept of complete equality of marital roles has gained some ground, it is still a minority view held by only four in ten Europeans. The contrasting view that the woman's place is in the home is still strong, accounting for approximately a quarter of all attitudes, and approximately three in ten believe that the wife should have a less absorbing job and take on more of the housework than her husband. Comparative data suggest that the United Kingdom and Denmark are the most advanced countries in terms of attitudes, and Germany and Luxembourg the least advanced.

If attitudes alone were sufficient, then we should expect to find that objective measures of women's opportunities demonstrated greater advances in those countries where greatest liberalism prevailed. However, while attitudes are undoubtedly important in shaping women's lives, equally important in a climate in which women are still assumed

Table 5.2   **The dependent population in Europe**

Country	1980 actual	1990 actual	2000 projected	2010 projected	2020 projected
Belgium	52.4	49.2	50.9	49.3	57.0
Denmark	54.5	47.9	49.1	51.3	57.9
France	56.8	51.1	52.8	51.2	59.6
Germany	50.4	45.3	46.7	50.0	57.3
Greece	56.1	49.6	48.8	51.7	57.1
Ireland	70.0	61.4	49.8	51.3	52.6
Italy	54.9	45.5	47.8	51.5	58.8
Luxembourg	47.8	44.8	48.4	50.0	58.5
Netherlands	51.1	44.5	47.7	47.5	58.1
Portugal	58.6	50.7	46.4	46.6	50.0
Spain	58.1	49.3	45.3	46.9	52.7
UK	56.2	52.9	54.0	52.3	58.3

Notes:
The dependency ratio is the population aged 0–14 and 65 and over expressed as a percentage of the working aged population.

Source: OECD *Ageing Populations, Pension Systems and Government Budgets*, working paper no. 156, Paris, 1995

to have the dominant, if not exclusive, responsibility for domestic roles, are practical policies on childcare and support for the elderly and infirm.

In Europe, the young and elderly account for the major proportion of social expenditure. Across Europe, as shown in Table 5.2, there is a significant variation in the dependency ratio: that is, the proportion of young and elderly to working-aged people, with the current highest ratio in Ireland and the lowest in The Netherlands. With declining birth-rates across Europe except in Luxembourg, the dependency ratios are both declining and becoming more uniform across Europe. However, OECD projections envisage that by 2020 all member states will experience growth in the ratio, in some cases by a significant amount, as the proportion of elderly in the population increases with the transition of the post-war population bulge of Europe into retirement and out of the working population. In Ireland, Portugal and Spain, the proportion is not expected to rise significantly until after 2020, but elsewhere the dependency ratio is expected to edge close to 60 per cent and by the mid twenty-first century, the OECD average dependency ratio is expected to be 65.7. This dependent population is increasingly elderly: in 1980 approximately one-third of Europe's dependents were elderly; by 2050, the elderly will constitute over half of all dependents. If the current pattern of care for the elderly persists, then the burden falling on European women looks set to increase hugely unless there are significant policy initiatives and associated changes in expectations.

The elderly do not constitute the sole familial and community burden for women; children, in particular the preschool child, are for many women a significant factor. This burden is assumed differentially by the women of Europe, in part because of different cultural traditions, but also because of different national state policies. If attitudes alone were sufficient to determine women's choices and life chances, then with the greater liberalism apparent from the European Commission's studies we should expect that women in Britain and Denmark would experience greater workplace participation and more shared responsibility for childcare than elsewhere. However, as Oakley (1974) notes while modern industrial society has created opportunities for equality, it has carried over the ideology of women's innate difference from men, and their domesticity. The role of wife and mother, with very few exceptions, is incompatible with an occupational role and does not allow the individual woman to realise the dominant goal set by our culture. The main mechanisms which ensure this incompatibility are the provision of paid maternity leave and childcare, which also affect women's participation in other activities and their well-being, whether they are employed outside the home or not.

In reviewing the provision of childcare and maternity benefits in Europe in 1990, Peter Moss (1990) notes that between 1985 and 1988 employment rates for mothers increased in all European Community countries although it remains below 40 per cent, and of those who do work, a third are employed part-time. Britain was the last European country to implement universal maternity rights for employed women; as a result of the European Directive on Pregnant Workers, all employees earning at or above the lower earnings limit (set at £57 per week in 1994) have been entitled since October 1994 to statutory maternity pay regardless of the hours worked. The right to longer maternity absence and paid leave for antenatal care remain unchanged for British women and they have among the lowest entitlement in Europe. As shown in Table 5.3, in most countries, the full period of leave is covered by earnings-related payments, normally between 70–100 per cent, but in Britain only six weeks leave is covered by earnings-related pay, a further 12 weeks are paid at a lower rate, set at £52.50 in 1994, and most of the 29 weeks of postnatal leave are unpaid. Britain lags in the provision of parental leave as well, which is offered in seven other countries, and paid for in the majority of cases. Table 5.4 lists the extent to which there is paid provision for paternity leave, and with Table 5.3 provides a summary of the provision for parental leave across the European Community.

Even after the birth of the child, parents in Britain fare less well with a poverty of childcare provision that is only partially remedied by an earlier-than-average start to the process of full-time education: only in The Netherlands and the UK does full-time compulsory education begin at five years of age. In Spain preschool education is provided by the education authorities from birth, and in Belgium and France it begins

Table 5.3   **Maternity leave provision in Europe**

Country	Postnatal period	Payment
Belgium	8–14 weeks (6 prenatal)	82% of wage for 30 days then lower rate
Denmark	24 weeks (plus 4 prenatal)	90% maximum
France	16 weeks (6 prenatal) plus 2 for multiple births	85% of basic salary tax free
Germany	14 weeks (6 prenatal) plus 4 for multiple births	100%
Greece	105 days (53 prenatal)	100%
Ireland	14 weeks (4 prenatal)	70% tax free
Italy	5 months (2 prenatal) only if wage discontinued	80%
Luxembourg	16 weeks (8 prenatal) plus 4 for multiple births	100%
Netherlands	16 weeks only if salary discontinued	100%
Portugal	90 days (30 prenatal)	100%
Spain	16 weeks maximum, 18 for multiple births	75%
UK	18 weeks maximum (flexible start)	90% for 6 weeks then flat rate for 12 weeks

Source: *Social Protection in the Member States of the European Union*, European Commission, Luxembourg, 1995: 140

at two and two-and-a-half years respectively.[24] Unlike in Belgium, France, Luxembourg and Portugal, there is no tax relief for childcare costs, nor for domestic help, as in Germany. The Netherlands has ended its system of tax relief and instead has directed the monies saved to an increased provision of publicly funded services; and Belgium, France, Luxembourg and Portugal also have policies of increasing publicly funded services. In Spain, tax relief was introduced in 1991, and in Italy, while parents pay for publicly funded services for under three-year-olds, local authorities subsidise the costs to the level of two-thirds or more. By comparison, in Britain, there are only publicly funded places for about 2 per cent of children aged under three, mostly in mixed age daycare centres which are provided mainly by local authorities for children who are severely disadvantaged or at risk. They are not designed to cater for working mothers, and the vast majority of under three-year-olds are in private care, with the costs unsubsidised. Overall, there is considerable

Table 5.4 **Paternity leave provision in Europe**

Country	Nature of the leave arrangements	Payment
Belgium	No statutory leave: workers can take 6–12 months 'career breaks' subject to employers' agreement	Flat rate; higher rate if taken within 6 years of birth of 2nd or 3rd child
Denmark	10 weeks In addition, can take 13–35 weeks of leave subject to employer's agreement	At maternity rate. Additional leave paid at flat rate
France	Until child reaches 36 months	Unpaid for 1st and 2nd child then flat rate
Germany	Until child reaches 36 months	Flat rate for first 6 months, then income related benefit until child is 2; last 12 months unpaid
Greece		100%
Ireland	None	–
Italy	6 months	30% of earnings
Luxembourg	None	–
Netherlands	6 months of reduced hours per parent (minimum of 20 hours a week) not transferable between parents	Unpaid
Portugal	24 months	Unpaid
Spain	12 months	Unpaid
UK	None	–

Source: *Eurostat*, European Commission, Luxembourg, 1995

variation in the provision for preschool children: countries vary in relation to the age at which children are allowed to attend school, the hours of schooling available, and the age at which compulsory education ends. Each of these factors influences the demand for supplementary services by parents who are at work.

Denmark has undoubtedly the most well-developed and comprehensive system of childcare, but it is closely matched by that found in France and Belgium, and for children older than three, by Germany and Italy. At the other end of the spectrum are Britain, Ireland and to a lesser extent, The Netherlands where in all cases there is negligible provision for under-threes, and little extra-school provision for those over three. Privately run nurseries and playgroups are widely used in Britain. Recent research by the Equal Opportunities Commission (EOC 1995) notes that 52 per cent of women with a child under five years of age were economically active. The EOC report notes that:

the type of daycare used by mothers of pre-school children depends largely on the age of the child and employment status of the mother: 32 per cent of children aged two and under do not receive any form of daycare, compared with only four per cent of those aged three and four. Over two-thirds of the care provided by unpaid family and friends for pre-school children is for ten hours per week or less. In contrast, of those who are in the care of paid childminders or nannies, nearly one half are looked after for 21 hours or more a week, indicating the importance of this daycare service for working mothers. (EOC 1995: 3)

The report also documents a shortage of various types of childcare provision, with a shortfall of day-nursery places for all under-fives, and of nursery school places for those aged three and four. This lack of provision impacts particularly on working mothers and lone parents.

Moss (1990) suggests that most countries provide, or are in the process of providing, two to three years of pre-primary schooling or kindergartens to the majority of their children. In Denmark, France, Italy and Belgium, over 80 per cent of children and in Spain, Greece and Germany 60–80 per cent of children experience such care. In Britain, Ireland and The Netherlands, pre-primary schooling is limited or not provided at all, and instead children are admitted relatively early to primary school or they attend playgroups. The latter offer a very short period of provision, on average five or six hours a week, and in Britain and Ireland they are not publicly funded but reliant on parental support, both physical and financial. Not only is the extent of provision variable, but its rate of growth varies significantly. Between 1985 and 1988/89, publicly provided services increased by more than 10 per cent in Denmark, France, Luxembourg and Portugal, and the attrition in the support for tax relief in The Netherlands meant that from 1989 a massive increase in public service expenditure was enabled. In Britain, Belgium, Italy, Ireland and Greece the rate of growth has been significantly slower, and in some cases non-existent. In Britain, the recently introduced voucher system for the provision of preschooling for children aged four years[25] is to be revoked by the newly elected Labour government. It is not yet clear what arrangements may be introduced to reduce the gap between the preschool opportunities and experiences confronting British children and their European counterparts, although early childhood learning has been targeted as a priority policy area.

Official data on privately funded services are more hard to come by and less reliable. The most significant private carers are relatives and they, often grandmothers, provide more care for children under three than any other type of service. In Britain there has been a growth in private nurseries, occasionally funded by employers, between 1985 and 1990, and this period also saw an increase in attempts to regulate the provision of private childcare. In 1988 registered family daycarers provided places for approximately 5 per cent of children under five. While the number of children being cared for in their own homes is difficult to ascertain, it probably does not exceed 2 per cent. For the vast majority of women who wish or need to work – particularly for those whose work is part-time – the typical childcarer for their children is a relative, likely to be the children's grandmother,[26] and the burden of care is likely to inhibit effective participation in the labour market.

As Moss notes, childcare is an issue of the labour force, of family policy and of women's welfare. It is also an issue for employers, as Lewis (1990) notes. She suggests that there are two major barriers which inhibit the effective incorporation of women into the labour market. First, the lack of suitable childcare facilities combined with an inflexibility of working arrangements in the majority of employing organisations, whether private or public sector organisations; and second the lack of provision leads to the 'child-bearing career break', and to its conscious and unconscious invocation when a women seeks a job and/or promotion. Childcare is thus irrevocably tied in with employment, and employment opportunities are irrevocably tied in with lifestyle opportunities. Childcare is therefore at the heart of equal opportunities for many women in Europe, not the least British women.

Employment

European Community policy has been directed explicitly at equal opportunities at work. The principle of equal pay for equal work was established in Article 119 of the Treaty of Rome, and reinforced by subsequent Directives aimed not only at ensuring equal pay for men and women, but also equal treatment with respect to access to employment, training, promotion, working conditions, and matters of social security such as pension rights. In this environment it might reasonably be expected that greatest strides forward in terms of gender equality would have been achieved at the workplace. However, the evidence suggests that while some steps forward have been taken, there is still considerable differentiation between men and women at work.

The number of women who work has steadily increased over the past two decades. In 1970 less than 29 per cent of European women worked, but by 1980 this had risen to 30 per cent and by 1994 38.5 per cent of European women aged over 15 are working with a further 13 per cent registered unemployed. However, as the data in Figure 5.1[27] show, the participation rate has varied considerably from one country to another. In 1970 both Britain and Denmark had participation rates in excess of 30 per cent and both remain at the top of the league in terms of the

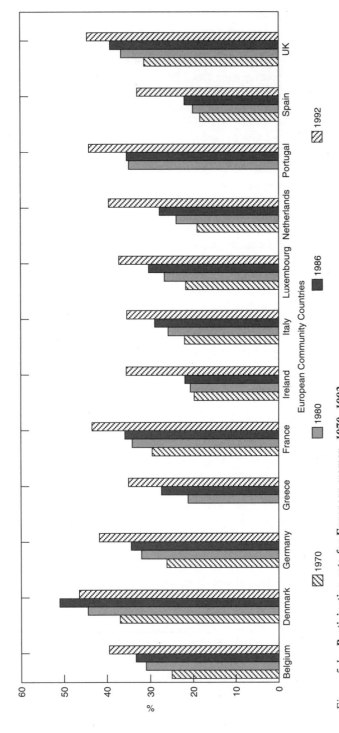

Figure 5.1   *Participation rate for European women, 1970–1992*

proportion of women who worked in 1986, with almost 40 per cent of British and 51 per cent of Danish women working. By 1992, the pattern had changed slightly with Denmark, Portugal and the UK all with participation rates of approximately 45 per cent and Belgium, Germany, France and The Netherlands at approximately 40 per cent. While Ireland and Spain remain at the bottom of the league, they now share this position with Greece, and the gap between these participation rates and those of the rest of Europe is decreasing. Throughout the last two decades there has been a surge of women into the labour market, and this is reflected in a relative growth of employment for women even during the recession, since when employment growth has slowed down. As Edye and Lintner (1996) note, during the period between 1985 and 1990, women took two-thirds of the 9 million jobs created across Europe. As they also note, women in the 25–49 age range are increasingly coming into employment as a response to the longer period of education and the earlier retirement patterns which are also characterising the European population as a whole. More than 80 per cent of the increased employment is in part-time jobs, and increasingly mothers are working. The pattern is, however, nationally different and among the several factors which account for this, the most important are marital status, childcare, and whether women work full-time or part-time.

As Figure 5.2 shows[28] Denmark (68.7 per cent) and Britain (58.6 per cent), together with France (51.7 per cent) and Portugal (55.4 per cent), have relatively high participation rates for married women, as they do for widowed and divorced women, with the rate rising fastest in Portugal. In Denmark and Portugal more than three-quarters of mothers are economically active; in Germany, France and Belgium approximately two-thirds of mothers work, and in Italy and the UK, over half of mothers are employed. In Germany, Greece, Spain, Ireland, Italy, Luxembourg and The Netherlands married women are significantly less likely to work than their single counterparts. Across Europe, the participation rate for women drops once they marry and less than a quarter of all married, widowed and/or divorced women work. In the majority of countries, the proportion of women in the labour force is higher for those without children than for those with, the exceptions being Belgium, Denmark, Greece, France and Portugal. Except in Denmark, the likelihood of a woman working decreases as the number of children under ten increases, although the impact of children is less if the woman works part-time.[29]

Although there have been some changes in recent years with the incidence of part-time working increasing for men, women are still much more likely to work part-time than men and, except in Greece, married women more likely to be part-time than their single counterparts, as is shown by Figure 5.3.[30] Overall only 18 per cent of unmarried women work part-time compared to 36 per cent of married women. Britain, Denmark and Germany have significantly higher than average rates, but it is not clear from the data alone whether this is an outcome of national

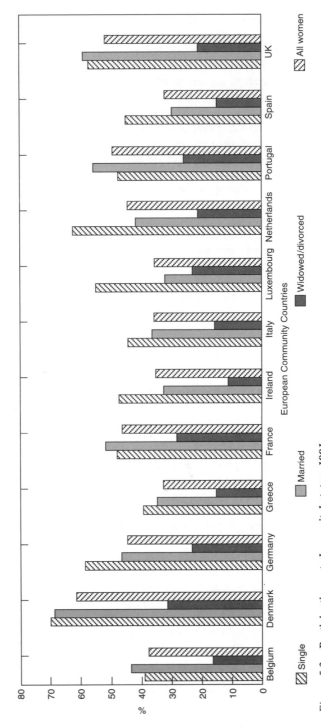

Figure 5.2 **Participation rate by marital status, 1991**

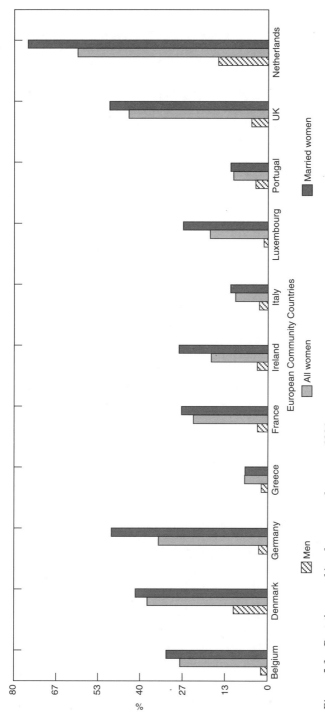

Figure 5.3 Part-time working by men and women, 1991

tradition or labour regulations, although in the case of Britain, the overall higher rates of part-time work for all women and for men suggests that there is a higher use of part-time employment than elsewhere in Europe. This may be a reflection of the growing pattern of flexibility in work, with a proliferation of casual, marginal and part-time work, including job-sharing. It is also the case that part-time work is concentrated in specific occupational sectors. For women in Italy, Greece, Portugal and Ireland it is in agriculture, whereas elsewhere in Europe, it is predominantly in the service sector. Little part-time work occurs in industry, and the concentration of part-time working in the agricultural and service sectors tends to enhance job segregation and inequality at work since these sectors are commonly poorer paid than industry.

Job segregation occurs where men or women are concentrated in different jobs, and across Europe gender segregation can be found both within the broad sectors of economic activity and between occupations within each sector. The majority of Europe's employed women, nearly three-quarters, work in the service sector rather than in either agriculture or industry, as Figure 5.4[31] shows, and they form an increasing proportion of all workers in that sector, accounting for 51 per cent of all service sector employees. However, women do not occupy the same jobs as men, even when working within the same sector, and within each occupation, women tend to cluster in the jobs and grades at the lower end of the spectrum where they experience lower pay and poorer working conditions.

Catherine Hakim (1979) suggests that segregation can be both vertical and horizontal. By horizontal segregation she refers to the separation of men and women into different types of occupation, so that men and women are found in different jobs. Vertical segregation refers to the tendency to find men in higher-grade occupations and women in lower-grade occupations, or vice versa. Segregation blurs into discrimination when the consequences of the segregation are inevitably unidirectional and disadvantageous. An OECD study in 1985[32] found that segregation continued to exist at a high level across all OECD countries. In particular the study found that the degree of segregation varied directly with the level of participation; those countries with the highest participation rate, such as the UK, also tended to have the greatest degrees of occupational segregation. It also found that segregation by industrial sector was less than segregation by broad occupational grouping, a reflection of the fact that women tend to be concentrated in a small range of occupations within different industries. However, economic restructuring, and in particular the growth of the service sector and a diminution in the size of the manufacturing sector, has tended, rather than reducing the aggregate level, to increase the extent to which segregation by industrial sector occurs.

There is a wealth of national data[33] documenting the nature and extent of gender segregation at work, but there are many difficulties in assessing the relative level of gender segregation in a comparative context, not the least of which is the lack of uniformity of measures and

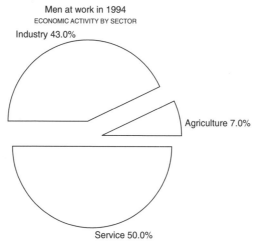

Figure 5.4 **Women and men at work in 1994**

the variation in the structure of national economies. Moreover, as Beechey (1989) points out, women's participation in the formal economy masks many variations in actual experience and pattern; simply put, similar patterns of participation may obscure widely different experiences, as for example is the case in Britain and France where similar rates are comprised in Britain of a high level of part-time and interrupted career employment, and in France of continuity and a work pattern not greatly dissimilar to male workers. Dex and Shaw (1986) have concluded from their comparative study of British and American workers that the higher level of upward occupational mobility of American women is in large part a consequence of their greater tendency to work full-time rather than part-time, although it may also be a function of the legislative context in that Britain has been slower to introduce equal pay and sex discrimination legislation. Crompton and Sanderson (1990) suggest that Italy illustrates clearly that while the early development of a policy on equal pay can have an important influence on women's employment opportunities, it is moderated by the cultural context. The active pursuit of equal pay for women since the 1960s has led to a greater protection of Italian women workers, but a low participation rate and the rapid growth of the informal sector, including homeworking, and small firms.

As Figure 5.4 has shown, there is clear evidence of differential participation in two of the three industrial sectors, and when we look within the sectors, we find that this segregation persists. In manufacturing, women are largely absent in the energy and water, engineering and petrochemical firms, while in the service sector, where they dominate overall, they are relatively under-represented in transport and communications and heavily present in the distributive trades and services, including banking, insurance and finance. Even in those sectors and jobs where women predominate, there is evidence of persisting vertical segregation. Jean Bocock (1991) analyses data on teaching in selected European countries and notes that within what is overall a significantly female occupation, women are concentrated in the lower echelons, and under-represented in the management grades. As Figure 5.5 shows, there is variation in the pattern across the ten countries chosen, with Portugal atypically showing almost equal representation of women in management and basic-grade primary teaching, and Greece showing this pattern for both primary and secondary teaching, but overall the percentage of female heads is about half that of basic-grade teachers. At the secondary level, characterised by generally higher status and better remuneration, the difference tends to be even greater, and there is a lower overall proportion of women teachers generally. This pattern in education holds for many other professions, services and industries, and is an illustration of what Hakim means by vertical segregation. Moreover, the 1985 study of women workers' attitudes found that the proportion of women holding executive or managerial jobs had dropped from 16 per cent in 1980 to 14 per cent in 1985. The 1980 study showed that most women work for male bosses or supervisors (68 per cent), and while 24 per cent of women worked in an exclusively female environment where their boss was female, only 4 per cent of women work in a mixed-gender environment with a female boss. As the study notes, and as Hakim's work highlights, in Britain the incidence of women working in an exclusively female environment is higher than in any other European country. Furthermore, as Hakim suggests, where segregation has been eroded at all in Britain, it is because men are entering jobs which traditionally have been the preserve of women, and not the reverse.

How can this pattern of segregation be accounted for and what are its implications? There is some evidence that historically women have

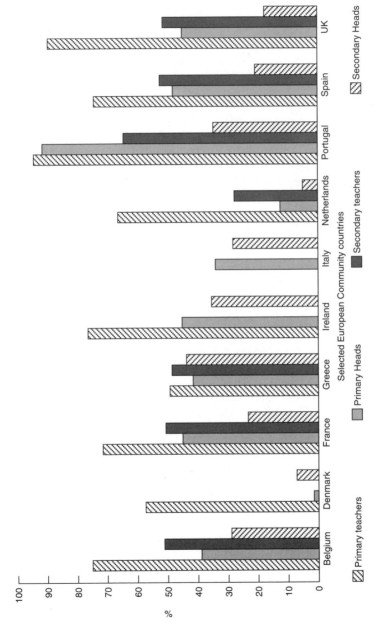

Figure 5.5 **Women in educational management 1985–1986. Relative proportions of teachers and head**

been regarded as constituting a different labour force from men. Several writers[34] have developed and applied the Marxist notion of a reserve army of labour and suggested that women have constituted a reserve to be drawn into the formal economy when there are labour shortages from traditional sources, as for example at time of war or mass male emigration, and to meet the needs of a changing economy. Because of their domestic role, women are relatively easily discharged from employment when their labour is no longer required.[35] While in the more established economies of Europe the reserve army thesis of the cyclical use of women's labour to meet the booms and slumps of production is seen as having decreasing relevance, in Portugal it has some currency. Here the rise in women's employment started significantly in 1970 with the introduction of a new industrial policy in the changed political context, and was undoubtedly also influenced by the massive emigration of male labour and the extension of the period of military service. Thus in Portugal it would appear that women have very recently acted as both a cyclical reserve, filling the vacancies created by unavailable male labour, and a secular reserve, through meeting the demands of a restructured economy. Despite this, women's concentration has tended to grow in those industries where they have traditionally predominated, in textiles, clothing and footwear, and to have grown at a slower rate in the more advanced sectors of industry, in non-electrical machinery, for example. Even in the service sector where they predominate, women's employment rate grew more slowly than men's. In terms of training programmes, women tend to predominate in traditional women's courses and to be absent, or present in only very low numbers, in mechanics, construction design, etc. There is therefore little evidence that segregation is breaking down, even under the pressure of radical restructuring and high levels of labour shortage.

In general, across Europe, and largely because of the general extension of education to girls and the growth of training programmes directed specifically at women, women have been a particularly useful reserve in meeting the needs of economic restructuring which has characterised European economies during the 1980s and 1990s. The service sector is often cited an a good illustration of this, and indeed women have been increasingly drawn in, but not equally to all areas of work, and in the main to the more marginal and poorer paid jobs. Overall, even where it does account in part for women's increased labour-force participation, the reserve army of labour thesis thus fails to account for the clustering of women at the lower echelons of occupations and within sectors, in the poorer quality jobs.

It has been suggested that technology and the more flexible work patterns which emerged throughout the Western economies in the 1980s and 1990s, would herald new opportunities for equality. Economic restructuring and the flexible use of labour are often seen as corollaries and are assumed to have positive implications for women in particular.

The growth of the service sector has undoubtedly benefited women, but it has had a greater benefit for men who have increased their relative presence in the sector. Elsewhere, technological change has been associated with new forms of work practice, of which flexibility is but a part. None of the evidence suggests that these new flexible patterns have done anything to redress the established gender imbalances in the labour force. The OECD study of 1985 found that a third of women are fearful that technological advances will lead to redundancy, and less than half of them (43 per cent) feel that they are equipped to meet the challenges of technological change. Women's level of education, types of employment, types of employer and degrees of responsibility are all factors which account for what in many cases are realistic assessments of their futures. In an earlier study, OECD (1976) it was found that because of their disproportionate concentration in the service sector women were insulated from the harshest effects of the recession, yet, except in the UK, women are more likely to be unemployed than men, as Figure 5.6 shows.[36] Even in the UK where women's employment appears superficially to be protected, Humphries and Rubery (1988) conclude that the adverse economic circumstances and associated government policies have impacted with particular severity on them, especially the unskilled, minority women, and single mothers. Women's availability to work for less than full-time hours is what in Britain has largely shielded them from higher levels of unemployment, together with a social security policy that effectively leads to an under-reporting of unemployment by women.

Overall the evidence suggests that occupational segregation persists in Europe, and that the experiences of women and men workers are different. There is no easy explanation for this common pattern of inequality, nor for the important differences which characterise women's work in the different countries of Europe. There is clearly a relationship between the availability of support for women's work and their ability to do so, but equally clearly, entrenched views about women's roles and their capacity to work influence their experiences. When asked directly, 30 per cent of women indicate that they have been discriminated against on at least one dimension.[37] Promotion is the area of greatest concern, but it is closely followed by pay, and then by training and access to bonuses and other perks. The persistence of these feelings of discrimination in a Europe committed to equal opportunities is disturbing.

Gender and politics

It has often been suggested that women have different orientations to work, indeed different political aspirations and consciousness altogether, and that these factors help to account for the nature of their experiences at work. It has long been argued that the marginal position of women in

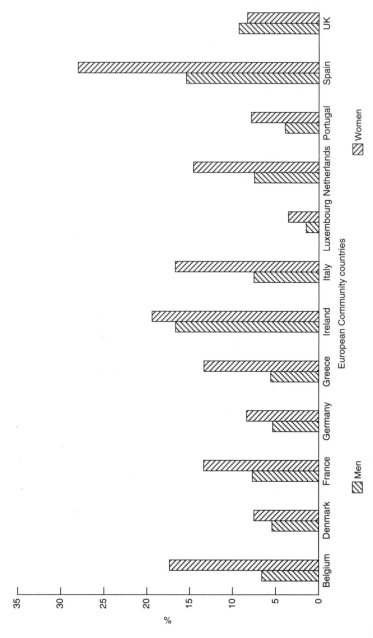

Figure 5.6 Unemployment rates for men and women, 1988

the workplace is reflected in their marginal position in the labour movement. Kate Purcell (1984) challenges this taken-for-granted assumption that women workers are less unionised, more placid, stable, and fundamentally more exploitable than men. For Feldberg and Glenn (1984) such views emanate from the sex-differentiated way in which work is studied by social scientists who operate with what they term a job model for men and a gender model for women which marginalises their work.[38] While historically there is some evidence to suggest that women have been less represented in trade unions, there is also contradictory evidence of the active pursuit of women's workplace interests, for example from the earliest days of the British labour movement, and of the exclusionary activities of male trade unionists.

Female trade unionism has grown considerably over the past few decades throughout Europe. Reporting on a survey of its membership the European Trade Union Institute notes that the proportion of women among the trade unions of the eighteen western European nations it surveyed has increased during the period between 1980 and 1985. Growth is particularly high in those unions which represent workers in the public sector and in retailing, while it has fallen in those unions representing employees in the decline sectors, such as the textile industry. However, there is great variation between European countries. In Britain, Italy, Belgium and Ireland women account for approximately 30–33 per cent of union members. In Germany the proportion is 22 per cent, while in The Netherlands and Luxembourg it is less than 15 per cent. The study also indicated a high correlation between the labour-force participation rate and unionisation. However, general union membership is not reflected in participation at the higher levels of trade unionism and, with the exception of France, women are considerably under-represented at national congresses where policy is established. This pattern is reflected in the figures for individual unions within each country despite in many cases apparent endeavours to increase the representation of women.

There has been a marked increase in the number of women's committees within specific unions across Europe, and there is some evidence that this has resulted in the adoption of more progressive programmes directed towards gender equality at work, and their incorporation into collective bargaining and agreements. However, it still remains the case that trade unions are not as active as they might be in relation to the pursuit of equality issues, and this is likely to be an outcome of their predominantly male membership profile. It remains the case that the majority of the membership is what shapes policy, which means that issues relating specifically to women and to part-time workers and other marginal categories will tend to be less forcibly pressed.

Outside the labour movement, in party politics, the picture is a little different although it is often also painted as one of female indifference. Vicky Randall (1987) suggests that the popular conception that women are less participative in the political process is based on a biased evaluation and perception of the facts. Indeed, she concludes that few dramatic differences exist between the political attitudes of men and women. While women do appear more conservative in some respects and less knowledgeable about and interested in conventional politics, the differences should not be exaggerated and are in any case diminishing. What then are these dimensions along which women's political behaviour is conventionally distinguished from men's, and what do the available data actually suggest to support or refute the popular view? Are European women less involved in and concerned with politics than their male counterparts?

It is frequently asserted that women are less likely to vote than men, and that when they do vote, they are more likely to vote for Conservative political groups. Baxter and Lansing (1980) reworked the British General Election data from the Butler and Stokes (1974) study to show that the differences between women's and men's turnout rate was minuscule: in 1964, 90 per cent compared to 92.5 per cent, and in 1970, 83.3 per cent compared to 87.1 per cent. Randall suggests that a similarly small gap characterised other European countries in the 1950s and 1960s, including not only France and Germany, but Norway, Sweden and Denmark. The exception has been Italy where, since enfranchisement in 1945, women have consistently turned out at a higher rate than men. In Britain by the 1979 General Election, 49 per cent of voters were women, and analysis of the 1983 Election suggests that if anything a slightly higher proportion of women than men voted. In Germany, by 1976, the difference was only 0.8 per cent.

Narrowly defined, women do appear to be less active in politics than men, and their formal membership of political parties is lower than men's. Randall notes that where data are available, they tend to confirm this view, although in Britain women are substantially represented in the two main parties, forming 40 per cent of Labour and 51 per cent Conservative Party memberships. In 1986, Lovenduski (1986) estimates that 40 per cent of the Social Democratic Party was female, and that the rates for membership of the Liberal and Scottish National Party were probably higher. In France she suggests that women comprised 36 per cent of the membership of the Communist Party, 27 per cent of the Socialist Party, 40 per cent of the Giscardian Conservative UDF membership, and 43 per cent of the Conservative Gaullist RPR Party. In Germany, women are significantly outnumbered by men as party members, in 1983 forming only 23 per cent of Christian Democrats, 14 per cent of Christian Socialists, 25 per cent of Social Democrats, and 24 per cent of Liberals. However, their membership of the Green Party which entered Parliament for the first time in 1983, was much higher at 50 per cent, and 37 per cent of the newly elected parliamentarians were women. As might be expected, women of the relatively newly established democracies of Greece, Portugal and Spain have been less organised than men but their participation in political parties is increasing rapidly. Women constituted 30 per cent of Centre Democrats, 9 per cent of Socialists and 11 per cent of Communists in Spain; and 40 per cent of the Socialists in Portugal.

Several factors help to explain this pattern of participation. Randall suggests that overall the evidence indicates that women's political activism is lower than men's, but that activism *per se* is a minority activity. Men are overall more likely to belong to organisations than women, but Scandinavian data from Hernes and Hanninen-Salmelin (1985) suggest that women are more likely than men to be involved in consumer, religious, and what Randall calls 'humanitarian and social' organisations. This pattern of participation has led some writers to suggest that women are interested in different kinds of politics from men. Marjorie Mayo (1977) suggests that women are actively involved in 'grass-roots' politics and campaigns, often centred on local housing and environmental issues, and Randall suggests that such studies as exist indicate that the women who participate in such campaigns are predominantly housewives. The Peace Movement has been very much a movement with which women have been involved. In Britain the early years of the Campaign for Nuclear Disarmament saw a female membership rate of about 40 per cent, and Randall suggests that women have played a prominent part in the revival of CND since the 1970s. Thirty thousand women took part in the first big demonstration at the Greenham Women's Peace Camp in 1982, and the association of Greenham with women is undeniably strong. Elsewhere, for example in France and Germany and as evidenced by the growth of the Green movement, women's political activism is visible.

There is some evidence, therefore, that women have a more active profile in some political organisations and activities than men, when the definition of politics is less circumscribed than that which focuses on parliamentary politics alone. Does it remain the case, however, that in parliamentary terms women are politically different in attitudes and orientations than men and, if so, how can this be accounted for?

The earlier data on membership rates has tended to suggest that women are more conservative in their politics than men. However, more circumspect analysis reveals that conservatism and longevity are closely associated, and in large part this accounts for the link between women and conservatism. Also influential on women's conservatism is the presence of a strong Roman Catholic Church, and Devaud (1968) suggests that it was Catholic women's votes which prevented the Communists coming to power in France, Germany and Italy in the 1960s. However, the other factor which appears to be at play is that it is not conservatism *per se* but rather adherence to the established social order that characterises women's political attitudes. This in itself may be largely accounted for by the fact that women appear to be less informed about political issues than men. A Euro-Barometer survey conducted after the European elections of 1984 found that women were less informed about the European Parliament than men, and a study the previous year suggests that the reason for this may be because women are less exposed to political news than men.[39]

Variables such as age, education, and knowledge of the political process and its associated issues are directly and indirectly linked with political participation. Once these factors have been taken into account, the influence of gender on voting habits in the formal parliamentary arenas appears to be negligible and declining. If women are not essentially apolitical, and if, as the evidence seems to suggest, they are developing a growing awareness of the importance of the political context as a mechanism for redressing issues of inequality and inequity, what evidence is there that women representatives better carry forward those ideas than men?

In two-thirds of the member states of the European Community less than 10 per cent of parliamentarians are women. However, in the European Parliament itself, women are better represented, although their proportion comes near neither to the proportion of the electorate that is female nor to the proportion of women who stood for election, except in the case of Denmark, Ireland and The Netherlands where women candidates were more likely to be elected than their male counterparts. In discussing whether women members of the European Parliament have made a difference to equality policy in the European Community, Elizabeth Vallance (1988) suggests that their ability to change traditional political priorities and preoccupations seems to be minimal, but their perception of themselves as women with particular experience and concerns does appear to have affected the emphasis of European politics, especially in the area of equality policy. While the presence of women alone is not a sufficient condition to ensure that women's political interests are taken seriously, it undoubtedly helps since, as Vallance comments, nobody fights other people's battles, and nothing is an issue until it has been shown to be electorally significant.

Sanzone (1984) similarly attributes advances in women's rights to the actions and influence of women in positions of political leadership, and believes that women in roles of executive political leadership will undoubtedly be instrumental in the creation of a more equal society.

Gender and age

Age is becoming an increasingly significant factor in understanding gender differences: today approximately one-quarter of all females are aged over 60: women are increasingly living into old age – often into very elderly years. Women are living nearly twice as long as their predecessors did at the turn of the century, and in 1994 the average life expectancy at birth for women in Europe is 80.1 years, compared with a man's expectancy of 73.7 years. A recent report from the Commission of the European Communities (1997) notes that women in Portugal have added 11.3 years to their life expectancy over the past thirty years, bringing it today to 78; it is French women who have the longest expectancy of life at 81.5 years at birth. While women's life expectancy at birth is higher than men's in every member state in Europe, the two rates are drawing closer to one another, although at advanced old age, women typically still outnumber men by over three to one. However, despite their numerical greater presence, older women are much less present in public life and leadership than men. A number of social and cultural factors account for this. First, enfranchisement came later for women in some member states than in others: in France, Italy and Belgium women were enfranchised in the 1940s, and in Greece not until 1958. Men of the retired generations are more likely to have received post-primary education, they are more likely to have held responsible positions in working life, and women are more likely to be restricted by personal factors such as limited finances and limited time. Older women have often experienced long careers as carers, and this often continued into old age. In Belgium, more than 25 per cent of women between 55 and 60 were found to be supporting sick, disabled or elderly persons and almost 30 per cent of carers over 55 were providing care for two or more people. The period and intensity of the care given varied widely from full-time over a period of years to crisis care over short periods interspersed with long intervals (Commission of the European Communities 1997). State provision of support for the carers of adult dependants is very patchy: in Britain, Ireland, Finland and Germany benefit schemes exist, and more limited provision is available in six other Member States, but in Spain, Luxembourg, The Netherlands, Austria and Portugal, no provision for benefits exists at all. Since the carers for elderly people are not usually in paid employment, the burden is doubly heavy. In Germany, Luxembourg, France and Greece families are held legally responsible for meeting the basic needs of older family members; in Denmark the younger generations are explicitly legally absolved of this responsibility.

Today, older women are in general significantly worse off financially than their male counterparts, although there are considerable differences in their situation depending on their nationality, marital status and previous work history. While current pension arrangements vary from state to state, in general, and with the exception of the Scandinavian countries, they rest on a model of the male family wage. As a result, in Italy women's pension income is typically only two-thirds of men's, in Britain it is less than 60 per cent of men's and in Germany it is 42 per cent of men's. In part this reflects the fact that in the majority of cases pensions are related to the length of the working life, but it also reflects lower wage levels and the frequent interruptions which working women tend to experience as a result of maternity. Thus, even in one of the key areas where women are often alleged to have benefits which outweigh those of men – longevity – the quality of the experience suggests that inequities earlier in their lives still persist.

Conclusion: a continuing gender divide?

The data presented earlier suggest that across Europe, the experiences and life chances of European women have improved in quality over the past few decades. However, gender remains a significant dimension in determining opportunities and experiences. What is clear in looking at the data is that there are important differences in the position of women within Europe, and that specific cultural contexts shape women's prospects. Christine Woesler de Panafieu (1991) describes British women as 'the laggards of Europe', suggesting that they are more obedient to traditional female role expectations. Yet the European Commission's survey of the evolution of opinions and attitudes conducted in 1987[40] concludes that the United Kingdom, together with France, Denmark and The Netherlands, is markedly above the European average with respect to egalitarian ideas concerning the role of men and women in the family, working life and politics. Moreover, Britain has one of the longest of European histories with regard to the formal emancipation of women, markedly ahead of France, Italy, Belgium and the three new democracies. How can these apparently contradictory views be reconciled?

Woesler de Panafieu suggests that under the veneer of egalitarianism in Britain, a rigid middle-class attitude to the ideal of family life, centred around the mother, persists. This she suggests affects women's independence in two important ways: work is still mainly considered essentially as an economic necessity and there are continuing negative connotations associated with the term 'career woman'; and the pivotal focus of the woman's activities is still centred on the home. She suggests that this is because of the apathy of a third of British women, mainly the young; the resistance to change of another third; and the impotence of the final third in transforming the current situation into a positive perspective for the majority of British women. Her analysis, however, neglects to discuss the structural context within which British women live and exercise rights and choices, and it is an understanding of this context that enables apparent inconsistencies in attitude and behaviour to be better understood.

The European Commission survey suggests that Britain shares with France third ranking in the Community for egalitarian ideas, following Denmark and The Netherlands, and all four nations are above or equal to the European average in the importance with which egalitarianism is rated. On these scales, Germany and Luxembourg come at the bottom, and they are particularly rigid with respect to the role of husband and wife within the family. Yet paradoxically the place of women in these societies does not appear to be a serious problem. The Irish are found to be less often in favour of equal roles within the family, but on the other hand they are relatively willing to accept women in politics. In Ireland, while the problem of women's place in society is not seen as very great, and is below the European average, the gap between men's and women's views on this question is very great: men minimise the problem whereas women think it very important. In Italy the paradox is even more acute: occupational roles are still believed to be very different for men and women, yet the principle of equality in the family and the role of women in politics is strongly accepted. Here the problem of women's position in society is judged more important than anywhere else in Europe. In Belgium there is most resistance to the notion of equality of roles in the family, and in Greece resistance focuses on women's entry and competence to perform specific occupational roles. In Spain and Portugal, while opinion is generally very close to the European average, the role of women in politics is less readily accepted, especially in Portugal, and certain traditional role models, as in Italy, remain very strong.

Attitudes alone do not appear to determine opportunities for women nor to relate directly to the significance of gender as a factor explaining experiences. However, when considered together with the nature of specific institutions and infrastructural support, a clearer picture can be built up. As Jacqui Lewis's discussion of childcare provision suggests, there are marked differences in the extent to which women's working is supported across Europe. On all the measures discussed earlier in this chapter, British women lose out: they have poorer entitlement to maternity benefit, and a significant absence of crèche and childcare facilities prior to the start of formal primary education. They experience weaker protection of their careers, so that for the majority of British women maternity comes to mean not a career break, where continuity is a prospect, but a career rupture. Once in the labour market, British women are therefore more likely to work part-time than their European counterparts, and the structure of British employment ensures that the great divide between the rights and perks of full-time and part-time work remains, further disabling working women not only during their working lives but during their long senior citizenship.

We have seen that there has been a pattern of active national and European legislation aimed at reducing the extent of gender inequality. Elizabeth Vallance and Elizabeth Davies (1986) question the extent to which the law can change attitudes, and hence experiences. There is ample evidence, not least from the rulings of the Commission on breaches of its conventions, that discrimination and inequality can persist even after the passing of a law. Vallance and Davies suggest that many factors limit the effectiveness of legislation, among others, the attitudes of women themselves, the reactions of employers and trade unions, the economic climate, which may inhibit the claiming of existing rights, and the complexity of the law itself. We can add to these factors the implementation of policy which, as we have seen in the case of abortion law reform, can inhibit the effectiveness of the law. Changes in the law should not be undervalued, however. As Vallance and Davies suggest, the law is an expression of policy and intention and few industrial and business interests are willing to give the impression of being discriminatory and thus at the least they make genuflections in the direction of equality.

The prospect for women of Europe in the future shows some promise, but there are no grounds for complacency and there remains a role for those active in consciousness-raising in pushing at the boundaries of established practice and in pressing for the effective implementation of policy to protect and enhance the position of women of all ages. In Britain, for the first time, not only is a significant proportion of women in the national Parliament, but we have a Cabinet with a strong female presence. It remains to be seen to what extent the next five years will, as a consequence, see a changed political agenda that will have a radical impact on the lives of British women. Today gender remains very visibly a dimension of European society, but a dimension with different facets in the different member states. Overall the conclusion suggests that structural factors are of greater importance than cultural/attitudinal factors. The prospects for change are therefore promising if member state governments and the European Commission direct change not simply at policy formation but at its implementation and monitoring.

Notes

1 *Women of Europe Supplement 14*, 1984a. In each of the ten member nations of the European Community, except Ireland, women constitute a numeric majority. Throughout the text references to the *Women of Europe Supplements* are abbreviated to *WoE*.

2 The emancipation of women was spread across several decades: Denmark (1915); Germany (1918); The Netherlands (1919); Luxembourg (1919); Ireland (1922); UK (1928); France (1944); Italy (1945); Belgium (1948); Greece (1952); Portugal (1976); and Spain, formally in 1930 but rarely able to use their votes before 1977.

3 This is not to suggest that the European Community, rising as it did from the pursuit of military and strategic nationalistic interests which characterised the 1930s and 1940s, was the sole platform for the pursuit of issues of gender inequality, but it has undoubtedly and explicitly addressed the issues, especially those associated with employment.

4 Article 119 states:

Each Member State shall during the first stage ensure and subsequently maintain the application of the principle of equal remuneration for the same work as between male and female workers.

For the purpose of this Article, remuneration shall be taken to mean the ordinary basic or minimum wage or salary and any additional emoluments whatsoever payable directly or indirectly, whether in cash or in kind, by the employer to the worker and arising out of the worker's employment.

Equal remuneration without discrimination based on sex means:
  (a) that remuneration for the same work at piece-rates shall be calculated on the basis of the same unit of measurement;
  (b) that remuneration for work at time-rates shall be the same for the same job.

Treaty Establishing the European Economic Community, Rome 25 March 1957; London: HMSO, 1962, p. 45.

5 The first Action Programme is presented in full, with a commentary, in 'Equal Opportunities Action Programme 1982–1985', *Women of Europe, Supplement 9*, 1982.

6 'Equal Opportunities for Women – Medium-Term Community Programme 1986–1990' was launched by a Council resolution in 1985, and is summarised together with a commentary in 'Equal Opportunities: 2nd Action Programme 1986–1990', *Women of Europe Supplement 23*, 1985b.

7 Women's rights under Community Law are well summarised in *Women of Europe Supplement 12*, 1983, *Women of Europe Supplement 19*, 1985a and *Women of Europe Supplement 25*, 1986, each of which is entitled 'Community Law and Women'.

8 As Randall notes, a mid-term conference to review progress was held in Copenhagen in 1980, and a final reviewing conference was held in Nairobi in 1985. Many of the delegations attending the latter conference were exclusively male, and few of the participants were centrally informed about women's issues.

9 See for example Banks (1981), Bouchier (1983), Deckard (1979), and Wilson (1980).

10 Banks (1981) suggests that the British movement, for example, can be separated into three 'faces': equal rights feminism, present also in the USA but particularly strong in Britain; evangelical feminism, concerned with the reform of the 'less fortunate' and espousing an essentially conservative philosophy; and socialist feminism, questioning the forms of marriage, family, childcare and housework.

11 The famous strike by women machinists at Fords in Dagenham is a prime example, cited by many such as Randall (1987).

12 See Coote and Campbell (1982) for a full account of these demands.

13 Randall (1987) suggests that the French term 'groupuscule' indicates well the fragmented nature of the early movement which had three discernable strands: Femmes Revolutionnaires (radical feminists) formed in 1970; Psych et Po (Psychoanalysis and Politique) which concentrated on psychocultural mechanisms for women's oppression; and socialist feminists as exemplified by the Cercle Dimitriev, founded in 1972. Lovenduski (1986) adds to the trio: a fourth group representing reform or rights interests, and exemplified by the Choisir Party of Gisèle Halimi.

14 These were the Movimento di Liberazione della Donna, concerned with educational opportunity, divorce, abortion and non-sexist education; and Lotta Feminista, concerned with the campaign for wages for housework.

15 This was a natural outcome of the agenda which emerged from the dissatisfaction of many women with the organisational politics of the student groups of the 1960s. Lovenduski (1986) suggests that four dominant agenda items emerged from this context: autonomy from established organisations and ideologies; separatism from men, thus enabling a realisation of women's culture and history; new small organisational structures (piccoli gruppi) without hierarchy; and consciousness-raising to develop an understanding of women's lives.

16 Colombo (1981), Ergas (1982) and Eckmann (1978) are all cited by Lovenduski as mentioning this change in focus.

17 In 1960 and 1965, before any legal reform, there were 918 286 and 997 275 live births across the member states respectively. In 1970, the number of

live births had declined to 918 819. By 1975 when abortion was available legally in the UK, Denmark, France, and The Netherlands, the number of births reached a low at 697 518.

18 Outshoorn (1988) labels the first the 'grounds' or indication type. Here, she suggests, abortion is legal if certain criteria are met, such as a grave danger to the health of the women (England), or if certain procedural rules are observed (The Netherlands). Second, there is what she calls the 'term' type where abortion is legal if performed before a certain time-limit in the duration of the pregnancy, such as ten or twelve weeks (France and Italy). Finally there is the 'mixed' type where indications are combined with given terms or procedural rules, as is found in the Federal Republic of Germany.

19 Vicky Randall (1987) provides a detailed discussion of abortion rights and reform in the policy context detailing how this happened. Janine Mossuz-Lavau (1988) provides a more succinct account in her discussion of women's private lives, but equally shows the strong political context of abortion law reform.

20 She comments:

> Long symbolized by a married couple accompanied by their two or three children, the family now takes on various shapes, including unmarried couples with children and single parents (usually women, more seldom men) with their children. There are more and more children born out of wedlock ... The number of single-parent families is also increasing. These changes, combined with the demands of women seeking legal guarantees of equality with their spouses or companions on the one hand and government concern over falling birth rates on the other, led to the adoption in many countries of new measures adapted to these new families. (1988: 13)

21 Some of the consequences are well-discussed in 'The graying of Europe: as the population ages, social pressures build', *Business Week*, 6 February 1989, pp. 12–16.

22 The discussion in this section focuses on aspects of childcare, but equally important to a full understanding of the impact of the changing structure of the family on women's and men's lives and experiences in Europe are issues associated with the care of the elderly. Hall (1977), Walker (1989), Hunt (1978) and Leonard and Speakman (1986) are but some of the useful sources for a discussion of these issues.

23 See 'Women and Men of Europe in 1978' *Women of Europe Supplement 3* (1978), 'Women and Men of Europe in 1983' *Women of Europe Supplement 16* (1984c), and 'Men and Women of Europe in 1987' *Women of Europe Supplement 26* (1987).

24 A summary table is presented in *Eurostat Yearbook '95: a Statistical Eye on Europe, 1983–1993*, Office for Official Publications of the European Community, Luxembourg, 1995. Because of comparability problems, the table provided excludes data on pre-primary education. However, it does provide a clear picture of the nature and stages at which educational provision is made by each nation state, indicating the range from the lowest level of state provision at 11 years in Greece, Ireland and Italy to the most prolonged at 16 years in Spain, 15.5 in Belgium and 15 in The Netherlands. Britain sits at the mid-point in providing 13 years of education to the end of the compulsory minimum leaving age.

25 The Nursery Voucher Scheme was introduced by the Conservative government in April 1997. Under its arrangements, all parents received vouchers
for three terms of early years education. These vouchers could be exchanged
for education in a range of settings, including state nursery schools and
reception classes at infant schools as well as private nurseries. In practice
the scheme did little to increase the take-up of state-provided places and
gave a small number of parents very small subsidies for their childcare
costs for four-year-olds in private nurseries.

26 A detailed breakdown of the use of different kinds of daycare for preschool-
aged children is provided in *Women and Men in Britain: the Life Cycle of
Inequality*, Equal Opportunities Commission, Manchester, 1995. The data are
derived from the OPSC Daycare Survey, the General Household Survey, Department for Education, Welsh Office, and Scottish Office Education Department.

27 The table is created from data presented in 'Women in Graphics', *Women of
Europe Supplement 30*, December 1989, and drawn from EUROSTAT data.

28 Data drawn again from 'Women in Graphics', *Women of Europe Supplement
30*, December 1989.

29 Data are presented in the Commission of the European Communities *Employment in Europe*, Office for Official Publications of the European Communities, Luxembourg, 1989. In most countries having a third child causes the
chance of being employed to fall to about the same extent as having a second
child. In Belgium, Denmark and France, however, a third child has a much
greater impact; in France, for example, a woman with two children is only
three-quarters less likely to work than a woman with one child, whereas a
woman with three children has an employment rate of only 34 per cent of
that of a single-child parent.

30 Data drawn from 'Women in Graphics', *Women of Europe Supplement 30*,
December 1989, which was based on data from EUROSTAT *Labour Force
Survey*, 1986. Neither The Netherlands nor Spain provided data on part-
time working and hence are not included. Further information can also be
found in 'European Women in Paid Employment: Their Perception of Discrimination at Work', *Women of Europe Supplement 20*, 1985, and Commission of the European Communities *Employment in Europe 1989*, Office
for Official Publications of the European Communities, Luxembourg, 1989.

31 Data taken from the EUROSTAT *Labour Force Survey*, 1986.

32 OECD *The Integration of Women in the Economy*, OECD, Paris, 1985. The
study was an up-date of earlier research, OECD *Women and Employment*,
OECD, Paris, 1980 which was a first attempt by the OECD to measure
international differences in occupational segregation by gender using indexes
of segregation.

33 For example, see the discussion of German women at work in Shaffer
(1981); the chapters on Italy, Germany and Sweden in particular in Jenson,
Hagen and Reddy (1988); the special supplement on women in Spain, *Women
of Europe Supplement 8* (1981c) and the supplement on women in Portugal,
Women of Europe Supplement 11 (1982b) for the Iberian peninsula; and for
Britain, Hakim (1979) and Walby (1988).

34 See for example Braverman (1974), Beechey (1977), Brueghel (1979) and
Simeral (1978).

35 Simeral makes an important distinction between the functions served by a
reserve army of labour (RAL). She suggests that first, capitalism depends

on a surplus population or RAL to supply its growing spheres. This reserve is formed over time by technological change and transformations in the structure of the economy. There is a need therefore for what she terms the 'secular' reserve. Second there is the cyclical role for an RAL, to absorb the unemployed and to 'take up the slack' during economic crises and hold down wages during periods of economic growth and prosperity. This reserve she terms the 'cyclical' reserve.

The ease with which women are discharged back into the home is also a function of the cultural values of a specific country. Where the state is perceived as having a high level of responsibility for childcare and formalised state provision of education and welfare more generally, and where traditional gender segregated roles have been somewhat eroded, the ability to discharge women easily back into the home is undermined.

36 Data are taken from 'Women in Graphics', *Women of Europe Supplement 30*, 1989b.

37 See the 1985 survey of working women's attitudes, summarised in 'European Women in Paid Employment', *Women of Europe Supplement 20*, 1985.

38 The male job model assumes that economic activities provide the basis for social relationships within the family and society generally, and that employment is a central life interest. The female gender model assumes that family caretaking activities determine social relations and that the family is the central life interest. Each model assumes homogeneity among members of the same sex, and recognises neither race nor class differences, nor differences over time.

39 See 'Women and Voting: Elections to the European Parliament', *Women of Europe Supplement 21*, 1985, and 'Women and Men of Europe in 1983', *Women of Europe Supplement 16*, 1984c, for further discussion of these attitudes.

40 'Men and Women of Europe in 1987', *Women of Europe Supplement 26*, 1987.

References

Banks, O. (1981) *Faces of Feminism: A Study of Feminism as a Social Movement*, London: Martin Robertson.

Baxter, S. and Lansing, M. (1980) *Women and Politics: the Invisible Majority*, Michigan: University of Michigan.

Beechey, V. (1989) 'Women's employment in France and Britain: some problems of comparison', *Work Employment and Society*, 3(3).

Bocock, J. (1991) 'Equal opportunities in a cold climate', *NATFHE Journal*, February.

Bouchier, D. (1983) *The Feminist Challenge: the Movement for Women's Liberation in Britain and the USA*, London: Macmillan.

Braverman, H. (1974) *Labour and Monopoly Capital*, New York: Monthly Review Press.

Bruegel, I. (1979) 'Women as a reserve army of labour: a note on recent British experience', *Feminist Review*, 3: 12–33.

Buckley, M. and Anderson, M. (eds) (1988) *Women Equality and Europe*, London: Macmillan.

Business Week (6 February 1989) 'The graying of Europe: as the population ages, social pressures build'.

Butler, D. and Stokes, D. (1974) *Political Change in Britain*, London: Macmillan.

Colombo, D. (1981) 'The Italian feminist movement', in *Women's Studies International Quarterly*, 4(4).

Commission of the European Communities

1981a Equal Opportunities: Action Programme 1982–1985. *Women of Europe Supplement* Brussels

1981b Women at work in the European Community: 50 questions, 50 answers. *Women of Europe Supplement 7* Brussels

1981c Women in Spain. *Women of Europe Supplement 8* Brussels

1982a Women in Statistics. *Women of Europe Supplement 10* Brussels

1982b Women in Portugal. *Women of Europe Supplement 11* Brussels

1983 Community Law and Women. *Women of Europe Supplement 12* Brussels

1984a Women in Statistics. *Women of Europe Supplement 14* Brussels

1984b Women at Work in the European Communities. *Women of Europe Supplement 15* Brussels

1984c Women and Men of Europe in 1983. *Women of Europe Supplement 16* Brussels

1985a Community Law and Women. *Women of Europe Supplement 19* Brussels

1985b Equal Opportunities: 2nd Action Programme 1986–1990. *Women of Europe Supplement 23* Brussels

1986 Community Law and Women. *Women of Europe Supplement 25* Brussels

1988 Women of Europe: 10 Years. *Women of Europe Supplement 27* Brussels

1989a *Employment in Europe* Directorate General, Employment, Industrial Relations and Social Affairs, Office for Official Publications of the European Communities, Luxembourg COM(89)399final

1989b Women in Graphics. *Women of Europe Supplement 30* Brussels

1990 Child Care in the European Communities 1985–1990. *Women of Europe Supplement 31* Brussels

1991 Equal Opportunities for Women and Men: the Third medium-term community action programme 1991–1995. *Women of Europe Supplement 34* Brussels

1997 Age Becomes Her: Older women in the European Union, *Women of Europe Dossiser 45* Brussels

Coote, A. and Campbell, B. (1982) *Sweet Freedom: the Struggle for Women's Liberation*, Oxford: Blackwell.

Crompton, R. and Sanderson, K. (1990) *Gendered Jobs and Social Change*, London: Unwin Hyman.

Dahlerup, D. (1988) 'Feminism and Politics', in *Scandinavian Political Studies*, 11(4).

Deckard, B. (1979) *The Women's Movement: Political, Socio-economic and Psychological Issues*, New York: Harper & Row.

Devaud, M. S. (1968) 'Political participation of Western European women', *Annals of the American Academy of Political and Social Science*, 375.

Dex, S. and Shaw, L. B. (1986) *British and American Women at Work*, London: Macmillan.

Duchen, C. (1986) *Feminism in France: from May '68 to Mitterand*, London: Routledge & Kegan Paul.

Eckmann, E. (1978) 'The new conception of the politics of the modern feminist movement: with special reference to the new Italian feminist movement'.

Paper presented for the Joint Sessions of the ECPR Workshops, Grenoble: 6–12 April.

Edye, D. and Lintner, V. (1996) *Contemporary Europe*, New Jersey: Prentice Hall.

Equal Opporunties Commission (1995) *Women and Men in Britain: the Lifecycle of Inequality*, Manchester: EOC.

Ergas, Y. (1982) '1968–79 – Feminism and the Italian party system: women's politics in a decade of turmoil', *Comparative Politics*, 14.

Feldberg, R. and Glenn, E. N. (1984) 'Male and female: job versus gender models in the sociology of work', in J. Siltanen and M. Stanworth (eds) *Women and the Public Sphere*, London: Hutchinson.

Field, M. J. (1979) 'Determinants of abortion policy in the developed nations', *Policy Studies Journal*, 7.

Hakim, C. (1979) *Occupational Segregation*, London: Department of Employment.

Hall, P. (1977) *Europe 2000*, London: Duckworth.

Hernes, H. M. and Hanninen-Salmelin, E. (1985) 'Women in the corporate system', in Haavio-Mannila *et al.* (eds) *Unfinished Democracy: Women in Nordic Politics*, Oxford: Pergamon.

Humphries, J. and Rubery, J. (1988) 'Recession and exploitation: British women in a changing workplace 1979–85', in J. Jenson *et al.* (eds) *Feminization of the Labour Force: Paradoxes and Promises*, Cambridge: Polity Press.

Hunt, A. (1978) *The Elderly at Home*, London: HMSO.

Jenson, J. *et al.* (1988) *Feminization of the Labour Force: Paradoxes and Promises*, Cambridge: Polity Press.

Leonard, D. and Speakman, M. A. (1986) 'Women in the family: companions or caretakers', in V. Beechey and E. Whitelegg (eds) *Women in Britain Today*, Milton Keynes: Open University Press.

Lewis, J. (1990) 'Breaking the crèche barrier', *Management Today*, February.

Lovenduski, J. (1986) *Women and European Politics: Contemporary Feminism and Public Policy*, London: Wheatsheaf.

Lovenduski, J. (1988) 'The women's movement and public policy in Western Europe: theory, strategy, practice and politics', in M. Buckley and M. Anderson (eds) *Women, Equality and Europe*, London: Macmillan.

Mayo, M. (ed.) (1977) *Women in the Community*, London: Routledge & Kegan Paul.

Moss, P. (1990) *Women of Europe Supplement 31*, Brussels.

Mossuz-Lavau, J. (1988) *Women of Europe Supplement 27*, Brussels.

Oakley, A. (1974) *Housewife*, London: Allen Lane.

Organisation for Economic Cooperation and Development (1976) *The 1974–1975 Recession and the Employment of Women*, Paris: OECD.

Outshoorn, J. (1988) 'Abortion law reform: a woman's right to choose?', in M. Buckley and M. Anderson (eds) *Women, Equality and Europe*, London: Macmillan.

Purcell, K. (1984) 'Militancy and acquiescence among women workers', in J. Siltanen and M. Stanworth (eds) *Women and the Public Sphere*, London: Hutchinson.

Randall, V. (1987) *Women and Politics: an International Perspective*, 2nd edn, London: Macmillan.

Roberts, Y. (1992) *Mad About Women: Can There Ever be Fair Play Between the Sexes?*, London: Virago.

Rossilli, Mariagrazia (1997) 'The European Community's policy on the equality of women', *The European Journal of Women's Studies*, 4, London: Sage.

Sanzone, D. S. (1984) 'Women in positions of political leadership in Britain, France and West Germany', in J. Siltanen and M. Stanworth *Women and the Public Sphere*, London: Hutchinson.

Shaffer, H. G. (1981) *Women in the Two Germanies: a Comparative Study of a Socialist and a Non-socialist Society*, New York: Pergamon.

Simeral, M. (1978) 'Women and the reserve army of labour', *The Insurgent Sociologist*, 8:2, 3.

Vallance, E. (1988) 'Do women make a difference? The impact of women MEPs on Community Equality policy', in M. Buckley and M. Anderson (eds) *Women, Equality and Europe*, London: Macmillan.

Vallance, E. and Davies, E. (1986) *Women of Europe: Women MEPs and Equality Policy*, Cambridge: Cambridge University Press.

Walby, S. (1988) *Gender Segregation at Work*, Milton Keynes: Open University Press.

Walker, A. (1989) 'The consequences of an ageing population for the social security system', *Contemporary European Affairs*, 2(1).

Wilson, E. (1980) *Only Half-way to Paradise: Women in Post-War Britain 1945–1968*, London: Tavistock.

Woesler de Panafieu, C. (1991) 'British women: the laggards of Europe', *RSA Journal*, 139(5417) (April) Royal Society of Arts.

CHAPTER 6

Race and ethnicity in Europe

JOHN REX

Arguably the most important problem in the political sociology of Europe today is that of the relationship which develops between the various nation states and the immigrant communities which have settled within their boundaries. Indigenous class struggles within the various European countries had, by the 1970s, led to the establishment in all cases of some sort of political consensus around the ideas of the welfare state, a mixed economy with public and private sectors, the establishment of mechanisms for collective bargaining by trade unions and employers, planning for full employment and the provision of basic services in such spheres as housing, health, education and personal and family social welfare. Moreover, although this consensus came under attack in the 1980s with more emphasis on privatisation, a reduction in trade-union power, the tolerance of higher levels of unemployment, and generally greater reliance on the free market, this did not mean a return to class struggle, and what emerged were societies based on the notion of a 'social market' with an incorporated working class. During the period between 1945 and 1970, however, economic expansion led to the settlement of some 16 million immigrants. Such immigrants were recruited to fill the jobs which indigenous workers were unwilling to do and, though they joined trade unions, were often inadequately protected by those unions and the state (see Castles and Kosack 1973; Piore 1974). Some immigrant leaders claimed that they indeed constituted the new European proletariat.

The statistics of immigration to the various European Union countries are somewhat difficult to interpret. The best comprehensive source is to be found in the *Demographic Statistics* published by Eurostat. These give the numbers of foreign residents in various countries. Table 6.1 is drawn from the 1990 report of Eurostat. Slightly increased figures are to be expected in the later (1995) edition. The 1990 figures do not include Sweden, Finland and Austria which joined the European Union at a later date, or Norway which remained outside.

What this table does show is that Germany, France, the United Kingdom, Belgium and The Netherlands have been the largest importers of labour, while Denmark, Greece, Ireland, Italy, Portugal and Spain have relatively small inflows. If, moreover, we look at the emigration from European countries to other countries within the community, as shown

*Table 6.1   **EC and non-EC migrants in EC countries***

Country of Residence	EC migrants	Non-EC migrants
Belgium	536 836	321 814
Denmark	26 875	109 302
France	1 577 900	2 102 200
Germany (Federal Rep.)	1 275 858	3 213 247
Greece	107 781	108 860
Ireland	66 400	17 100
Italy	89 844	206 012
Netherlands	156 901	434 946
Portugal	25 296	69 157
Spain	193 312	140 424
United Kingdom	766 000	1 019 000

Source: *Demographic Statistics*, Eurostat (1990)

by the breakdown of the EU migrant figures by country, it is clear that there are considerable outflows from Greece, Ireland, Italy, Spain and Portugal. Referring to the later adherents to the EU we should add that Sweden had relatively large numbers of immigrants, that Finland had considerable outflows, while Austria, on the Eastern borders of the EU, had considerable numbers of refugees or other political migrants from the former Yugoslavia.

According to the latest figures for the stocks of foreign citizens living in the main European countries given in the annual report of SOPEMI *Trends in International Migration* (OECD 1995) the most significant groups of migrants from one EU country to another were, in the united Germany, 563 000 Italians and 352 000 Greeks, in France 650 000 Portuguese, 253 000 Italians and 216 000 Spanish, in the United Kingdom 465 000 Irish, in Belgium 216 000 Italians and in Sweden, 109 000 Finns. (The figures give here are rounded to the nearest thousand.) It may be noted that all these numbers actually declined between 1988 and 1993 because of returns and naturalisation.

From outside the European Community, the principal sources of immigration, as shown by stocks of foreign residents, the principal sources of migration listed are Yugoslavia Turkey and the Maghrebian countries. The united Germany had 1 918 000 Turks and 930 000 from the former Yugoslavia. France had 1 325 000 Maghrebians (including 614 000 Algerians and 573 000 Moroccans) and 198 000 Turks. The United Kingdom had 1 281 000 foreign residents from non-EU countries of whom 130 000 were from Africa and 322 000 from India, Pakistan and Bangladesh Belgium had 145 000 Moroccans and 88 000 Turks. The Netherlands had 203 000 Turks and 165 000 Moroccans. Italy, traditionally a country of immigration, had 97 000 Moroccans and 73 000 from the former Yugoslavia (OECD 1995).

There are three important points, however, to be noted about these figures. One is that they do not adequately record the numbers of asylum-
seekers and other political refugees, some of them illegal, who have
entered Europe since the end of the Cold War in 1989 and the break-up
of Yugoslavia since 1993. The second is that they do not include those
who acquired citizenship in the country of settlement or who had it on
arrival. These foreign-*born* residents who are not listed as foreign citizens include all who have been naturalised in any of the EU countries
and most of the million New Commonwealth immigrants in the United
Kingdom, Indonesians and Surinamese in The Netherlands and immigrants from France's overseas departments such as Guadelope and Martinique. Finally, they do not record the children of immigrants who,
where the *jus soli* prevails, automatically acquire the citizenship of their
birthplace.

Some of the problems involved here can be illustrated in the case
of the United Kingdom. According to the 1981 census there were 1.41
million immigrants from the New Commonwealth including 412 000
from India, 272 000 from the Caribbean, 177 000 from Pakistan, 133 000
from East Africa (mostly East African Asians), 91 000 from the Mediterranean (mainly from Cyprus) 80 000 from the Far East and 47 000
from Bangladesh. In this census, however, the number of those living in
a household with a New Commonwealth head were recorded in order to
obtain a rough approximation of the numbers of New Commonwealth
immigrants and their British-born children. The total numbers recorded
in this way was 2.2 million, of whom 674 000 were from India, 546 000
from the Caribbean, 295 000 from Pakistan, 181 000 from East Africa,
170 000 from the Mediterranean, 120 000 from the Far East and 65 000
from Bangladesh (Commission for Racial Equality 1985).

A further development in the 1991 census was the attempt to dis-
cover the size of ethnic minority communities including any descendant
of an immigrant who identified with the ethnicity of their immigrant or
other ancestor. To this end a question was included in the 1991 census
asking respondents to which of a number of so-called ethnic groups
they belonged. The options offered were White, Black Caribbean, Black
African, Black Other, Indian, Pakistani, Bangladeshi, Other Asian and
Other Other.

The political and, indeed, logical basis of this classification has been
the subject of much debate, but it proved possible for the Office of
Population Census and Statistics to record numbers identifying with the
ethicities stated and to consider their various life chances. Of a population of 54.86 million in Great Britain 3.01 million chose the categories
other than White (i.e. 5.5 per cent of the population of Britain) 885 000
(1.6 per cent) saw themselves as Black, of whom 499 000 chose Black
Caribbean, 207 000 Black African and 178 000 Black other; South Asian
categories were chosen by 1 475 000 (2.7 per cent) of whom 840 000
chose Indian, 475 000 chose Pakistani and 160 000 Bangladeshi; 157 000

of the Other Asians identified themselves as Chinese; there were 196 000 who identified as other Asian and 290 000 who identified as Other/ Other (Owen 1991; Peach 1996).

Official figures equivalent to these are not available for other European countries, although the publication *Immigrant Policy*, a Report to the Government by the Netherlands Scientific Council for Government Policy (1990) gives estimates of the numbers of those from 'non-indigenous groups with Netherlands citizenship'. The total number of these is 327 000, of whom 194 000 are from Surinam, 66 000 from Aruba and the Antilles, 40 000 who are Moluccans and 23 000 Chinese. In the case of the other European countries, the fact that relatively few of those from certain groups have sought naturalisation does mean that the statistics for the numbers of foreign citizens does give some indication of the size of minority communities. This is particularly true of the Turks in Germany, France and Belgium as well as in The Netherlands, and it is probably also true of the Moroccan minority in Belgium. The number of Maghrebians or the number from Guadeloupe and Martinique in France, however, is not deducible from the numbers having citizenship in those countries. Many Algerians who settled in France before independence had French citizenship, and many have been naturalised, while, so far as Guadeloupe and Martinique are concerned, immigrants from these territories are simply counted as French. There are no reliable estimates of the numbers of Maghrebians, West Indians or Africans in France, although the number of Maghrebians and their children is variously estimated at between 3 and 4 million.

Problems and policies

The problems of race and ethnic relations with which we are here concerned arise in the major countries of settlement, and each has its own distinctive profile. The primary preoccupation of Germany has been with its Turkish population, that of France with its Maghrebians, that of the United Kingdom with its Black and Asian immigrants, that of Belgium with its Moroccans and that of The Netherlands with its Turks and Moroccans as well as with Surinamese and Indonesians. This is not to say that Portuguese and Spanish immigrants in France, Italians, Yugoslavs and Greeks in Germany, the Irish in the United Kingdom and Italians in Belgium have not faced problems, but, given their cultural similarity to the peoples of their host societies, they have been and are likely to continue to be assimilated within three generations, with the internal EC migrants assimilating most readily of all. Significantly, too, the question of race and colour has not emerged as strongly in France as it has in Britain, immigrants from the overseas departments being seen as Black Frenchmen.

Although most of the migrants discussed above have been labour migrants, a small number of those from non-EC countries are refugees from the Middle East, from Africa and Asia, and from the communist countries. The collapse of communist regimes in 1990 will also add large numbers of east Europeans who are no longer likely to be refugees but may well become labour migrants. West Germany now also faces an inflow of east Germans following German unification. Problems arising from labour migration might well, therefore, be pushed into the background as the traditional countries of immigrant labour face new problems of dealing with refugees and east Europeans.

British policy for dealing with its immigrants was discussed and dealt with in a way quite different from other European countries. Although well over half of those born overseas were White, discussion of 'immigrants' was commonly focused on those who were thought of as 'Black'; that is, those from the Caribbean and those coming directly or indirectly from the Indian subcontinent. The collection of separate statistics of those coming from the New Commonwealth seems to have been designed to achieve this without making overt reference to race or colour. Moreover, the ethnic question in the 1991 census offers a choice between 'White', 'Black (West Indian, African or other)' or 'Asian (Indian, Pakistani or Bangladeshi)'.

Before 1962 all Commonwealth immigrants whether from the old and largely White Commonwealth or from the new and largely Black Commonwealth could settle freely in Britain. In 1962, however, controls were introduced. At first these applied equally to those from the old and new Commonwealth but, when the Act was amended in 1971, so-called 'patrials' (those with parents or grandparents who had lived in Britain) were given few rights of settlement, whereas even more severe restrictions were applied to 'non-patrials'.

Such distinctions were coupled with special policies of integration for the non-patrials, and a series of bodies culminating in the Commission for Racial Equality in 1976 were set up to combat 'racial' discrimination. These were based on American models for dealing with the problems of Black Americans, but were thought of as dealing not merely with the problems of West Indians, whose condition to some extent paralleled that of American Blacks, but also with the immigrants of Asian origin, who outnumbered the West Indians in a proportion of 11 to 5. The Commission had powers to help individual complainants who claimed they had suffered racial discrimination, and to carry out its own investigations of organisations against whom there was a prima-facie case of discrimination whether the discrimination was of a direct or indirect sort. The Commission was also empowered to do promotional work to promote good 'race relations', and the Act called on local councils to set up their own machinery for promoting equality of opportunity and good race relations.

The purpose of rehearsing these developments in Britain here is not, however, simply to describe the British situation, but rather to draw attention to the fact that British practice was not replicated in continental Europe. Some of those working in the race-relations field have suggested that Britain should lead the way and offer a model to European countries for setting up machinery to overcome racism and racial discrimination. What this ignores, however, is the fact that European countries do not necessarily conceive of their immigration problems in terms of race and colour at all.

Discussion of the problems of immigrants and ethnic minorities in terms of race was discredited in most of western Europe by the experience of Nazism. The very use of the term 'race' has, in fact, been to a large extent taboo, and there is a fear of a revival of racism which is often focused on the question of anti-Semitism. This is particularly true in Germany, where there is very considerable majority opposition to neo-Nazi movements, while in France colour-consciousness has never played the same role in political thinking that it has in Britain.

French thinking about immigrants and ethnic minorities is based on central political ideas deriving from the French Revolution. All citizens, it is thought, should be entitled to the full rights of citizenship regardless of race and of national, ethnic or religious origin. The state is thought of as being secular and, crucially, educational policy is based on the notion of the '*école laïque*'. Involved in this is a relative absence of colour consciousness of the British sort together with a fear that alien and immigrant cultures will undermine French political ideals. The major tensions in French society, so far as immigrants are concerned, tend to be ethnic and cultural rather than racial. It focuses especially on the fear of Islam and of what is referred to as 'Muslim fundamentalism', and the most pressing problem of ethnic relations in France today concerns the way in which the native majority and the secular state on the one hand and immigrant Muslim communities on the other come to terms with each other.

In Germany the situation is quite different. Its central political ideals involve not the sort of universalist political and republican conception of citizenship to be found in France, but rather an exclusive ideal of an ethnic group or '*Volk*'. Thus the constitution of the Federal Republic provided automatic citizenship for a spouse or descendant of persons who were settled in the German Reich on 31 December 1937, as well as refugees or deportees with German '*Volkszugehörigkeit*' (ethnicity), and this category has been extended to take in a wide range of ethnic Germans from the east, including, for instance, Germans who had settled in Romania between the twelfth and seventeenth centuries (Wilpert 1990). Non-Germans can also acquire citizenship by naturalisation, but the guest-worker ideology and policy insists that Germany is not a country of immigration and that, unless they do become naturalised, the guest-workers and their families may be workers and residents, but not citizens.

The combination of the ethnic nationalist and the guest-worker ideologies therefore makes for a kind of racism or, perhaps one should say, ethnicism, more sharp than in any other European country.

Policy in The Netherlands was directed to dealing with two major problems. One was the assimilation of various groups from the Dutch colonies; the other dealing with migrants from outside the former Dutch Empire. Prior to both these problems, moreover, was the fact that The Netherlands had already developed on pluralistic lines to accommodate the religious division of Dutch society. Relatively progressive policies were adopted towards those coming from the former colonies, the more so because they included many Dutch or half-Dutch immigrants from Indonesia. But, so far as Turks and others coming from outside were concerned, the first reaction was to treat them as guest-workers. Eventually, however, it was recognised to an extent which was not possible in Germany that what was needed was a policy for the integration of immigrants of both kinds. The government became concerned to promote equality of opportunity for immigrants, even though it did not set up elaborate institutional machinery to this end as in Britain. Yet at the same time it did not adopt the sort of assimilationist position to be found in France and, in accordance with Dutch tradition, was prepared to give recognition to minority cultures in a multicultural society.

Belgian experience was affected by the fact that Belgium is the most pluralist society in Europe. The country is divided in terms of language, religion and politics, and government depends on a balance between the linguistic groups, the different religions and differing class-based parties (Deprez 1989). The main early source of immigration was Italy, and the various indigenous political and cultural groups sought to assimilate the newcomers to themselves. Much more difficult is the assimilation of Moroccan immigrants. They have remained in relatively poor jobs and poor housing conditions, and their religion keeps them from assimilating to the predominant groups.

Finally, we should note the case of Italy. Italy was, until recently, primarily a country of emigration, a sending rather than a receiving society. At the same time, however, the Italian borders were exceptionally open, and the 1980s saw the arrival of many legal and illegal immigrants from eastern Europe as well as Africa and Asia. For the first time in 1989, Italy was becoming concerned both about the threat of large-scale immigration and about the dangers of the growth of racism and the resurgence of fascism. A new government edict in 1989 gave an amnesty to existing illegal immigrants and sought to promote their social rights without actually according them citizenship. It remains to be seen how Italian policy towards its immigrants will develop. Recently there have been spontaneous outbursts of racism and racist attacks against Blacks, and racism has found some political expression. At the same time, however, there is concern in the political parties and the unions to promote the interests and the rights of immigrant workers.

Multiculturalism

One particular feature of the British situation has been the gradual acceptance of the notion that Britain has become a 'multicultural society'.
This was not the first reaction to the coming of West Indian and Asian
immigrants. In 1964 the Commonwealth Immigrants Advisory Council
stated that 'a national [educational] system cannot be expected to per-
petuate the different values of minority groups'. In 1968, however, the
Home Secretary, Roy Jenkins, defined integration as 'not a flattening
process of uniformity, but cultural diversity coupled with equal opportunity in an atmosphere of mutual tolerance'. It is to be doubted whether
all those who accepted the idea of a multicultural society really based
the idea on this definition. For many it meant simply an acceptance of
the fact that there was a large immigrant population whose appearance,
language, religion and customs were different from those of the British.
Some also saw such diverse peoples and cultures as inferior, but eventually the Swann Committee, which was appointed to investigate the
problems of ethnic minority children in schools (Department of Education and Science 1985) concluded that all children should have their
education enriched by learning about ethnic minority culture and that
the practice of the schools and the content of the school syllabus should
be anti-racist.

The actual problems facing West Indian and Asian children, however,
differed from one another. West Indian children, although differing in
race and colour from their English peers, spoke English as their home
language and had a cultural background which was largely British. None
the less, there was a considerable body of evidence to suggest that they
were not doing well at school (Rex and Tomlinson 1979). Children from
Asian homes, on the other hand, spoke different languages at home and
came from different cultural and religious backgrounds, and Indian children at least were doing as well as their English peers (Department of
Education and Science 1981). West Indian parents and teachers claimed
that their children's relative failure was caused by racism both in the
school and in the wider society. Asians, on the other hand, had linguistic
problems, and some, primarily Muslims, were concerned that the schools
might undermine their religion and culture.

Because the education system in England is a highly decentralised
one, the actual developments which occurred varied from one local area
to another, but there was considerable development of multicultural
policies in many local authority areas and most teachers were expected
to develop their teaching in a multicultural way as well as being aware
themselves and making their pupils aware of the dangers of racism.

Such developments as these have not occurred in France. The French
educational system is both highly centralised and secular. It might well
include as part of its civics teaching the inculcation of democratic, egalitarian and anti-racist values, but it could have no place for the perpetuation
of minority cultures and religions. It is no way surprising that Muslim

girls at a French school with a Black French headmaster should have been sent home merely for wearing the scarf which was a normal part of Algerian Muslim dress. This contrasts quite sharply with the British situation, in which some local authorities have accepted religious instruction in minority religions in schools, the provision of *halal* meat in school meals, the right of Muslim girls to opt out of physical education and swimming lessons and the maintenance of some single-sex schools out of deference to the views of Asian parents.

The education of Turkish children in Germany has been considerably affected by the guest-worker system. Not merely are these children concentrated in the poorer schools, but there is also uncertainty on the part of the schools and of parents as to whether their children would not be best served by trying to achieve the sort of education which would help them on return to Turkey, rather than that which equipped them for competing in German society. No doubt this position is changing as more and more Turkish families become committed to remaining in Germany, but there is little doubt that so long as the parents are simply regarded as temporary workers there will be little in the way of educational development which will give Turkish children equality of opportunity and still less for the development of any sort of multiculturalism in the schools. Any development of the latter sort would also run counter to the ethnic nationalist ideology we have discussed above.

The European country most open to the idea of multiculturalism, other than Britain, is The Netherlands. Even there, however, the report *Immigrant Policy*, written as recently as 1990, envisages only that 'education in own language and culture henceforth be provided outside the regular curriculum but within the school' (Netherlands Scientific Council for Government Policy 1990). Clearly there is some acceptance here of the obligation of the schools themselves to provide for education in minority cultures rather than simply leaving it to voluntary effort by the parents and the community, but any such education is clearly to be kept 'outside the regular curriculum'. This contrasts with the recommendation of the British Swann Committee that all children should receive education in minority cultures as part of the curriculum, although it should be noted that the Swann Committee also suggests that the teaching of minority mother-tongue languages should actually occur outside the school.

It would seem, then, that the various European countries are far from being committed to multicultural education or to the idea of the multicultural society. The more normal response is either to base education on a shared culture in the public domain or simply the maintenance of traditional nationalist cultures. Even in Britain, moreover, it is to be doubted whether the notion of 'cultural diversity' coupled with 'equality of opportunity' is being realised. What actually occurs in many schools may involve no more than a token recognition of minority cultures.

Looking beyond the schools to the wider issues involved, it must be said that all European countries fall short of realising the two ideals of promoting both multiculturalism and equal opportunity for ethnic minorities. French critics of British policy sometimes accuse the British of actually achieving the 'ghettoisation' of minorities under the guise of multiculturalism, and rightly so, because, too often, diverse cultures are accepted only on unequal terms. On the other hand, British social scientists, looking at French practice, see the pressure towards giving the same rights of social citizenship to all, as actually being based on an assimilationist philosophy which allows no space for cultural diversity. In the German case, moreover, given the commitment to both German ethnic nationalism and to the notion of guest-workers, neither equal opportunity nor multiculturalism are likely to be attained.

Ghettoisation also occurs, in actuality, in all countries. We only have to look at British inner cities to see a process whereby most members of ethnic minority communities are increasingly isolated from their British born fellow-citizens as 'White flight' from the inner areas increases. But similar developments occur in other European cities. In France the ethnic minorities are often concentrated, not in the inner city, it is true, but in cheaply built suburban estates, while in Germany Turkish quarters emerge where apartments are available to immigrants. Such processes of segregation may in part be due to the choice of the ethnic minorities who need to be near their own mosques and temples, their own shops and their cultural centres. But they are also due to the constraints imposed by discrimination both in the private housing market and in publicly provided housing. No serious attempt has been made in any country to ensure that, while ethnic communities are encouraged to develop their communal facilities, they also have equal access to the better types of housing. Ghettoisation of the minorities is therefore likely to remain as a feature of western European cities for several generations.

A similar process of ghettoisation occurred in the field of employment when immigrants originally arrived to fill jobs unwanted by indigenous workers, and little was achieved by way of training or education on the job for these workers, so that they often remained in an industrial ghetto. When unemployment increased in the 1980s, moreover, immigrants bore more than their fair share, and trade unions were more inclined in these circumstances to defend the interests of indigenous workers. In Britain the position of the children of Black workers was particularly acute, since they were neither acceptable in the jobs which their parents had done, nor, because of discrimination, in the jobs for which they were qualified. Not surprisingly, Britain led the way in the occurrence of urban riots as the young Black unemployed came into conflict with the police, but recently there have been similar developments in France.

Refugees and EC controls

Worst placed in all the European countries are refugees, who have been given leave to remain while awaiting the outcome of their applications

for asylum, and unknown numbers of illegal immigrants. While technological developments made large-scale legal labour-immigration unnecessary and undesirable and led to the immigration stop in the early 1970s,
and capital moved to labour in the Third World rather than importing it,
there was still a need, even in the new technological conditions, for casual
unskilled labour in restaurants, in domestic service, in agriculture and
in some unpleasant manufacturing jobs, and this need was largely filled
from this new illegal and semi-legal population (Heisler and Heisler
1986). In Britain, Sivanandan has recently pointed out that 'hotel and
catering workers, the contract cleaners in hospitals, airports and so on,
the security guards in the private security firms, petrol pump attendants,
domestics, fast-food assistants, hospital auxiliaries and porters and . . .
many others come increasingly from Colombia, Chile, Turkey, Sudan,
Sri Lanka, Eritrea, Iran'. He says that these workers 'with no rights to
housing or to medical care, and under the constant threat of deportation
. . . are forced to accept wages and conditions which no indigenous worker,
Black or White, would accept' (Sivanandan 1990: 156). The numbers
of workers in these categories are probably greater in the continental
European countries and are also to be found there in other industries (as
in Italy where they play a larger part as itinerant agricultural workers).
Thus, if guest-workers are seen as a kind of relatively rightless 'underclass' compared with established immigrant workers, this new category
of workers would appear to form a kind of underclass beneath the underclass (Layton-Henry 1990).

In the preparation for 1992, the EC countries have sought to maximise the rights to EC citizens migrating from one EC country to another,
while at the same time restricting the rights of non-EC migrants. This
means that among those already settled, a distinction will exist between
mobile migrants who, because they have acquired citizenship, can move
from one country to another, and non-mobile migrants like the guest-
workers, who will not be entitled to move in this way. The implementation of such distinctions, moreover, will mean that minorities who are
visible by virtue of their skin colour or culture will, at best, be called on
to provide documentary evidence of their status and, at worst, will be
subject to harassment by the police and other authorities.

So far as new refugees and migrants are concerned, the position will be
even more difficult. Already groups of civil servants from the EC countries have been meeting to discuss the harmonisation of their policies at the borders, taking in as well as the questions of immigration and
the rights of refugees to asylum, the question of drug traffic and terrorism.
One group consisting of representatives of France, Germany and The
Netherlands (with the later adherence of Italy) has met at Schengen to
consider the creation of a common external border for those countries,
while an all-EC group meeting at Trevi has dealt with the problems of
the EC countries as a whole (Minority Rights Group 1990). From what
is already known of the findings of these groups, it seems likely that

immigration and refugee policy will be harmonised at the level of the greatest possible restriction, an outcome which is the more inevitable when it is noted that immigration and refugee questions are being discussed in the same fora as the questions of drug traffic and terrorism. Although there are lobbies in all countries concerned with defending the rights of immigrants and refugees, the overall ideology which at present informs policy-making is that of 'Fortress Europe', with the strongest possible defences against outsiders.

A new environing element in this situation has been created by the collapse of communist regimes in eastern Europe and, indeed, the Soviet Union itself. The likelihood is that within the next ten years millions of east Europeans will seek to move to the greater prosperity of the West. In the immediate euphoria surrounding the end of the Cold War, migrants and refugees from this quarter will enjoy a certain prestige, and there will be pressure for their admission. Even though this euphoria will abate as cheap east European labour comes to compete with that of western Europe, it seems likely that such labour will be more acceptable than that coming from the Third World, or even from Turkey. Already in West Germany, ethnic Germans from the East may readily acquire German citizenship, while Turkish and other guest-workers remain relatively rightless. It is likely that in other countries, east Europeans who are thought of as being 'like us' will be regarded as being like the ethnic Germans, while existing guest-workers, refugees waiting for asylum, and illegals of all sorts will form a relatively rightless underclass.

It is clear that, even though there remains a fear of immigration as such in Europe, during a period of economic recession, the declining birth rate in west Europe, coupled with future economic expansion, will mean there will inevitably be a considerable new immigration in the 1990s. The countries which have a demographic surplus and which can potentially meet this need are in east Europe, Africa and Asia, though any one of them could meet the whole need. It is conceivable that immigration policies could be based on actual economic needs, regardless of nationality and race, but the likelihood is that the consciousness of kind of the west Europeans will lead them to opt for their fellow-Europeans from the East. The fact that these east Europeans are White could well mean the emergence of a new type of European colour racism which, as well as closing the boundaries to Africans and Asians, could rebound on Europe's existing Black and Asian populations.

In these circumstances it is likely that those immigrants and their children who are relatively rightless will organise themselves along ethnic lines across European boundaries, and there is some evidence that this is happening. Such transnational organisation is a source of considerable concern in some European countries, particularly in France, but at the level of the European Commission steps were already being taken in 1990 to set up a consultative mechanism for such organisations. Although the theory behind this development is that, because non-EC migrants are not represented in the European Parliament, their interests should be taken care of through a consultative mechanism, it is interesting to notice that the Commission has included British Black and Asian organisations in their consultation even though they represent EC citizens. This reflects the fact that Black British and Asian workers share *de facto* the political and economic position of the non-EC migrants in Europe; but, in any case, it is clear that the Commission recognises it has to deal with classes of immigrants who are not represented through normal political channels (Hammar 1985; Gordon 1989).

All in all, the new European society which is likely to come into being will include a politically stratified system of groups. The majority will be citizens of the EC countries entitled to mobility between these countries and having representation in the European Parliament. Included in this group, however, there will be some like British Blacks and Asians, who, despite their citizenship, may be confused with non-EC migrants, and *de facto* fail to enjoy the same rights and freedoms as other EC citizens. There will also be immigrants and refugees from east Europe who, although not enjoying full citizenship at first, may be recognised by virtue of their shared skin colour and culture, as being especially entitled to rights and as having an easy path to naturalisation. There will still be many contract labourers and guest-workers who will be, as Hammar (1990) has put it, 'denizens' rather than citizens, and who will not enjoy the rights of citizens. And, finally, there will be a residue of refugees and illegals, whose presence is tolerated so long as they are in employment, but who can readily be deported and dispensed with. Given such distinctions of political, legal and social status, these different groups of European inhabitants will have differing access to employment and social rights and will in effect be distinct classes. In a Marxist interpretation, the existence of such classes might be seen as a necessary consequence of the needs of European capitalism (see, for example, Sivanandan 1990: Ch. 9). In other interpretations, their emergence may be seen as an historic accident, but one which none the less provides the environment within which the capitalist economic development of Europe is likely to occur.

At least at the level of rhetoric, however, the new Europe is unlikely to accept this picture of a politically and economically stratified society within 'Fortress Europe' as a fair and final definition of itself. Thus it may be expected that, entrenched though the guest-worker ideology may be in some countries and the ideology of racism in others, there will be some pressure to alleviate the position both of guest-workers and of those who suffer racial and ethnic discrimination. There will also be pressure to harmonise future immigration and refugee policy on a non-racist basis. It would be wrong, however, to imagine that rhetoric in these areas actually describes the structural reality of Europe.

Conclusion

In more general terms, European countries and the EC as a whole will need to, and probably will, develop policies to promote equality of opportunity and to prevent racial and ethnic discrimination on the one hand, and to deal with cultural diversity on the other. At the moment the debate about these issues has, however, hardly begun; different countries have different ideologies and different institutions; harmonisation of policy will be by no means easy, and the likelihood is that the first steps towards harmonisation will be at the level of the lowest common denominator; that is to say, at the level which does least to protect inferior groups.

So far as equality of opportunity and the prevention of racism is concerned, what is most likely to occur is a rhetorical denunciation of 'racism' as in the European Parliament's *Declaration against Racism and Xenophobia*, without any serious attempt to require the setting up of institutions to prevent discrimination and overcome racial and ethnic disadvantage. In this matter, Britain, having established elaborate institutions on an American model, might be thought of as leading the way. In many European countries, however, it will be argued that such machinery has been developed in Britain precisely because colour-racism is endemic there to an extent that it is not in other countries. It remains to be seen, though, whether these other countries will move beyond the level of rhetoric and develop appropriate forms of enforcement to prevent racial and ethnic discrimination.

Clearly, without effective enforcement machinery of this kind (and it should be noted that as the most recent studies of the Policy Studies Institute show – (Brown 1984) – even the elaborate institutional machinery established in Britain has been far from fully effective), any move towards multiculturalism, taken on its own, will mean only ghettoisation at best and apartheid at worst. None the less, the issue of multiculturalism or assimilation to a unitary culture is one which has to be faced.

It is not to be expected that most European societies will wish to become pluralistic in the way which Belgian society and, in a lesser way, Dutch society is. Belgian society is pluralistic because of the relative equality of power of two linguistic groups, and the so-called 'pillarisation' of The Netherlands arose to meet the needs of two religious communities. What is possible, however, is that, while maintaining a unitary political culture in the public sphere, these societies might develop policies for the tolerance of minority cultures in the private and communal sphere.

A real obstacle to the emergence of this kind of limited multiculturalism, however, lies in the ethnic nationalism of majority groups, as represented most clearly in the German case. It is one thing to proclaim a culture based on political values of liberty, equality and fraternity, as the French do, or to recognise the existence of common social rights, as has been suggested by T. H. Marshall (1950) in Britain, since all groups can be invited to share in such a culture, while preserving their own communal cultures. It is quite another to proclaim a culture based on ethnic nationalism, from which minorities are by definition excluded.

Even if a national political culture rests on political values which all groups can share, however, the problem remains as to how far private communal cultures should be, or are likely to be, maintained. In this matter, the French tend to be the most assimilationist, the Dutch and the British the most inclined towards multiculturalism. Probably, in the long run, the dogmas and ideologies surrounding these notions may be modified in practice, with assimilationists recognising that there has to be some at least temporary recognition of minority cultures in the private sphere and the multiculturalists recognising that the problem they face may become less urgent over several generations. Possibly, the major problem which may arise is about the place of Islam in European society, since there are now, probably, some 6 million Muslims in Europe and Islam is unlikely to disappear. But even here dialogue is beginning about the place which Islam claims and can be accorded in European society.

Thus there are many problems which still have to be resolved relating to the position of immigrant ethnic minorities in Europe. They concern both the question of equality of opportunity and of cultural coexistence. They may, indeed, be the major problems of the political sociology of Europe in the 1990s.

References

Brown, C. (1984) *Black and White in Britain: the Third PSI Survey*, London: Heinemann.

Castles, S. and Kosack, G. (1973) *Immigrant Workers and Class Structure in Western Europe*, Oxford: Oxford University Press.

Commission for Racial Equality (1985) *Ethnic Minorities in Britain*, London: Commission for Racial Equality.

Department of Education and Science (1981) *Committee of Enquiry into the Education of Children from Ethnic Minority Groups: Interim Report: West Indian Children in our Schools*, Cmnd 8272, London: HMSO.

Department of Education and Science (1985) *Education for All: Report of the Committee of Enquiry into the Education of Children from Ethnic Minority Groups*, vol. 2 (Chairman, Lord Swann), Cmnd 9453, London: HMSO.

Deprez, K. (ed.) (1989) *Language and Intergroup Relations in Flanders*, Dordrecht: Foris Publications.

Eurostat (1990) *Demographic Statistics*, Brussels.

Gordon, P. (1989) *Fortress Europe: the Meaning of 1992*, London: Runnymede Trust.

Hammar, T. (ed.) (1985) *European Immigration Policy*, Cambridge: Cambridge University Press.

Hammar, T. (1990) *Democracy and the Nation State*, Research in Ethnic Relations Series, Centre for Research in Ethnic Relations, University of Warwick, London: Gower.

Heisler, M. and Heisler, B. (1986) 'From foreign workers to settlers: transnational migration and the emergence of new minorities', *Annals of the American Academy of Political and Social Science*, 485.

Layton-Henry, Z. (ed.) (1990) *The Political Rights of Migrant Workers in Western Europe*, London: Sage.

Marshall, T. H. (1950) *Citizenship and Social Class*, Cambridge: Cambridge University Press.

Minority Rights Group (1990) *Refugees in Europe*, London: Minority Rights Group.

Netherlands Scientific Council for Government Policy (1990) *Immigrant Policy*, The Hague: Netherlands Scientific Council for Government Policy.

OECD (1995) *Trends in International Migration*, SOPEMI Annual Report.

Owen, David (1991) *Ethnic Minorities in Great Britain: Settlement Patterns*, Central Statistical Paper No. 1, National Ethnics Minority Data Archive, Central for Research Warwick, in Ethnic Relations.

Peach, C. (ed.) (1996) *Ethnicity in the 1991 Census, vol. 2, The Ethnic Minority Populations of Great Britain*, Office of National Statistics, London: HMSO.

Piore, M. (1974) *Birds of Passage: Migrant Labour and Industrial Society*, Cambridge: Cambridge University Press.

Rex, J. and Tomlinson, S. (1979) *Colonial Immigrants in a British City*, London: Routledge & Kegan Paul.

Sivanandan, A. (1990) *Communities of Resistance: Writings on Black Struggles for Socialism*, London: Verso.

Wilpert, C. (1990) 'Racism – the blind spot of migration research in the Federal Republic of Germany', Unpublished paper delivered to the Congress on Racism and Migration in Europe, Hamburg.

PART TWO

Responding Social Institutions

CHAPTER 7

A crazy quilt: education, training and social change in Europe

LYNNE CHISHOLM*

At first glance, institutional and policy arrangements for education and training across Europe are bewilderingly diverse. These complex patterns win coherence if we regard European societies as responding to sets of common problems with a range of different solutions, which themselves are structured by divergent forms of social and cultural organisation and relationships (Jallade 1989: 103). This means that we need to identify unifying features which can anchor variations in educational and training policies, provision and participation within wider debates about social change in advanced economies.

The economic development and prosperity of EU member states obviously differs, and so the education and training problems faced by Greece or Portugal as opposed to France or Germany are not entirely common. Portugal, for example, established the legislative basis for a modern educational system only in 1986, the year it joined the European Union. Now, a decade later, compulsory education lasts nine years and over half of Portuguese 18-year-olds are still in some form of education and training, which is well within the broad pattern for the member states as a whole (see Tables 7.1 and 7.2). At the other end of the scale, in 1993 only 13 per cent of Portuguese employees had received some form of continuing training; jointly with Greece, this was the lowest level among the member states (European Commission 1997a: 32). Similarly, in 1995 only 23 per cent of those aged between 25 and 59 in Portugal had been educated to at least upper secondary level, against an EU average of 68 per cent (Eurostat 1997: 15).

However, it is equally so that in EU comparison, Portuguese education and training participation rates for the 15–24 age group rose fastest of all between 1987 and 1995: from 35 per cent to 57 per cent (ibid.: 19). The drive to modernise Portugal's education system has focused especially on its role in assisting economic development, with the country 'setting off in pursuit of other European countries in an attempt to make

---

* This contribution represents the personal professional judgements of the author. It does not necessarily represent European Commission policy positions, nor does it implicate the Commission in any field of its activities.

up for lost time' (Tavares Emídio 1988: 195). This raises the more general issue of whether contemporary change in Europe might bring greater convergence in education and training policies, systems and behaviours: a question to which we return later in this chapter.

Nevertheless, the links between education and economy are neither automatically linear nor simple, as the experience of central and eastern European countries shows, who developed particular kinds of solutions for their specific contexts (for examples, see Adamski and Grootings 1989). In planned economies, young people all found, or were allocated to, training courses and jobs. These did not necessarily match their aspirations or potential, but then no one necessarily expected them to do so. Qualifications were adapted to the occupational structuring of planned labour markets, and were, in that context, both transparent and reliable in use. After 1989, many found themselves working towards qualifications which suddenly lost their labour-market exchange value and with occupations in view that rapidly ceased to exist in the transition to modernised market economies. These dislocations in established education–economy relations, and the high unemployment rates that have accompanied them, signify personal and social ruptures difficult fully to appreciate in western Europe (for example, see Koklyagina 1995; but also Roberts 1996, which equally focuses on the similarities between contemporary youth transitions in eastern and western Europe).

Once more, we can ask whether, despite different pasts and dissimilar presents, European societies as a whole are now facing similar challenges as processes of economic and cultural globalisation take hold. What do these challenges imply for the structures, processes and contexts of learning which have become part of the taken-for-granted of growing up in industrial societies and relatively insulated national cultures?

In the discussion which follows, the key underlying concepts are those of transitions and critical turning points. The term 'transitions' emphasises processes of moving between social locations. Young people, for example, are in the process of moving between childhood and adulthood, and their progress through education, training and into the labour market is one of the central and socially legitimated means by which they do so. 'Critical turning points' direct attention both to the institutional arrangements and to the decisions which privilege and enact different kinds of routes through to adult life. Youth transitions are therefore highly socially structured experiences. Education and training policy, provision and practice, whatever forms these may take in particular countries, contribute very significantly to that structuring. At the same time, the conditions of young people's lives are shifting, too, as part of wider patterns of social change in Europe.

The next section of this chapter looks at some of the changing patterns of youth transitions, placing these in the broader context of social change, which is beginning to reformulate intergenerational relations and the place of learning across the life-course as a whole. The following two sections describe some of the diversity among solutions to increasingly shared problems, by looking at how member states organise their education and training systems and by asking whether they are becoming more similar in certain basic respects. The final section then considers the challenge of creating a learning society for Europe, which is perhaps the central policy issue for the coming years.

The changing patterns of youth transitions

In comparison with the patterns of youth transitions that had established themselves in western societies by the mid-twentieth century, the last twenty years or so have seen marked change. The youth phase has become longer in duration, is now dominated by schooling rather than employment, and the classic milestones of transition no longer necessarily follow what was the normative sequence (education to training to employment to marriage, an independent household, and finally children). These changes are usually described in terms of the destandardisation and individualisation of the youth phase.

Adulthood is still socially defined as being economically independent and setting up one's own household and family, although the contexts of people's lives increasingly indicate some redefinition of life-course phases. The boundaries between youth and adulthood are fuzzier than they used to be, with a series of 'quasi-statuses' opening up between dependence and independence as well as a loosening of normative prescriptions about what kinds of identities, images and behaviours are appropriate for people of different ages and stages. This has led some researchers to argue for a 'new' phase of life called either post-adolescence or simply young adulthood (Zinneker 1990; Walther 1996). The high rates of youth unemployment which began to appear from the mid-1970s in most parts of western Europe and which have now become a persistent feature of European labour markets accelerated these changes.

Howsoever interpreted in life-course terms, it takes longer to reach economic independence than it used to do twenty years ago, and much of the 'extra' time is now spent learning rather than gainfully doing – or, indeed, in mixtures between the two. These new transition patterns also include living in diverse kinds of household and partnership arrangements, but in most of Europe young people are now staying rather longer in the parental home than they did two decades ago, largely for financial reasons but also in response to the widespread liberalisation of intergenerational relations in the family. In essence, negotiating the journey between youth and adulthood has become altogether more complicated. Opportunities for formulating one's own life-plan may have expanded, but the corollary is that the risks of failing to carry this through successfully in personal and social terms have also intensified (for an extended discussion of the literature on this topic, see Furlong and Cartmel 1997).

Evidence for these changes is readily identifiable in all member states, although there are significant differences in the extent to which they have taken hold, how they are expressed in people's lives, and the cultural meanings attached to them. So, for example, while the idea of broken transitions caused by the collapse of the youth labour market gained early currency in British debates, the idea of a more fundamental restructuring and retiming of the youth phase caused by broader economic and social change in Europe was not widely discussed until the mid-1990s. This idea was debated much earlier in those parts of Europe where the extension of youth transitions had appeared earlier on, in particular in western Germany, The Netherlands and the Nordic countries. In these countries, post-compulsory education and training-participation rates had risen to much higher levels by the end of the 1970s than in Britain, where the majority of young people continued to enter the labour force at a much earlier age through to the late 1980s. This was part of a broader-based cultural pattern in which an earlier transition to autonomy and independence was favoured in Britain, even if it was not necessarily realisable and had become distinctly less realisable since the mid-1970s (Chisholm 1993).

It is also important to bear in mind that youth transitions are not solely about transitions between education and employment. When family-based transitions are taken equally into account, this can change the perspective on what extended transitions mean and where they are most typically to be found. It has been argued, for example, that there is a basic cleavage between patterns of youth transitions in northern versus southern Europe, with patterns in France occupying a bridging role (Le Bras 1996). Based on an event analysis that covers four classic milestones (completing education/training, finding regular employment, getting married and having a first child), Lagrée (1996) shows that youth transitions in northern Europe begin later and finish earlier, i.e. all four events occur over a shorter period of the lifetime, making for a 'denser' transition process. Dense transitions do not necessarily mean chronologically early transitions: from this kind of perspective, young people in Denmark and The Netherlands experience the densest transitions, but the events themselves take place later – because of longer periods of education and training, for example. In contrast, 'stretched' youth transitions are most likely to occur in Italy and Portugal. In Italy, family-based transitions take place chronologically late; in Portugal, education and training still finishes relatively early for the majority of young people. Looked at in this way, it is young men living in southern Europe who experience the longest-drawn-out youth transitions. Over the last twenty years, the differences between northern and southen Europe have narrowed, and this is primarily a consequence of the rising rates of post-compulsory education and training.

Extended participation in education and training: trends and contrasts

The trend towards longer periods of education and training by ever higher proportions of young people can be traced back to the 1960s, when economic affluence and expanding labour markets provided the basis for educational expansion and reform – although the onset and the intensity of these changes clearly differed between European countries. By the 1980s, extended education and training participation had become a universal response to youth unemployment and contracting labour markets, engendered both by policy measures (such as youth training schemes) and by individual decisions to continue (in the hope that improved qualifications would bring better employment chances).

In the 1990s, these problems have certainly not disappeared, but they are being increasingly overlain by the implications of demographic change towards an ageing society and the demands of transition to a post-Fordist, knowledge-based economy. In differing ways, both place a renewed emphasis on education and training as the foundation and guarantee of individual and social well-being. Raising levels of qualification and skill for all citizens has become an important policy priority with a double focus – not only initial education and training for young people, but also continuing education and training for people of all ages and circumstances.

While continuing education and training participation remains singularly underdeveloped (and see OECD 1996), those member states in which young people's participation rates were particularly low in the early 1980s (such as Portugal and Spain, but also the UK) are those in which intense efforts at improvement have been made, including structural and curricular reforms in order to facilitate and encourage greater participation.

Leaving the education and training system completely at the end of compulsory schooling is now a minority pattern (at the national level) everywhere in the European Union, and in many member states it is no longer exceptional for 20-year-olds still to be engaged in some form of education and training (see Table 7.1). The generality of this picture has emerged only in the course of the 1990s, with significant upward shifts having taken place from the late 1980s. From each hundred 15–24-year-olds living in one of the present member states, those in full-time or part-time education and training numbered 49 in 1987 and 58 by 1995. Over the same period, the age at which at least half of young people have entered the labour force on at least a part-time basis has risen from 18 in 1987 to 20 in 1995 (Eurostat 1997: 22, 41).

At the same time, this general picture conceals significant differences between the member states, and national level statistics themselves do not display regional and social differences in participation patterns; on the latter, we lack systematic European comparative data, but the extent of the differences at national level alone indicates the need to develop more closely focused comparisons.

First, the scale of the generation gap in cohort participation/qualification levels is considerably wider in southern member states than in northern ones (with the exception of Ireland and Luxembourg). In 1995, at least four-fifths of Danish, Dutch and German 25–59-year-olds (the main body of the active labour force) had completed at least upper secondary level education, whereas this was so for under two-fifths of those in Italy, Spain and Portugal. However, the differences in education/qualification level between those aged 25–29 and 55–59 are much greater in southern European countries, where the oldest cohorts are least well-qualified of all and the younger cohorts have moved ahead very swiftly since the 1970s. Between 1987 and 1995 the biggest leaps in the proportion of 15–24-year-olds in education and training took place in Portugal and Spain, but also in Luxembourg, where high participation rates are also a relatively recent pattern (Eurostat 1997: 15, 19).

Second, participation rates of 15–24-year-olds in the mid-1990s are still spread across quite a wide range. At least two-thirds of this age group were in some form of education and training in Denmark, France, Finland and The Netherlands; something under half were doing so in Sweden and the UK (ibid.). Understanding why particular countries fall where they do on such participation continua requires more information. For example, Sweden actually has high participation rates through to age 18, and only after the age of 19 are young adults more likely to be in the labour market than to be in education and training; subsequently, relatively high proportions of mature students find access to higher education. This means that Sweden's education and training system today succeeds in bringing the bulk of its population through to successful completion of upper secondary level qualification followed by some form of further training, but not necessarily university studies; subsequently, opportunities to return to higher education and to participate in continuing education and training alongside employment are among the best in the Union (European Commission 1997a: 32).

The probability of Swedish employees having received training within the past year rose from 15 per cent in 1982 to 38 per cent in 1994; participation rates rose in the UK, too, but at 15.4 per cent, were still at a much lower level in 1990 (OECD 1996: 55–6). And although the proportion of those aged 30+ registering as first-year undergraduates in the UK is higher than elsewhere in the Union, participation rates continue to drop more sharply than in most member states after the age of 16 and once more after the age of 21 (Eurostat 1997: 32; and Table 7.1). This means that the UK continues to be less successful than Sweden in bringing the bulk of its population through to the benchmark stage of upper secondary completion: after the age of 17, British young people are more likely to be in the labour market than in education and training.

Table 7.1 now summarises 1994 participation patterns for 15–24-year-olds on the basis of OECD data for the EU member states (except for Italy and Luxembourg, for whom data are not available). Countries are shown in descending order of participation rates across three bandings: the ages at which rates drop below 75 per cent, 50 per cent and 25 per cent respectively. These boundaries are also indicated on the table.

Table 7.1 **Participation towards the end of compulsory schooling and beyond: total participation in all levels of education and training for ages 18–24 in public and private institutions, 1994, %**

	15	16	17	18	19	20	21	22	23	24
Belgium	103	104	101	87	72	61	45	35	24	18
Germany	98	96	93	85	66	46	34	39	21	18
France	98	96	92	84	69	54	40	30	20	12
Sweden	97	96	95	83	34	28	28	28	26	22
Finland	100	96	92	83	37	40	46	46	39	33
Netherlands	99	98	91	80	67	57	46	36	29	22
Denmark	98	94	81	70	53	41	37	34	31	27
Ireland	95	93	83	82	48	35	28	13	8	5
Austria	95	92	86	61	34	23	19	16	15	13
Spain	94	82	75	63	52	49	40	34	24	18
United Kingdom	99	87	74	53	44	37	28	20	16	14
Portugal	85	74	67	55	44	37	31	27	20	15
Greece	81	82	57	59	53	39	33	17	13	8

Notes:
1 OECD statistics for Italy and Luxembourg not available.
2 Figures have been rounded up/down to the nearest whole number.
3 These figures are not comparable with earlier OECD statistics; they are
based on head counts only and do not distinguish between full-time and
part-time involvement. For some countries, part-time enrollments may
be underestimated. All vocational training courses are included except those
which are workplace-based but not supervised by educational authorities.
4 There is an error in the OECD publication for participation rates in Ireland
at age 18: the correct figure is shown in this table.

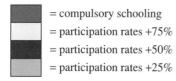

= compulsory schooling
= participation rates +75%
= participation rates +50%
= participation rates +25%

Source: CERI 1996: Table P3.1, p. 122 (amended)

The participation patterns shown in Table 7.1 suggest a broad clustering into three groups of countries, with two 'outliers'. In the first group,
Sweden, Finland, Denmark and The Netherlands, participation rates remain
highest for longest. A third of Finnish 24-year-olds are still in education
and training and all four countries record the highest levels for this age.
Further down the age scale, all four countries maintain high participation rates, although these begin to dip markedly at different points: in
Denmark between 18 and 20, in Sweden and Finland at 19, but not until
21 in The Netherlands. Group 1 is characterised, then, by relatively high
participation rates that also extend well into people's mid-twenties.

The second group, Belgium, Germany and France, are notable for very high participation rates through to age 20. Rates for those aged over 20 remain comparable with those in the Nordic countries and The Netherlands, but decline more noticeably after the age of 22. Belgium and Germany have the longest compulsory systems (see Table 7.2), and the 1980s in France saw a major policy campaign – including the introduction of new *baccalauréat* options – with the goal of bringing 80 per cent of each age cohort through to an 18+ qualification level. It is Germany's dual system of vocational education and training that ensures high participation rates through to age 19, rather than maintaining high levels of participation in school-based upper secondary education, as in the case of Belgium and France. In sum, group 2 is characterised by the maintenance of high participation rates, but which then begin to fall away by people's early twenties.   .

The third group, Spain, the United Kingdom, Portugal and Greece, form a cluster because participation rates fall off earliest, and most especially at the earliest ages. By age 17, at least a quarter of young people in these four countries are no longer in education and training; and participation falls off to below 50 per cent at age 19 in the United Kingdom and Portugal and at age 20 in Spain and Greece. Participation rates between the ages of 20 and 22 are comparable with those in group 2 (though rather lower in the UK) and then decline in a similar way (and most sharply in Greece). So group 3 is characterised by comparatively low participation rates which fall off quite early on.

Ireland and Austria are the two outliers. Ireland's participation pattern is in fact similar to group 3, with the difference that participation rates through to age 18 are much higher. In Austria, however, participation rates decline earliest of all throughout the 15–24 age range. By age 20, fewer than a quarter of young people remain in education and training, which is the lowest level in the member states. However, participation rates for the 15–18 age range are noticeably higher than in group 3 countries. Participation levels beyond age 23 are also higher than in Ireland, which reflects their differently organised higher education systems. We could nevertheless summarise that in Ireland and in Austria, participation rates are relatively high, but these fall off quite early on.

Differing combinations of participation levels and durations are the outcome of complex interactions between the established structures of national systems, policy measures to raise and shift participation profiles, and the collective effects of individual decision-making about which education and training strategies are possible, desirable and useful as perceived in a given social and economic context. One visible current trend, for example, sees greater numbers of young people choosing to combine their studies with paid work. In some member states, such as Denmark and The Netherlands, this is an established and widespread pattern. The 1995 European Labour Force Survey records 29 per cent of 15-year-olds in these two countries as combining the two in some fashion. By the age of 18, two-thirds of Danes and two-fifths of the Dutch are doing so; and they are joined by between 30 and 40 per cent of Germans, Austrians, Finns and the British (Eurostat 1997: 43).

Another increasingly popular strategy is to accumulate qualifications by consecutively following two or more education and training courses; in Spain and in Germany, a fifth of the relevant age group is doing so (OECD 1996: 121). So, for example, over the 1980s it has become more common for young Germans completing their *Abitur* (the equivalent of A-levels for the UK, and guaranteeing access to university) to take an apprenticeship in the dual system before going on to higher education (in 1992, 18.4 per cent did so; Statistisches Bundesamt 1995: Ch. 2). This is now seen as an extra bonus point for career opportunities later on, and recent research has been able to show that in some occupational sectors and for young people at some qualification levels, dual-system apprenticeships are used strategically as a stepping-stone to higher-level training/qualification access and to different occupations altogether from those for which they originally trained in the dual system (Heinz 1998).

Selection and participation in national education systems

All European countries face sets of fundamental tensions about the purposes of modern education. General education concerns itself with cultural socialisation, but also, together with the more specific contributions of vocational education and training, with economic sustenance through the provision of appropriately skilled and knowledgeable individuals for the labour market. Education and training as a whole is orientated towards the optimal development of a wide range of human potential, but also to selection and allocation into social and economic positions according to the demands of the collectivity rather than personal capacities and preferences. Education and training systems aim in principle to offer equal access and opportunity to all, but in practice outcomes reflect the structured inequalities of the wider society. Policies and patterns of provision reflect these tensions in one way or another.

Most contemporary educationalists would favour broad-based and open-ended learning for all, centred on the concept of a common curriculum. Indeed, today's 13-year-olds all study the same compulsory subjects at school, even if the proportional weight given to each subject varies between member states; and the evidence indicates that across Europe, secondary schooling is moving towards providing a broad and common curriculum for all pupils (including those with special needs; European Commission 1996a: 52; Green, Leney and Wolf 1997: Ch. 3).

Nevertheless, specialisation will and must occur at some stage in the educational process. Young people's capacities, preferences and motivations are diverse, too, quite apart from the considerable influences exerted on the shape of educational options by labour markets themselves. How and when specialisation is introduced into education systems by the provision of different kinds of routes – together with the ways in which these routes are valued and rewarded – are key markers in charting national (and in certain cases regional) responses to these various tensions. By the stage of post-compulsory education and training at the latest, specialisation into different routes and levels becomes virtually axiomatic. For this reason, the extent to which it is possible to develop choice and diversity at this stage while keeping to a minimum the well-known negative effects of differentiation becomes a key and perennial question (OECD 1989: 10).

The relationships and distinctions between 'education' and 'training' routes are of particular importance in this connection. In most parts of Europe, academic routes are still valued more highly than are technical or vocational ones and, when pursued through to higher education qualification level, usually bring higher rewards in terms of income and career development (one partial exception has been Germany). Many barriers continue to exist for those wishing to combine the two branches or switch from one to the other, especially from the vocational to the academic.

The division between academic *knowledge* and vocational *skills* is deeply coded into European teaching and learning systems. In the English language, this division is mirrored in the very terms 'education' and 'training', which have traditionally been seen as quite separate activities which, rephrased as *philosophia* and *technica*, also stand in a hierarchical relation to each other. In practice, curricula gradually separate out into subjects commonly understood as theoretical and practical; examination tracks and selective school systems branch into general-academic and technical-vocational pathways. Pupils are selected, and select themselves, on to these different routes. These selection processes are mediated and legitimated primarily through formal attainment, but fundamentally they are social in nature, thereby largely reproducing the gender, ethnic/race and class divisions that already exist in the society concerned. Those who do well at school mainly move on to general-academic tracks; technical-vocational tracks absorb those who do not or cannot do so.

Indeed, resolving these problems has been identified as one of the major challenges facing the European Union in the coming decades (Study Group on Education and Training 1997: Ch. 3). The argument that all students should study both the academic and the vocational, both the theoretical and the practical, has been forcefully argued for some time (for example, see Finegold *et al.* 1990). In the UK, the opening up of upper secondary qualification routes by the introduction of GVQs during the 1990s illustrates one country's attempt to break the academic/vocational dichotomy; the introduction of the *baccalauréat professionnel* in the mid-1980s in France is another.

There are signs of moves in most parts of Europe to develop a more integrated relationship between academic and vocational education, but it may be that this is now contributing to what could be termed 'academic drift'. Young people are opting increasingly for upper secondary general education routes, while simultaneously vocational education and training is becoming increasingly school-based and less occupationally specific in nature (Green, Leney and Wolf 1997: Ch. 4). In Germany, where technical-vocational routes are traditionally strong and respected, there is also evidence that companies are beginning to recruit university graduates into jobs formerly held by those trained and qualified in the dual system. This is not simply a feature of credential inflation, but is rather encouraged both by the changing nature of skills demands (placing more emphasis on abstract/symbolic competences) and by the changing cost-benefit equations made by employers struggling to maintain competition (schools and universities are funded from the public purse, whereas vocational training requires significant employer investment; see Büchtemann and Vogler-Ludwig 1997: 19). Nevertheless, the ways in which education and the workplace are integrated remain dissimilar between those countries where apprenticeship plays a major and respected role, and those where it does not (Green, Leney and Wolf 1997: 126).

The axes along which particular countries find their specific solutions to the differentiation and specialisation dilemma include the following: comprehensive versus differentiated secondary schooling; common curricula for all versus differentiated tracks and options; general-academic versus technical-vocational knowledge; education-led versus employer-led teaching and learning; school-based versus workplace-based vocational education and training; and unilinear access and progression versus modular and interlinking participation and accreditation systems. Table 7.2 uses some of these distinctions to identify critical turning-points in education systems; that is, institutionalised moments at which young people select themselves and are equally selected into (or out of) particular kinds of transitions routes. These are by no means the only kinds of critical moments in the educational shaping of social biographies, but they are important ones. They offer a skeleton, and thus a starting point, for thinking about how transitions systems between education, training and paid work may develop in the future in the European Union.

Table 7.2 shows that compulsory schooling begins between the ages of four and seven, most typically at the age of six. Where compulsory education begins early, the first year or so is more like kindergarten (educationally oriented preschooling). In addition, almost all member states provide some form of preschooling or nursery education, although this is not always formally regarded as part of the mainstream education system and children do not necessarily have the right to a place. Preschooling is typically available from the age of three, in some parts of the Union much earlier. Figures for 1992/3 (European Commission 1996a: 25–32) show that in France, where *écoles maternelles* are accessible for all two-year-olds, over one-third were attending by the early 1990s; by the age of three, attendance is almost universal. In Belgium, where there

Table 7.2 Critical turning points in the education systems of European Union member states

Age at which	Compulsory schooling begins	First branch in system occurs	Compulsory ft general education ends	Compulsory ft/pt VET ends	Entry to HE can occur	First HE qualification can occur	N years of compulsory ed./tr.
Belgium	6	12/14	15/16	18	18/19	20/24+	12[1]
Germany	6/7	11/12	15/16	18/19	18/19	22/23+	11[1]
France	6	13/15	16	16	18	20/22	10
Sweden	7	16	16	16	19	22	9
Finland	7	16	16	16	19	22/24+	9
Netherlands	5	12	16	17/18	18	22+	12[2]
Denmark	7	16/17	16	16	19+	22/23+	9
Ireland	6	12	15	15	18	21/22	9
Austria	6	10	15	15	19	22/23+	9
Spain	6	16	16	16	18	21/23	10
United Kingdom	4/5	11/14	16	16	18	21/22	11/12[3]
Portugal	6	15	15	15	18	21/22+	9
Greece	5½	15	15	15	18	22	9½
Italy	6	14	14	14	19	23	8
Luxembourg	4	12	15	15	19+	20+	11

Explanatory notes are to be found at the end of the chapter.

Note: For some countries, ages at given stages may be typical or expected rather than accurate for each individual. The further one moves through the system, the more likely it will be to find students of somewhat different ages at the same stage; Denmark is a particular case in this point.

[1] of which 2/3 years may be part-time
[2] or 11 full-time + 2 part-time
[3] 12 in Northern Ireland

Source: Eurydice/Cedefop 1995; European Commission 1996

is a similar preschool system, fully three-quarters of two-year-olds attend; but virtually no Dutch children attend kindergarten until they are four years old, by which time almost all attend the non-compulsory first year of *Basisonderwijs* (primary school). In Denmark, Finland and Sweden, daycare and kindergarten provision is everywhere available from a very early stage, in line with established philosophies on the importance of children's early education and socialisation into the community, and participation rates are high (see Dencik 1995). In the UK, few children are in education-oriented preschool until the age of three, by which time at least a third are attending; by the time children are 'rising five', they are almost all in preschool or have been accepted into the primary reception class. There are, then, wide variations in the provision and take-up of preschool education, but nevertheless a clear majority of four-year-olds in the European Union are now attending kindergarten.

Compulsory full-time schooling ends at either 15 or 16 in all member states except Italy, where young people may still leave at 14. In addition, part-time vocational education and training for those who do not continue on to full-time upper secondary education is compulsory in Belgium, Germany and The Netherlands. This means that across the European Union, it is possible for today's young people to experience a minimum of eight and a maximum of 12 years of compulsory education and training of some kind. At first sight, it might be assumed that lengthier compulsory systems result in higher and lengthier post-compulsory participation. Taken together, Tables 7.1 and 7.2 would seem to suggest this in the case of France, Germany and Belgium, for example. And certainly, school-leaving ages have been recently raised in Portugal and Spain as part of their respective educational modernisation and reform, which *inter alia* aim to improve participation rates overall. However, of those countries with high and extended participation rates for the 15–24 age group (previously labelled group 1 countries), Sweden, Finland and Denmark prescribe only nine years of compulsory education.

Three kinds of features impact on post-compulsory participation rates. First, the operation of labour markets (national, regional and local), together with the effects of policies directed specifically at guiding the transitions behaviour of 16–19-year-olds, exert contextualising push-and-pull effects. This is obviously an important reason why post-compulsory participation rates have risen everywhere in Europe in the past 20 years.

Second, the internal structuring of education systems exerts stronger or weaker influences on young people's trajectories through tracks, options and routes which may have very different prospects for further/higher education, training and on the labour market. Highly differentiated secondary systems may result in lower post-compulsory participation rates in the absence of a lengthier compulsory education system and of a dual system supported by such arrangements. This used to be the case in England and Wales, for example, and may partly account for the rapid fall-off in post-compulsory participation in Austria. Equally, however, Sweden, Finland and Denmark do not begin to differentiate and specialise until the upper secondary level; they maintain high and extended post-compulsory participation, all of which becomes essentially voluntary from the age of 16 onwards.

This points to the third feature that shapes participation profiles: the national cultural traditions that have informed the ways peoples and their governments think education and training is best provided and used, and of which today's teaching and learning systems have become their institutionalised reflections. It is for this reason that, despite the many areas in which such systems are facing common forces and pressures, in response to which national policymakers are pursuing similar general aims, there remains little evidence of an overall pattern of substantial convergence between systems themselves – although, as shown by the statistics included in this chapter, it is becoming easier to identify clusters of similarity and difference. And, as Table 7.2 indicates, there does seem to be increasing agreement on where critical turning-points in young people's learning trajectories are best placed. There is least agreement in relation to differentiation and specialisation in the lower secondary education phase (typically, for 11–16-year-olds), but the past 20 years have witnessed a majority and continuing trend towards delaying their onset, both in curriculum and institutional terms (Green, Leney and Wolf 1997: Ch. 3).

Evidence and argument tend to suggest that education and training systems based on the twin principles of late selection and high participation hold the most potential for achieving social justice and assuring inclusion, but no less so for reaching the higher levels of competence and employability required in a post-Fordist and globalised world. Such systems, however, demand high levels of resources that are distributed evenly across the different levels and sectors. Comparatively speaking, the Nordic countries fund their systems most generously and more evenly than elsewhere in Europe, and this is not a recent development. Some member states are not accustomed to spending so much on education and training, and clearly others may not be able to afford to do so. There is, then, increasing concern that investment in education and training may no longer be sufficient to provide the foundation for high-quality systems that offer open, flexible and appropriate access and progression not only for young people, but also for adults of all ages as part of a lifelong learning strategy (Study Group on Education and Training 1997: 33, 141–52).

Moving towards a learning society

This chapter has been almost wholly rewritten for the second edition of *Social Europe*, although the first edition was only published in 1992. Not only have the empirical patterns changed, but the European Union now has 15 member states. In addition, the provisions of the Maastricht Treaty, while affirming the fundamental responsibility of the member states for the organisation and content of their teaching and learning arrangements, established a firm basis for Community action in the fields of education, training and youth to complement and support national level policies and actions. This has lent renewed impulse and purpose to European cooperation in this domain.

The basic argument of the chapter remains the same: European societies respond to common problems in different ways; similar national or regional policy aims are implemented in diverse institutional contexts. Together with the impact of specific cultural traditions, these factors continue to produce different patterns of educational selection and participation. Nevertheless, some basic aspects of national systems do appear to be becoming more compatible, if not necessarily converging in the strict sense of the term. Critical turning-points in educational systems are patterned more closely together than they were ten years ago, and there is a majority trend towards delaying differentiation and specialisation until the upper secondary phase. A generalised upward trend in post-compulsory participation is clearly in evidence, and has been particularly strong in countries where participation traditionally declined swiftly and early. The UK belongs to this category, but so do Portugal and Spain. It remains the case that those countries which are most successful in keeping many young people in some form of education and training for longest are those which delay differentiation and specialisation longest and whose systems are comparatively generously resourced. Most particularly, this means the Nordic countries.

The economic, social and cultural landscape of the European Union has now entered a new era of change, one with deep implications for education and training policies and practices. The challenges of transition to a knowledge-based economy, to an ageing population, and to a culturally pluralist society pose a new set of common problems for European countries to resolve.

First, the combination of technological advance and increasing global competition in trade and production means that European economies are moving towards new forms of work organisation and new kinds of products and services, in particular 'immaterial' ones which demand high levels of competence and innovative capacity. This demands not only a better qualified and more flexible, problem-solving oriented workforce, but also implies the continuous renewal of knowledge and skill to keep pace with rapid technological change and the pressure of a globally competitive environment.

Second, the new demographic transition means that in the next 25 years Europe's overall population will stabilise and possibly begin to fall, and in particular the proportion of younger people will certainly fall significantly. By about 2010, those aged over 60 will outnumber those aged under 20; workers aged over 50 will outnumber those aged under 30 (European Commission 1997b: 6–8). This means that upgrading and renewal of qualification in the workforce cannot primarily be assured by generational renewal, as in the past. It also implies the need for new forms of education and training provision to respond to a rising demand for learning by a much more differentiated population in terms of age, experience, needs and circumstances. Smaller numbers of young people also offer an opportunity to raise the quality of teaching and learning processes on a broad front; new information and communication technologies offer an opportunity to introduce more innovative, and in some cases potentially more cost-effective, teaching and learning methods.

Third, European societies themselves have, for the most part, become increasingly and more consciously pluralist in nature, through both in-migration from other parts of the world and the re-emergence of regional and group-based linguistic and cultural diversities within Europe itself. The process of European integration lends a new dynamism to this development, because it is founded on the principle of maintaining and valorising diversity as a positive resource in learning to live and work together. The will and the capacity to live and work constructively together in a pluralist and intercultural environment very much depend on gaining the skills and experiences to do so with confidence: this is a quintessentially educational agenda, and one which speaks not simply to economic concerns but, most pertinently of all, to the intrinsic aims of democratic education.

These are, in fact, some of the key issues currently being debated at European level in the context of moving towards a learning society (European Commission 1996b; Study Group on Education and Training 1997; European Commission 1997c). The points raised above all suggest that lifelong learning provides the most promising framework for rethinking the structures, contexts and processes of teaching and learning in the economic, social and cultural world on our doorstep. Ensuring access to education and training opportunities on a continuous basis for people of all ages and circumstances, and providing those opportunities in ways that are able to release and foster the full range of individual capacities and potentials people possess, is an enormous challenge. Its realisation is likely to involve the development of new architectures for learning in which the boundaries and separations of the education and training practised in western industrial societies – between age groups, providers and institutions, curricula and pedagogies, tracks and specialisms – will become much more fluid. Certainly, describing and analysing selection and participation patterns in the way this chapter has done would become much more difficult and probably much less meaningful. Critical turning points would be differently structured, academic and vocational tracks would be difficult to separate, and participation patterns by age would hold much less interpretive sense.

Just what might emerge, and how, are fields for speculation and debate (in the case of the UK, for example, see Coffield 1997). One of the most important aspects to consider is the extent to which moving towards a learning society offers renewed prospects to create a more inclusive society in which all can feel they have a genuine stake and in which they can develop their potential to the full. Building an integrated Europe with this aim in mind cannot afford to leave teaching and learning at the margins, for even if education cannot compensate for society, it is by no means powerless in shaping individual lives and the quality of social life. Contemporary change processes also hold significant risks for individuals and communities, expressed in an increasingly entrenched social marginalisation and exclusion in which the negative effects of educational differentiation and inequality are known to play a formative and perhaps decisive role. The social and economic consequences are neither desirable nor, in the longer term, affordable: the best available option, then, is to work towards making learning a positive and rewarding activity for all concerned.

Table 7.2: explanatory notes

Belgium

Primary-secondary transfer occurs at age 12 throughout the country. The Flemish Community then has a unified secondary system through to 18, but which branches into four tracks from 14. The French and German Communities begin complex institutional branching from 12, but all schools must follow a common curriculum in the first year. Everywhere, students may not leave full-time schooling at 15 unless they have spent at least two years in secondary education; leavers at 15 and 16 must continue with part-time education until they are 18. A year of pre-university studies may precede higher education entry. University courses can be completed in 2/3 years for a first qualification, followed by 2/3 years for a higher qualification.

France

Since 1992/3, the final year of lower secondary schooling (*collège*) offers special 'transition to working life' courses for those planning to move on to vocational training at 16. The second half of the four-year *collège* branches into general and technological specialisms, but 16+ progression routes are not affected thereby. A first university qualification is awarded after two years; two further years give two further levels of qualification.

Sweden

Since 1991, parents have the right to send their children to school at the age of six if they wish. Comprehensive upper secondary schooling was introduced from 1992, which offers a wide range of courses, most of which have a vocational focus.

Finland

Students may stay on for an optional tenth year of comprehensive secondary schooling. In higher education, it still takes 5/6 years to complete the traditional first degree, but from 1994 new degrees were introduced, designed for completion in about 3 years.

Denmark

Students may stay on for an optional tenth year of comprehensive secondary schooling.

Ireland

Primary schools may accept pupils after they become four, but on average children are five when they start. Three-fifths of secondary students attend Voluntary Secondary Schools, traditionally academically oriented but now, like other schools, increasingly comprehensive in their aims and methods.

Spain

The table shows the arrangements gradually being introduced in conformity with the 1990 reform legislation. Under the new system, up to one-third of curriculum time will be taken up by options by 14, but with the aim that these choices should not limit subsequent progression opportunities. Higher education courses follow a two-step 3 + 2 years qualification model.

UK

In Northern Ireland, primary school begins at age four; in the rest of the UK, many children begin school before they are five. In Northern Ireland, children transfer at 11 to a bipartite selective system. In Scotland, in Wales and for most students in England, secondary schooling is comprehensive through to 16. Curriculum specialisation begins from 14, but this is limited by the National Curriculum in England and Wales, and by national guidelines in Scotland.

Portugal

Varying according to course, qualification and institution, first university qualifications are completed in between three to six years.

Greece

Thirteen per cent of young Greeks pursue higher education in another member state (European Commission 1996a: 66).

Luxembourg

The first two years of primary education take the form of preschool. At the other end of the spectrum, only the first year of university study can be undertaken in Luxembourg itself; afterwards, all students must go elsewhere to complete their qualifications. Luxembourg provides non-degree-level higher education courses in technology, primary teaching and management.

Source: Eurydice/Cedefop 1995

Note

Information on the European Union and its action programmes in the field of education, training and youth can be accessed via the Internet site *http://europa.eu.int*.

References

Adamski, W. and Grootings, P. (eds) (1989) *Youth, Education and Work in Europe*, London: Routledge.

Büchtemann, C. and Vogler-Ludwig, K. (1997) 'Das deutsche Ausbildungsmodell unter Anpassungszwang: Thesen zur Humankapitalbildung in Deutschland', *IFO Schnelldienst*, 17–18/97: 15–20.

Chisholm, L. (1993) 'Youth transitions in Britain on the threshold of a New Europe', *Journal of Education Policy*, 8(1): 29–42.

Coffield, F. (1997) *Can the UK become a learning society?* Fourth Annual Education Lecture, King's College London School of Education, 26 June.

Dencik, L. (1995) 'Modern childhood in the Nordic countries: "dual socialisation" and its implications', in L. Chisholm, P. Büchner, H.-H. Krüger and M. du Bois-Reymond (eds) *Growing Up in Europe. Contemporary Horizons in Childhood and Youth Studies*, Berlin/New York: Walter de Gruyter, pp. 105–20.

Eurydice/Cedefop (1995) *Structures of the Education and Initial Training Systems in the European Union*, Luxembourg: Office for Official Publications of the European Communities, 2nd edn.

European Commission (1996a) *Key Data on Education in the European Union 95*, Luxembourg: Office for Official Publications of the European Communities.

European Commission (1996b) *Teaching and Learning: towards the learning society*. White Paper, DGXXII/DGV, Luxembourg: Office for Official Publications of the European Communities.

European Commission (1997a) *Report on access to continuing training in the Union*, Luxembourg: Office for Official Publications of the European Communities.

European Commission (1997b) *Demographic Report 1997*, COM(97)361 final, 9 July, Brussels.

European Commission (1997c) *Agenda 2000: Pour une Union plus forte et plus large*, COM(97)2000 final, 15 July, Brussels.

Eurostat (1997) *Youth in the European Union from Education to Working Life*, Luxembourg: Office for Official Publications of the European Communities.

Finegold, D., Miliband, D., Raffe, D., Keep, E., Spours, K. and Young, M. F. D. (1990) *A British Baccalauréat. Ending the division between education and training*, Education and Training Paper 1, London: Institute for Public Policy Research.

Furlong, A. and Cartmel, F. (1997) *Young People and Social Change. Individualisation and Risk in Late Modernity*, Buckingham/Philadelphia: Open University Press.

Green, A., Leney, T. and Wolf, A. (1997) *Convergences and Divergences in European Education and Training Systems. Final Report*, Study DGXXII/9/96, European Commission, Brussels, July (mimeo).

Heinz, W. R. (1998) 'Job entry patterns in a life-course perspective', in W. R. Heinz (ed.) *From Education to Work: Cross National Perspectives*, Cambridge: Cambridge University Press, Section 2.

Jallade, J.-P. (1989) 'Recent trends in vocational education and training: an overview', *European Journal of Education*, 24(2): 103–25.

Koklyagina, L. (1995) 'From school to work in a transitional society: changing patterns in Russia', in L. Chisholm, P. Büchner, H.-H. Krüger and M. du Bois-Reymond (eds) *Growing Up in Europe. Contemporary Horizons in Childhood and Youth Studies*, Berlin/New York: Walter de Gruyter, pp. 145–52.

Lagrée, J. C. (1996) 'Youth in Europe: cultural patterns of transition', *Berkeley Journal of Sociology*, 41: 67–101.

Le Bras, H. (1996) 'Le jeunesse en Europe: de la compétence à la performance', *Agora: Débats/Jeunesse*, 5: 11–22.

OECD (1989) *Pathways to Learning: Education and Training from 16 to 19*, Paris: OECD.

OECD (1996) *Lifelong Learning for All*, Paris: OECD.

Roberts, K. (1996) 'Individualisation and risk in east and west Europe', in H. Helve and J. Bynner (eds) *Youth and Life Management*, Helsinki: University of Helsinki Press, pp. 226–40.

Statistisches Bundesamt (1995) *Datenreport 1994*, Bonn: Schriftenreihe der Bundeszentrale für politische Bildung 325.

Study Group on Education and Training (1997) *Accomplishing Europe through Education and Training*, Luxembourg: Office for Official Publications of the European Communities.

Tavares Emídio, M. (1988) 'The process of modernisation and secondary education in Portugal', *European Journal of Education*, 23(3): 195–202.

Walther, A. (1996) 'Junge Erwachsene in Europa: Eine neue Lebensphase oder Ubergang auf Dauer?' in A. Walther (ed.) *Junge Erwachsene in Europa. Jenseits der Normalbiographie?* Opladen: Leske + Budrich, pp. 9–38.

Zinneker, J. (1990) 'What does the future hold? Youth and sociocultural change in the FRG', in L. Chisholm, P. Büchner, H.-H. Krüger and P. Brown (eds) *Childhood, Youth and Social Change. A Comparative Perspective*, Lewes: Falmer Press, Ch. 2.

CHAPTER 8

Trade unions in Europe

IAN PROCTER

European trade unionism has long been marked by national diversity in structure, degree of workplace organisation, ideology, and place within industrial and political relations. In this chapter no attempt at a geographically comprehensive review of unionism in western Europe is attempted. Rather, the focus is on Germany, Italy and France. These are the largest societies of continental western Europe but they also represent different historical traditions of unionism. Germany exemplifies a highly legalised, centralised and cooperative form of labour representation, Italy and France the alternative pattern of politically differentiated unionism with a conflictual relationship to employers.

One theme of this chapter is the maintenance of national diversity over the recent past. The period since the mid-1970s has posed considerable problems for unions. The era of postwar economic growth, high employment rates, developing welfare provision and expanding unionisation came quickly to an end. Union movements were faced with rising unemployment, retreats from welfarism and calls for wage restraint despite price inflation and demands from employers for concessions in labour deployment. Yet despite this common set of circumstances, the chapter will show that national variations remain. A second theme is that one reason for this is the relationship between unions and the state. Variation is partly a result of historical origins, but these are renewed through the interaction of unions and the state, a process particularly highlighted in times of national economic crisis such as the recent past. Then the political legitimacy and institutional robustness of unions comes to the fore. Unlike in Britain, no fundamental challenge to the legitimacy of unions has been displayed in these three societies. In Germany the state has largely maintained its distance, while in Italy and France the state has been interventionist but in markedly different ways – in Italy seeking to incorporate unions into economic management, in France by legally reshaping the form of worker representation. Finally, the chapter is written for a British audience, schooled in an experience of political exclusion and legal constraint of unionism. The intention is to display how other kinds of unionism fared under conditions of economic change.

In order to avoid overloading the text with a myriad of organisational names, abbreviations are used throughout the chapter and a glossary is provided at the end.

Germany

This section discusses unions in what was West Germany. The reverberations of the reunification of Germany in 1990 will not be discussed in detail as these are currently unclear. However, despite the upheaval of labour migration to the West and the economic liberalisation of the East, it might be ventured that reunification will not materially affect the German system of industrial relations. This is because a united Germany was achieved by the incorporation of the former GDR into the FRG, thus extending the federal legal system to the East. As, in matters of industrial relations, legal institutions are extensive, this should extend what was the federal system to the East. Second, the federal system has been marked by its stability over the economic troughs of the last two decades and thus should be capable of adapting to the politically induced change of reunification.

There are four trade-union confederations in Germany: the DGB (7.9 million members), the DBB (0.8), DAG (0.5) and CGB (0.3) (Upham 1994: G-37, figures for 1989). As these membership figures show, the DGB is by far the dominant union organisation and will be the focus here. The DGB is a federation of 17 industrial unions. This small number indicates that each union covers a broad sector. This applies particularly to the largest and most significant, the Metal Workers Union (IGM), which includes workers in steel, machine tools, ship-building, aerospace, electrical and mechanical engineering and car manufacture. IGM, with 3.4 million members, accounted for 31 per cent of DGB members in 1992 (*European Industrial Relations Review* (1993) 236: 8–9).

The employers also form a national confederation (BDA) which Furstenberg (1984: 618) estimates includes 80 per cent of all enterprises. Both the DGB and BDA are essentially supportive organisations for their constituent members, providing research, coordination and representation. Although the DGB has historical and ideological links to German Social Democracy (SPD), these are not institutionalised. For example, the DGB always has two members of the Christian Democrats on its nine-person executive (Berghahn and Karston 1987: 35). However, it is the constituent industrial unions and employers' associations in industrial sectors which are the effective units of industrial relations outside the workplace. These relations are regulated by an elaborate code of labour law which defines the scope and procedures of collective bargaining generating legally binding agreements, which include a peace obligation to avoid conflict over the contract's duration. Industrial conflict is also legally controlled with mediation mechanisms built in and specific requirements for legal strikes and lock-outs (Berghahn and Karston 1987; Weiss 1987: Ch. 3).

Unions are characterised by their centralism, the leading role of full-time officials and the coordination of heterogeneous industries and workplaces into an industrial union. The justification for this is a 'solidaristic wages policy' whereby wages and conditions across regions, industries and firms are regulated by nationally coordinated agreements which do not discriminate between workers in weaker or stronger market positions. These features are illustrated in Streeck's (1984: Ch. 2) account of bargaining by the IGM with particular reference to the car industry. The union's national executive, which is dominated by officers, initiates the process several months before the expiry of an agreement, with a statement of issues and demands. These are extensively discussed at lower levels and modifications incorporated, this phase culminating in resolutions from regional pay committees which cover the range of industries and occupations in the sector, their composition carefully regulated by the national executive. The executive has final say in the claim. Bargaining takes place regionally, by teams dominated by officers. Any proposals for industrial action, conciliation or arbitration must be agreed nationally. When the bargain is struck it must cover the 'industry' as a whole, be consistent with other regions and be approved by the national executive.

Legal controls on strikes/lock-outs and the centralised control of bargaining are two reasons for the low level of industrial conflict in Germany, consistently among the lowest in the industrialised world. However, adherence to the law and central control are not unproblematic. Rather, they are dependent on the form of worker representation *within* the workplace, the system of 'codetermination' via Works Councils and worker directors (Streeck 1984; Neal 1987: Ch. 3).

Works Councils are legally required in all firms and public organisations with more than five employees. All employees of the firm are entitled to vote in four-yearly elections of a Council to represent the workforce's interests on a wide range of issues. These are formalised as a works agreement, which includes disciplinary procedures, hours of work, holidays, health and safety, pay schemes, bonuses and piece rates, the hiring and dismissal of labour, worker transfer, training, work reorganisation and the introduction of new technology. In all these, employers have to gain the assent of the Council or face legal action. The Council is also responsible for monitoring the legality of the firm with respect to the legal rights of workers and the firm's compliance with agreements entered into with unions. What Councils do not do is negotiate such agreements, nor are they permitted to engage in industrial action. The recourse of Councils is to law; unions maintain the monopoly of the strike weapon.

As legal entities Councils are formally separate from unions which, in many industries, have no organisational presence within the firm. However, in reality, the Council is 'the extended arm of the union movement' (Schregle 1987: 325–6). Unions put up slates of candidates and nominate union officers as candidates. In fact, the great majority of councillors are unionists. Jacobi and Muller-Jentsch estimate that 85 per cent of councillors in the industrial sector are union nominees (1990: 134). As such, union policies are represented within the statutory system of the firm.

However, as Councils are independent entities, unions cannot simply impose their policies; they have to be acceptable within this context. The legal independence of Councils thus imposes an important check on the central powers of unions. Councils also enable unions to overcome a perennial problem of solidaristic wage policies – allowing some leeway for better-placed workers to exploit their market position without undermining agreements across an industry. Councils cannot enter negotiation on wages but can influence actual wages by codetermining piece rates and hours (Streeck 1984: 34–6).

The unions' effective monopoly of representation within Works Councils was challenged by amendments to the legislation in 1988 to strengthen the access and rights to minority groups within the firm. For example, the number of supporters required for a councillor nomination was reduced, and Councils' control of their appointments of officers and committees was shifted from simple majority to proportional representation (SLB 1989(1): 29–30). However, unions' experience in using Councils is expected to incorporate these changes and, as Jacobi and Muller-Jentsch point out, given the extensive powers of Works Councils, 'the employers fear losing competent, reliable and predictable bargaining partners' (1990: 140).

The second aspect of codetermination is the presence of worker directors on the supervisory boards of companies which appoint and monitor the firm's management board. The composition of supervisory boards varies according to industrial sector and size of firm. Broadly, in medium-sized companies, workers have one-third representation on the board, while in companies with more than 2000 employees, half the supervisory board are worker directors. They are elected by the workforce but are generally union nominees and often officials not employed by the firm (Berghahn and Karston 1987: Ch. 4).

The German system is thus centralised industrial unionism outside the firm and codetermination, in which unions have a substantial *de facto* role, within the workplace. This system remained remarkably stable in the 1980s. This was despite shifts in the political and economic context. The era of Social Democratic hegemony, originating in 1966, ended in 1982 with the election of the Christian Democrats. Although this marked a shift in ideological tone, it amounted to little change in substance in industrial relations. Three legislative changes have been introduced. The 1985 Act on Improvement of Employment Opportunities was intended to loosen worker security by permitting temporary contracts in which the worker was not protected by legal procedures for dismissal (Weiss 1987: 46–8). But it is noticeable how temporary contracts are hedged around by legal safeguards. The limitations of the 1988 amendments to the Works Constitution Acts have been noted. Finally, the government has impeded the unions' use of the strike by restricting unemployment benefit to those laid off as a result of a strike in another area. This was intended to frustrate the effectiveness of the strategy of the 'focal' strike

(Furstenberg 1984: 628) deployed by the IGM. Strikes were called in key firms, which quickly led to the disruption of production elsewhere. The government intervention means that laid-off workers are not compensated. Although this is an impediment, the success of the IGM's use of the focal strike to move to the 35-hour week (see below) shows it to be still effective.

German employers have joined the movement for greater flexibility in the hours and deployment of labour. Quality circles have been introduced, raising the possibility of an alternative line of communication and representation to the Works Council (Jacobi and Muller-Jentsch 1990: 132–4). But, crucially, such changes go through not around codetermination and thus unions have a degree of control over their implications. Again this will be illustrated below by the 35-hour week.

Unions maintained their numerical strength in the 1980s, at around 42 per cent of the workforce. What is noticeable is that this not only remained stable in the 1980s but has been around that figure for the last 30 years. Although the composition of members has shown shifts to increased white-collar, female and public-sector workers, this is not so extensive as elsewhere (see below) and has not led to structural change in the balance of unions.

These various points can be illustrated by what was the major employment issue of the 1980s: hours of work. Here the leading role of the IGM has been confirmed with concessions won in metal-working, setting the example for others such as public-sector workers (1988) and shop workers (1989) (SLB 1988(1): 214; 1989(3/4): 266). IGM pressure came to a head in 1984 with a series of focal strikes in the car industry (Jacobi and Muller-Jentsch 1990: 144–6). The dispute lasted seven weeks, with over half a million workers on strike or (the majority) locked out. The strike achieved a reduction in hours to $38^1/2$. This was followed by further action culminating in the winning of the 35-hour week in 1990 (SLB 1990(2): 161–2). To some commentators, however, the hours of work issue marks a crack in the German system, as they rightly point out that the shorter working week has been achieved in return for concessions on the flexibility of hours (Katz and Sabel 1985; Schroder 1989; Windolf 1989). The 1989 agreement, for example, allowed the standard working week to vary between 37 and 40 hours, and the $38^1/2$ hour average had to be achieved over a two-month period. Furthermore, these practical arrangements were not fixed in the agreement but left to negotiation by Works Councils. Windolf, in particular, argues that 'In the long run, this arrangement may weaken industrial unions and their centralised bargaining system' (1989: 12).

What this judgement overlooks is that union bargaining in the workplace through the Council system is not new. Streeck (1984) describes how short-time and overtime were key areas of codetermination in the Volkswagen plants in the 1970s. The delegation of detail to Councils is, in his judgement, one way in which the unity of industrial unionism is maintained. Clearly, German unions face problems with structural changes in the labour market and the workplace, but as yet the dual system of industrial unionism and codetermination has proved durable both in institutional continuity and the maintenance of workers' strength.

Italy

Unions in Italy need to be set against the background of the decade after the 'hot autumn' of 1969, a period of very rapid membership expansion, from 28 to 44 per cent of the workforce (Santi 1988: 154). The basis for this was the organisational renewal of 'delegates' councils', which became active media for worker representation in the workplace. A second trend was towards organisational unity. Italy has three main national union confederations, the communist-inclined CGIL, the Christian Democratic CISL and the socialist UIL. In the 1970s this ideological and institutional pluralism seemed to be in decline, with the establishment of the 'Unitary Federation' (Giugni 1984) in 1972. The three confederations worked together and put aside their political allegiances in advancing the common interests of the working class. This does not mean that the unions became apolitical.

The 1970s saw the mobilisation of the union movement not just in negotiation with employers but in the exertion of political influence. Union power, expressed in the willingness to take militant action in the strike or demonstration, achieved considerable gains. Rising living standards were accompanied by some egalitarian redistribution, especially through the *scala mobile*, whereby a proportion of wage increases was indexed to price rises to favour the lower-paid. Extension of the 40-hour week throughout manufacturing, improvements in working conditions and legislative reform of pensions, health care and public housing represented the unions' political accomplishments.

Unions in the 1970s could legitimately claim to represent a wide spectrum of the population through the direct action tradition, which remained alive within the Italian movement (Golden 1988) and through the unity of a grass-roots-based unionism.

These qualities of unity, a democratic base, egalitarianism, political influence and class representation were all called into question in the crisis years from the mid-1970s. Like other economies, Italy's experienced soaring inflation, rising unemployment and widening balance of payments as well as public expenditure deficits. In response to the crisis, the state did not ignore the power and legitimacy of unions but rather incorporated unions. One key aspect of this was the politicisation of collective bargaining by an active state involvement in industrial relations (Negrelli and Santi 1990: 169–73). Tripartite negotiation focused on regulating wages, especially curbing the automatic, price-indexed rises of the *scala mobile*. But they also included state policy on employment and social welfare. State resources were deployed to counter the effects of recession and restructuring. One important example was the Short-Term Earning Compensation Fund (CIG), originally designed as a bridge to help workers in cyclical downturns, in the 1980s deployed to compensate workers made redundant from industries in structural decline. Another example was the extension of early retirement provision to whole industries, as in steel in 1984. The state also intervened actively in conflict mediation, not only in recourse to the Ministry of Labour's conciliation service but the spread of political involvement to other ministries such as Education, State-Controlled Companies, and Industry.

The extent of tripartite 'concertation' in the early 1980s was such that a distinguished analyst of Italian industrial relations suggested that a neo-corporatist future was a distinct option for Italy (Giugni 1984: 613). In fact, a permanent institutional role for Italian unions in state economic management did not materialise (see below).

In terms of absolute numbers, union membership increased in the 1980s. In 1979 unions claimed 8.7 million members; Upham (1994: G52–53) puts the figure at 10 million around 1990. But in terms of the proportion of the workforce unionised, membership fell from 44 to 37 per cent (Negrelli and Santi 1990: 188, 190). Furthermore, as Santi (1988) points out, there was a significant change in the composition of membership. Italian unions do not only organise employees but also pensioners. The increase in pensioner members was remarkable: their confederation has 2 million members and is one of the largest unions in Europe (SLB 1988(3): 326). But this area of growth substituted for a decline in employee members, a fall of $1^1/_4$ million members, 17 per cent of the 1980 membership (Santi 1988: 159). This decline was concentrated in agriculture and manufacturing, with a slighter decrease (but not increase) in services. A key feature is the falling proportion of union members who work in large factories – the bastion of union power in the 1970s.

These changes are linked to the restructuring of the Italian economy, the decline in agricultural and manufacturing employment and increase in service jobs. Two features are particularly prominent: the rising number of small businesses and the 'underground economy'. Casual workers, temporary and seasonal workers were estimated to amount to 23 per cent of the regularly employed workforce in 1984 (Negrelli and Santi 1990: 161). Italian unions have failed to recruit in these areas to compensate for loss of membership in agriculture and manufacturing.

As well as this, Kriele (1988) argues that two other factors weakened the union movement. The first was the unintended effects of the very successes of the unions in the 1970s. One such success was the 1975 agreement on the *scala mobile* which provided a standard flat-rate increase to all workers as inflation rose. This had been intentionally redistributive in favour of lower-paid workers but the extent of this and the negative response of the better-paid were not foreseen. A second area of strength had been the increase in union control of labour deployment, in which delegate councils had considerable say in the hiring, allocation, transfer and firing of workers. Although this was of considerable benefit to union members protected by it, it worked to the detriment of others, especially young workers coming into the labour market and those working in the underground economy. Finally, participation by the unions in tripartite negotiations led to a shift in union power to the centre, which then had to police militancy in the delegate councils.

Kriele's second factor relates to the political party affiliations of the three union confederations. Throughout the late 1970s and early 1980s the struggle for party advantage in Italy's ever-changing coalition governments ramified into the unions. Time and again disputes within the unions were interpreted as expressions of their political allegiances. The 1983 tripartite agreement on incomes policy was hailed by CISL as a move to northern European corporatism, which the communists of CGIL rejected. CGIL communists refused to sign the 1984 agreement, a decision the other unions interpreted as the result of the Communist Party's opposition. The Unity Federation was formally dissolved in 1984 and the trend to a unified movement brought to an end.

So by the mid-1980s the trends of the 1970s seemed to have been reversed. The vitality of the delegates' councils appeared to have been suppressed by the shift to centralised participation in tripartite negotiations. Party political competition had brought the move to a unified movement to a halt. The claim of organised labour to represent the interests of the whole working class was undermined by discontent among rank-and-file members, the growth of independent unions among technicians and professionals (Garonna and Pisani 1986: 160–2), and lack of interest among young workers and in the service sector. Steeply rising unemployment and the unions' policing role spiked the strike weapon.

Such a turn-around leads Kriele to refer to the 'crisis' of Italian trade unionism, a crisis not simply of declining organisational strength and power but in the unions' sense of identity and legitimacy as the expression of working-class interest and aspiration (1988: 54). This is perhaps an exaggeration, as Negrelli and Santi put it: 'More than a profound, decisive "turning point" . . . the changes constitute an adaptation to new conditions' (1990: 192). In sustaining such an assessment three points can be made: maintenance of membership, continuity of political credibility and the sustained vitality of plant-level bargaining.

The observations above about the declining rate of unionisation and changing composition of unions are significant, but the fact remains that, in absolute terms, Italian unions, unlike many others, maintained their membership in the 1980s. The rise of 'non-active' members also has another side: through the medium of trade-union organisation pensioners have successfully mobilised to protect their pensions (SLB 1988(3): 326).

The trend to neo-corporate tripartisanism came to an end, the 1984 agreement being the last. The experiment was in no way a success from the point of view of organised labour, yet through difficult years the unions maintained a presence and defended the interests of labour. Because of their pressure, a host of measures such as CIG and early retirement schemes eased the cost of restructuring on labour. Although much weakened, Italy still has a measure of wage indexation protecting the lower-paid. In social welfare, although workers have suffered some losses, union pressure also led to gains. Family allowances, for example, had fallen in value by 1984 because of inflation. In reforming the system the state introduced means-testing. In the autumn of 1986 union-government negotiations led to a substantial rise in means-test thresholds (Negrelli and Santi 1990: 171). This indicates that the legitimacy of unions as expressions of broad worker interests has not been fundamentally challenged. Italy has not introduced anti-union legislation to undermine the legal protection of workers and unions in the 'Workers' Statute'. To speak, as Garonna and Pisani (1986) do, of a 'crisis of political unionism' seems to be an exaggeration.

The emphasis on early 1980s centralism tends to obscure the continuing vitality of plant-level bargaining. Although this is not the assertive neo-syndicalism of the early 1970s, the union within the workplace is still a potent force. Employers have demanded greater flexibility of labour time and work organisation but, other than in the small firm and private services, have had to *bargain* for them. Greater flexibility in hours of work has been conceded but in return for a reduction in hours.

Italian unions have changed significantly since the 1970s, but this represents an evolution rather than a change in fundamentals. The trend to centralism emerging in the early 1980s has not led to a neo-corporate system; rather, the unions remain an important and independent lobby on the state. The trend to a single-union movement has dissolved with a return to politically defined pluralism. Yet, in conjunction with an active grass-roots presence, it is arguable that this fosters democratic processes (Regalia 1988). This condition is met, the delegates' councils, the bedrock of 1970s unionism, seem to be firmly in a bargaining relationship with employers.

France

In 1981 the French elected their first left-wing government since the inception of the Fifth Republic in 1958. The Socialist-Communist coalition government quickly introduced a wide range of reforms (Hanley, Kerr and Waites 1988), including a comprehensive recasting of labour legislation, collectively known as the Auroux laws. This package of five laws and several government ordinances came into effect in 1982–83 and can serve as the focus for review of French unionism. Their manifest intention was to strengthen unionism and introduce a degree of democracy within the workplace. Their actual effects, in the context of economic recession and industrial restructuring, seem to be very different. But before describing the Auroux laws and their impact, an overview of the character of French unions and industrial relations is necessary.

There are five major union confederations in France. With one exception they are differentiated by their political allegiances rather than their appeal to separate sections of the workforce. Until recently, by far the strongest union was the CGT, with its Marxist-Leninist allegiance. From the 1960s the CFDT became the second most powerful confederation. Politically the CFDT was also Marxist-inspired but with an ideology of workers' control rather than the statist emphasis of the CGT. The FO and CFTC are social democratic in politics, while the CGC is a centrist union of managerial, technical and supervisory employees (Goetschy and Rojot 1987).

The leading unions in postwar France have thus had an explicitly class-struggle conception of their role and objectives. This was matched by the stance of French employers, with their reputation for jealousy of managerial prerogatives and a virulent anti-unionism. The 'patronat' formed a powerful federation, CNPF, which Kendall described as 'highly representative, well-staffed, well-equipped, disciplined and above all unified. The unions are outmatched in each respect' (1975: 73). The class-struggle orientations of both unions and employers have been mediated by an elaborate system of legal regulation. The law stipulates the working week, holidays, a job-classification scheme of skill levels, the minimum wage. The law provides mechanisms for arbitration and the designation of unions as 'representative'. Except in small firms, companies are required to form enterprise committees for consultation between management and workers. After the events of 1968, unions were (at last) legally protected in the workplace.

French unionism has historically the lowest level of membership of the developed capitalist societies. In the 1970s it was generally reckoned to be around 20 per cent of the workforce, although precise figures were difficult to establish. Both the low numbers and the lack of precision were a function of the nature of unionism in France. Legal rights had a paradoxical effect on membership. While the right to union membership was legally established, so was its converse; the closed shop was illegal. Until the early 1970s union organisation in the workplace was legally inhibited, but a legal process was established in which unions were 'representative' of the workforce. Rather than this being based on actual membership, a labour court established union bargaining rights (Forde 1984). Workers thus had little incentive to join unions, especially in the context of anti-union employer practices. Kendall (1975: 83) and Gallie (1978: Ch. 11) note the routine victimisation of union members. But the union objective and strategy was never to establish high rates of membership and organisational strength at the workplace. Grassroots members were expected to be activists, committed to the political ambitions of the union (Smith 1987: Chs 3 and 5).

Gallie's (1978) study of British and French oil refineries brings out the distinctiveness of French unionism compared to British practice. British unions aimed to maximise membership and organisational strength at the workplace in order to negotiate routinely with the employer on day-to-day matters of wages and conditions. French unions put their effort into propaganda in order to raise the consciousness of the workers for a political role. Rather than representing the workforce in negotiation with the employer, French unions sought to mobilise workers in a wider context.

This context was two-fold. Industrial relations negotiations were conducted at an industry or national level, agreeable to employers in their maintenance of control of the workplace, and to unions to maximise their class rather than sectional representation. But on occasion, the objective of French unions of mobilising the working class politically was achieved – in 1936 after the election of the Popular Front, in the years immediately after the Second World War and in the 'events' of 1968. These were periods of mass radicalisation of the French population, and it was at these points in time that the legal rights of workers and unions were advanced. Unions thus sought to serve the interests of workers by political mobilisation rather than bargaining strength in the workplace.

This pattern of legally regulated class struggle was associated with a high level of unpredictable industrial conflict. The lack of local institutionalised bargaining meant that grievances exploded in wildcat strikes, often to the surprise of the unions (Smith 1987: Ch. 5). Union activists were successful in galvanising the workforce: in Gallie's oil refineries there were 24 strikes between 1961 and 1971, all of them one-day 'demonstration' strikes in support of a broad slate of objectives. Such politicisation culminated in the national upheavals symbolised by 1968, the nearest any western capitalist society has come to revolution.

The Auroux laws are complex and only their main thrust can be indicated here (a detailed description is given by Glendon 1984). The rights of unions in the workplace were strengthened to give greater protection to members. Employers and unions were required to negotiate annually at the firm level on wages and hours. But other forms of worker representation were also developed. The long-established works committees were granted greater powers to require information from employers, appoint expert assistance and call workforce meetings. Firms of more than 50 employees were required to appoint committees on health, safety and working conditions. Perhaps the most controversial innovation was the introduction of 'expression groups', giving workers the right to express their views collectively on the content and conditions of their work.

The government introduced Auroux in the language of workers' control, which had long been dear to the CFDT and to which the CGT had also inclined in the 1970s. The Auroux Report had declared, 'Citizens in the political sphere, workers must also be citizens in the workplace' (quoted in Smith 1987: 210). But the left-wing influence was by no means the only one. Gallie (1985) points out that during the 1970s large

French employers had developed rather different management strategies from the traditional autocracy of the 'patron'. These involved greater efforts to integrate workers in a way parallel to Auroux's emphasis on the worker's rights within the firm. Others note that throughout the 1970s (right-wing) governments were concerned to address the perceived 'chaos' of French industrial relations by encouraging a 'modern' system of institutionalised rights and obligations (Eyraud and Tchobanian 1985; Moss 1988a).

As well as these various motivations, the context of introduction of Auroux should be borne in mind. The Keynesian-inspired response to recession by the left-wing government was reversed from 1983, with a shift to state encouragement of profitability and flexibility in the use of labour. Unemployment rose, and the initiative passed to employers (Segrestin 1990). In this context a pessimistic diagnosis of the effects of Auroux predominates.

Auroux required annual bargaining at firm-level (Amadieu 1988). It did not, however, control for the economic context of bargaining nor provide the organisational basis for it. Moss (1988a, 1988b) thus charts the increase in plant-level agreements but argues that these have been made very much on the employers' terms. Aldir (1989) and Smith (1987) point out that, as well as economic weakness, union organisational strength within the workplace was weakened rather than bolstered by Auroux. The old pattern of legal rights inhibiting the need for *de facto* strength from organisation continued. Smith further develops the ambiguities posed for the traditional union militant. The Auroux reforms were introduced not in the manner of other legal rights, by mass mobilisation, but by legislation following electoral victory. Shop-floor interest was minimal. The militant could not, therefore, count on popular backing in establishing new patterns of workplace relations. Yet the union activists were faced with a plurality of forms of worker representation to administer: works committees, annual bargaining, expression groups, and health and safety committees. All this amounted to a bureaucratising of the activist's role. This jarred with the essentially political definition of union activity, leaving the militant stranded between their political aspirations and role as a cog in a complex bureaucratic mechanism.

The form and purpose of expression groups was left open by the legislation. Despite initial opposition, it appears that it was employers rather than unions who seized the opportunity to shape this innovation. Membership of groups, terms of reference, timing of meetings, control of the agenda and the chair have been determined by management. Personnel staff have been trained in small-group management to use the groups in a way parallel to quality circles, so that workers 'control' has been deflected to incorporating the worker into the firm (Borzeix, Linhart and Segrestin 1986; Jenkins 1987).

Auroux has certainly not stimulated union membership, the level of which is still a matter of informed estimate rather than a reliable measure.

Labbe puts the current rate at 10 per cent of the workforce (1994: 106). Overall decline has occurred through falls in CGT and CFDT membership and stabilisation of FO and CFTC support. This shift in the balance of confederations is reflected in works-committee elections with the CGT/CFDT losing their overall supremacy to FO/CFTC and non-union candidates (Segrestin 1990: 106). These election figures are often taken as the measure of worker support for unions, and the current trend suggests a shift away from worker allegiance to the political aspirations of the radical unions.

The term 'crisis' has been used to describe many European union movements in the 1980s. It seems most applicable to the French. This is paradoxical in that the French state introduced a comprehensive package of prima-facie pro-union legislation in the 1980s. Yet this legal intervention deflected rather than built on the strength of French unions. This lay in the unions' role in radicalising and mobilising the working class at local, workplace and national levels (Lash 1984). Auroux has completed a process of incorporating unions into a complex web of legal rights and mechanisms which contradicts this role. As Sellier and Silvestre comment, 'the weakness of unions in France is largely a state-created weakness' (1986: 173), but this is a function of legalisation rather than repression.

Conclusion

In this chapter the workings and recent development of unionism in three major European societies have been examined. In the postwar period these came to exemplify two very different types of labour representation system. In Germany, highly legalised, centralised and cooperative; in Italy and France politicised, pluralistic and conflictual. The evidence of the last two decades shows that these systems are not static but evolving. The economic circumstances of this period have not been propitious, so that the ascent of unions which marked the years up to 1975 has ended. Yet the responses of unions to these economic conditions has varied, and a key factor in this variation has been the complex relationship between unions and the state.

Germany represents the most stable of these three systems. Although highly legalised, the German state has but tinkered with the workings of industrial relations in the recent past. Neither has the DGB attempted to use political influence to achieve its main objective, relying on the solidarity of industrial unionism to bargain with employers to reduce working hours. This situation contrasts with those of Italy and France, yet the contrasts between the two are just as marked. The Italian state attempted to incorporate unions into policy implementation and intervened actively in industrial relations but without legal reform. This phase proved temporary, and Italian unionism has returned to its pluralism, politicisation and grass-roots organisation.

By contrast, in France, despite the socialist pretensions of the government of the Left, unions were not incorporated into state policy implementation. Rather, the state embarked on a massive reformulation of labour law. Pro-union and pro-worker in rhetoric, the indications are that the Auroux package has seriously and permanently undermined the tradition of French unionism.

The trend to maintenance of national variability in European unionism and the influence of union–state relationships is confirmed by developments in other European societies, to which brief reference can be made. Germany's stability is not generic to all highly institutionalised forms of unionism. In Sweden[1] the leadership of the predominantly private sector, male, manual worker labour organisation has been challenged by unions representing white-collar, public-sector and women workers. The former pattern of bipartisan collective bargaining without state involvement has been broken by the unions' use of statutory means to advance workers' interests, the parallel higher political profile of employers and state attempts to regulate industrial relations. National coordination of bargaining by a solidarity wages policy has weakened, with employer attempts to decentralise and union confusion over egalitarian objectives. Sweden, long the model for social democrats, is itself rapidly evolving.

By contrast, in Belgian unionism,[2] also a highly organised system, the state responded to the economic crisis of the early 1980s by a five-year suspension of the elaborate network of national, industrial and plant-level institutions. From 1986, however, the system was reactivated. Furthermore, the procedure whereby the state can suspend the system has been formalised, with the role of unions in that process legally specified.

Three European societies, Spain, Portugal and Greece, moved from dictatorship to parliamentary democracy in the 1970s, Spain[3] being the most significant here, as the underground union movement played a leading role in the downfall of Francoism. Unions expanded rapidly in the late 1970s, yet the political priority of Spanish society was the consolidation of parliamentary democracy and the unions subordinated themselves to the political objectives of their sister political parties. The late 1980s saw Spain's unions taking a more independent stance and unifying around a much tougher negotiating position. Once again the relationship between unions and the state leads to a distinctive national pattern being established.

The legal definition and political role of unions in the nation state means that unions face considerable problems in responding to their next economic challenge, the liberalisation of capital and labour markets in 1993. This economic shift may be accompanied by some legal and political harmonisation, as embodied in the 'Social Charter'. However, this is unlikely radically to shift the embeddedness of unions in national legal and political systems. On the basis of the union's response to recession, the prediction must be that they will respond to market liberalisation within the legal and political frameworks of their own national societies.

Notes

1 For discussion of the Swedish model and recent developments, see Ahlen (1989), Fulcher (1987), Hammarstrom (1987), Lash (1985), Peterson (1987), Rehn and Viklund (1990) and Svensson (1986).
2 An introduction to Belgium unionism can be found in Albertijn, Hancke and Wijgaerts (1990), and Fitzmaurice (1983).
3 For further detail on Spain, consult Balfour (1989), Estirill and de la Hoz (1990), Ferner (1987) and Lucio (1989).

Glossary of names

Germany

BDA   Bundesvereinigung Deutscher Arbeitgeberverbande
      (Confederation of German Employers' Associations)
CGB   Christlicher Gewerkschaftsbund Deutschlands
      (Confederation of Christian Trade Unions of Germany)
DAG   Deutsche Angestelltengewerkschaft
      (German Salaried Employees Union)
DBB   Deutscher Beamtenbund
      (Confederation of German Civil Service Officials)
DGB   Deutscher Gewerkschaftsbund
      (German Trade Union Federation)
IGM   Industriegewerkschaft Metall (Metal Workers' Union)

Italy

CGIL   Confederazione Generale Italiana del Lavoro
       (General Italian Confederation of Labour)
CIG   Cassa Integrazione Guadagni
       (Short-term Earnings Compensation Fund)
CISL   Confederazione Italiana Sindacati Lavoratori
       (Italian Confederation of Workers' Unions)
UIL   Unione Italiana dei Lavoratori (Italian Union of Workers)

France

CFDT   Confédération Française Démocratique du Travail
       (French Democratic Confederation of Labour)
CFTC   Confédération Française des Travailleurs Chrétiens
       (French Confederation of Christian Workers)
CGC   Confédération Générale des Cadres
       (French Confederation of Managerial Staffs)
CGT   Confédération Générale du Travail
       (General Confederation of Labour)
CNPF   Conseil National du Patronat Français
       (National Council of French Employers)
FO   Force Ouvrière (Workers' Strength)

References

Note

Throughout the chapter reference is made to recent developments as reported in the International Labour Office's *Social and Labour Bulletin*. In the text this is abbreviated to SLB, followed by the year of publication, the issue number and the page; e.g. (SLB 1990(1): 38).

Ahlen, K. (1989) 'Swedish collective bargaining under pressure: inter-union rivalry and incomes policies', *British Journal of Industrial Relations*, 27(3): 330–46.

Albertijn, M., Hancke, B. and Wijgaerts, D. (1990) 'Technology agreements and industrial relations in Belgium', *New Technology, Work and Employment*, 5(1): 18–30.

Aldir, L. (1989) 'The American model, unrealised: a re-evaluation of plant bargaining in France', *Comparative Labour Law Journal*, 10(2): 196–213.

Amadieu, J. (1988) 'Employment flexibility, unions and companies in France', *Industrial Relations Journal*, 19(2): 117–23.

Balfour, S. (1989) *Dictatorship, Workers, and the City: Labour in Greater Barcelona since 1939*, Oxford: Clarendon Press.

Bamber, G. and Lansbury, R. (1987) *International and Comparative Industrial Relations*, London: Allen & Unwin.

Berghahn, V. and Karston, D. (1987) *Industrial Relations in West Germany*, London: Berg.

Borzeix, A., Linhart, D. and Segrestin, D. (1986) 'Direct workers' expression in France: the voice of management?' *International Journal of Sociology and Social Policy*, 6(2): 22–9.

Estirill, J. and de la Hoz, J. (1990) 'The complexity of Spanish industrial relations', in G. Baglioni and C. Crouch (eds) *European Trade Unionism: the Challenge of Flexibility*, London: Sage.

Eyraud, F. and Tchobanian, R. (1985) 'The Auroux laws and company level industrial relations in France', *British Journal of Industrial Relations*, 23(2): 241–59.

Ferner, A. (1987) 'Industrial relations and the mesopolitics of the public enterprise: the transmission of state objectives in the Spanish national railways', *British Journal of Industrial Relations*, 25(1): 49–75.

Fitzmaurice, J. (1983) *The Politics of Belgium*, London: Hurst.

Forde, M. (1984) 'Trade union pluralism and labour law in France', *International and Comparative Law Quarterly*, 33(1): 134–57.

Fulcher, J. (1987) 'Labour movement theory versus corporatism: social democracy in Sweden', *Sociology*, 21(2): 231–52.

Furstenberg, F. (1984) 'Recent trends in collective bargaining in the Federal Republic of Germany', *International Labour Review*, 123(5): 615–30.

Furstenberg, J. (1987) 'The Federal Republic of Germany', in G. Bamber and R. Lansbury (eds) *International and Comparative Industrial Relations*, London, Allen & Unwin, Ch. 8, p. 165.

Gallie, D. (1978) *In Search of the New Working Class*, Cambridge: Cambridge University Press.

Gallie, D. (1985) 'Les lois Auroux: the reform of French industrial relations?' in H. Machin and V. Wright *Economic Policy and Policy Making under the Mitterrand Presidency 1981–84*, London: Pinter.

Garonna, P. and Pisani, E. (1986) 'Italian unions in transition: the crisis of political unionism', in R. Edwards, P. Garrona and F. Todtling (eds) *Unions in Crisis and Beyond*, London: Auburn House, Ch. 4, p. 114.

Giugni, G. (1984) 'Recent trends in collective bargaining in Italy', *International Labour Review*, 123(5): 599–614.

Glendon, M. (1984) 'French law reform, 1982–83: the struggle for collective bargaining', *American Journal of Comparative Law*, 32: 449–91.

Goetschy, J. and Rojot, J. (1987) 'French industrial relations', in G. Bamber and R. Lansbury (eds) *International and Comparative Industrial Relations*, London: Allen & Unwin.

Golden, M. A. (1988) 'Historical meaning and ideological orientations of the Italian workers' movement', *Politics and Society*, 16(1): 1–34.

Hammarstrom, O. (1987) 'Swedish industrial relations', in G. Bamber and R. Lansbury (eds) *International and Comparative Industrial Relations*, London: Allen & Unwin.

Hanley, D., Kerr, A. P. and Waites, N. H. (1988) *Contemporary France*, London: Routledge.

Jacobi, O. and Muller-Jentsch, W. (1990) 'West Germany: Continuity and structural change', in G. Baglioni and C. Crouch (eds) *European Trade Unionism: the Challenge of Flexibility*, London: Sage.

Jenkins, A. (1987) 'Work, new technology and the changing form of industrial relations in France', *Employee Relations*, 9(6): 17–22.

Katz, H. and Sabel, C. (1985) 'Industrial relations and industrial adjustment in the car industry', *Industrial Relations*, 24(3): 295–315.

Kendall, W. (1975) *The Labour Movement in Europe*, London: Allen Lane.

Kriele, M. (1988) 'The crisis of Italian trade unionism in the 1980s', *West European Politics*, 11(1): 54–67.

Labbe, D. (1994) 'Trade unionism in France since the Second World War', *West European Politics*, 17(1): 146–68.

Lash, S. (1984) *The Militant Worker: Class and Radicalism in France and America*, London: Heinemann.

Lash, S. (1985) 'The end of neo-corporatism? The breakdown of centralised bargaining in Sweden', *British Journal of Industrial Relations*, 23(2): 215–39.

Lucio, M. (1989) 'Union–worker relations in a transforming Spain', *Economic and Industrial Democracy*, 10(4): 423–46.

Moss, B. (1988a) 'Industrial law reform in an era of retreat: the Auroux laws in France', *Work, Employment and Society*, 2(3): 317–34.

Moss, B. (1988b) 'After the Auroux laws: employers, industrial relations and the right in France', *West European Politics*, 11(1): 68–80.

Neal, A. (1987) 'Co-determination in the Federal Republic of Germany: an external perspective from the United Kingdom', *British Journal of Industrial Relations*, 25(2): 227–45.

Negrelli, S. and Santi, E. (1990) 'Industrial relations in Italy', in G. Baglioni and C. Crouch (eds) *European Trade Unionism: the Challenge of Flexibility*, London: Sage.

Peterson, R. (1987) 'Swedish collective bargaining – a changing scene', *British Journal of Industrial Relations*, 25(1): 31–48.

Regalia, I. (1988) 'Democracy and unions: towards a critical analysis', *Economic and Industrial Democracy*, 9(3): 345–71.

Rehn, G. and Viklund, B. (1990) 'Changes in the Swedish model', in G. Baglioni and C. Crouch (eds) *European Trade Unionism: the Challenge of Flexibility*, London: Sage.

Santi, E. (1988) 'Ten years of unionisation in Italy', *Labour*, 2(1): 153–82.

Schregle, J. (1987) 'Workers' participation in the Federal Republic of Germany in an international perspective', *International Labour Review*, 126(3): 317–27.

Schroder, K. (1989) *The Trade Unions in a Changing Society*, Bonn: Inter Nationes.

Segrestin, D. (1990) 'Recent changes in France', in G. Baglioni and C. Crouch (eds) *European Trade Unionism: the Challenge of Flexibility*, London: Sage.

Sellier, F. and Silvestre, J.-J. (1986) 'Unions' policies in the economic crisis in France', in R. Edwards, P. Garrona and F. Todtling (eds) *Unions in Crisis and Beyond*, London: Auburn House, Ch. 5, p. 173.

Smith, W. (1987) *Crisis in the French Labour Movement*, London: Macmillan.

Spineaux, A. (1990) 'Trade unionism in Belgium', in G. Baglioni and C. Crouch (eds) *European Trade Unionism: the Challenge of Flexibility*, London: Sage, Ch. 2, p. 42.

Streeck, W. (1984) *Industrial Relations in West Germany: a Case Study of the Car Industry*, London: Heinemann.

Svensson, L. (1986) 'Class struggle in a welfare state in crisis: from radicalism to neoliberalism in Sweden', in R. Edwards, P. Garrona and F. Todtling (eds) *Unions in Crisis and Beyond*, London: Auburn House.

Upham, M. (1994) *Trade Union and Employer's Organizations of the World*, London: Longman.

Visser, J. (1989) *European Trade Unionism in Figures*, Deventer: Kluwer.

Weiss, M. (1987) *Labour Law and Industrial Relations in the Federal Republic of Germany*, Deventer: Kluwer.

Windolf, P. (1989) 'Productivity coalitions and the future of European corporatism', *Industrial Relations*, 28(1): 1–20.

CHAPTER 9

Crime and policing in Europe

MICHAEL LEVI AND MIKE MAGUIRE*

Introduction

In 1991, when we wrote the first edition of this chapter, issues relating to crime and crime control figured relatively low on the agenda of academic and policy debates about 'the new Europe'. However, the situation has changed substantially during the 1990s. The continued growth of crime and, perhaps more importantly, of fear of crime and feelings of insecurity – a phenomenon connected to broader features of late modernity such as structural unemployment and globalisation – has made crime and responses to it a major political issue in many countries. At the same time, the signing of the Maastricht Treaty has placed several important aspects of police and criminal justice cooperation between European member states on a formal footing, and hence brought transnational 'law and order' firmly on to the agenda of the European Union and associated debates.

British criminologists have as yet paid surprisingly little attention to these developments. At the same time, they have paid little attention to the work of any of their academic counterparts in continental Europe. This holds both for theoretical work – where, with a few notable exceptions such as Foucault and Gramsci, major European writers remain largely unknown to most 'mainstream' criminologists in Britain – and for policy-related research. Most mainland European criminology, it should be emphasised, is highly theoretically oriented and alien to the 'grounded' American sociological approaches which have dominated criminological training and thinking in the UK. The gap has been especially pronounced over the last 15 years, during which much British research has been influenced by the 'situational' and 'opportunity'-based approaches (for example, to the study of crime prevention) which have intentionally side-stepped broader analytical and ideological considerations. Moreover, even where empirical work is concerned, only the Dutch and, to a lesser extent, the Swedes are generally regarded as having

* Professor Maguire wishes to extend his thanks to the Leverhulme Trust for the award of a research fellowship which allowed him to undertake background research on this and other related publications.

similar enough conditions and, crucially, a willingness to write in English, to merit consideration and referencing in British work (though the Norwegian Nils Christie has had an effect on 'alternative thinking' about informal, non-punitive approaches to crime control and, latterly, German scholars such as Hans-Jorg Albrecht, appointed in 1996 as Director of the Max Planck Institute, have become increasingly influential). Southern Europeans have had a negligible impact on empirical or policy-related writing in Britain.

Equally, many of the innovations in policy which attract attention in Britain – recent examples are Neighbourhood Watch, Closed Circuit Television, 'zero tolerance' policing, electronic tagging and private prisons – originated in the USA. Major initiatives by other European countries, such as France's social policies aimed at reducing youth crime, and Germany's efforts to reduce its prison population, have been virtually ignored by policy-makers and academics alike (for rare exceptions, see Downes 1988; Graham 1990). Vice-versa, too, the impact of British policies and evaluation research on other Europeans has been modest.

As we noted in the first edition, the general lack of British scholarly interest in Europe reflects the fact that crime control was for many years an issue of relatively low priority among the mass of cooperative ventures associated with the growth of the European Community. The subject was not included in the Treaty of Rome, and most crime-related agreements between member states were made in a piecemeal, *ad hoc* fashion under what is now known as the 'First Pillar': rights and obligations that existed prior to the Maastricht Treaty. This is largely because member countries have usually regarded crime control as the exclusive prerogative of sovereign nation states. This is not an absurd view: most crimes probably are local, being typically committed within a few miles of the offender's home (Mawby 1979; Maguire 1982). Sophisticated travelling or 'cross-border' criminals are in a very small minority and, for the bulk of criminal investigations, police forces see little need for communication with neighbouring forces, let alone forces in other countries. Moreover, each country has its peculiar legal and penal traditions, often defended by powerful interest groups resistant to change. Although the European Committee on Crime Problems at the Council of Europe in Strasbourg has for many years collated information, promoted exchanges of ideas and produced broad recommendations on criminal justice issues, its impact on national policies – especially in Britain – has been modest.

Nevertheless, there is some clear harmonisation, now beginning to accelerate. Some of this is apparent in long-term trends: for example, growing international communication between practitioners in specialised fields such as crime prevention and victim assistance, helping to spread ideas about 'best practice'; the gradual expansion of small networks of European-minded criminologists and criminal lawyers which previously existed almost unnoticed (for early examples, see Hood 1989;

Heidensohn and Farrell 1991), including more frequent international conferences; and, assisted by some modest funding from the EU and elsewhere, increasing interest in comparative research, especially in the area of cross-border policing (see, for example, Fijnaut 1993; Anderson *et al.* 1995; Brants and Field 1995). Another sign is the appearance of new specialist academic journals and more articles on European crime and policing in existing journals. The *European Journal on Criminal Policy and Research* (which carried a special issue on cross-border crime in 1993) and the *European Journal of Crime, Criminal Law and Criminal Justice* are two relatively new English language journals, while *Crime, Law and Social Change* has throughout the 1990s carried numerous articles on organised crime with a European dimension.

Much more fast-moving developments, however, can be found in a small number of areas arousing major political interest. By far the most governmental attention, unsurprisingly, has been lavished on types of crime with a strong international or cross-border element which have been perceived as a serious threat to the 'fabric of the state'. These include large-scale drug trafficking, terrorism, illegal immigration and, still to a more symbolic than practical extent, fraud against the funds of the European Union and various other forms of business (or 'enterprise') crime. In such instances, although investigation and prosecution remain firmly in the hands of member states (there is as yet little support for the creation of a supranational police force), 'harmonisation' means far more than simply the adoption of similar policies. It may entail the construction of international intelligence-gathering systems and databanks; the regular international exchange of information and crime analysis; joint policing operations across borders; the allowance of 'hot pursuit' across frontiers; and, increasingly, the use of new methods of surveillance and undercover policing (Fijnaut and Marx 1995; Maguire and John 1996). It may also entail the use and extension of Community powers originally granted for purposes other than crime control. A good illustration, discussed below, is provided by efforts to control 'money laundering' by major enterprise criminals. These have led to the imposition of criminal liability on banks and other credit institutions if they knowingly assist money launderers, fail to keep specified information about their clients, or fail to inform the police about suspicious transactions – all of which challenge previously accepted principles of banking secrecy (Levi 1991, 1997; Taylor 1992; Gilmore 1995).

Such developments have not been restricted to major crime. Concern about football hooliganism also generated collaboration between European police and criminal justice authorities (Williams 1989), culminating during the 1990 World Cup in joint operations of a scale and intensity regarded by some commentators as wildly out of proportion to the problem (Armstrong and Hobbs 1995). Such operations, some of the undercover methods used and the heavy-handed pre-emptive actions taken (for example, restrictions on movement and summary deportations) raise questions about the control and public accountability of cross-border policing. Similar questions are raised by the growing surveillance of immigrants within 'fortress Europe'.

In this chapter, we can do no more than touch on a few basic issues relating to crime and its control in Europe. We look, first, at the degree to which levels of crime differ in the various European countries; second, at the nature and extent of 'cross-border' crime; and third, at trends in policing and criminal justice policies in different states and among transnational bodies, including the degree of 'harmonisation' so far apparent. Finally, we argue that, as cooperation between crime control agencies increases, civil rights issues and questions about accountability are likely to assume more prominence.

Variations in crime levels

To what extent do levels of crime vary between different European countries? This cannot be answered satisfactorily by simply comparing officially produced statistics in the various countries. Definitions of crime, police and court practices, and counting procedures differ widely. Moreover, whatever comparable statistical material can be obtained, it cannot be sensibly interpreted without looking at any major variations in, for example, levels of unemployment or social inequality, geography, population density, car ownership, alcohol and illegal drugs consumption, or any other factors which may affect levels of opportunity for the commission of crime or may help to generate particular patterns of criminal behaviour. We only have space to skirt these issues.

Official (police-recorded) statistics have indicated fairly uniform trends in crime levels throughout western European countries since the Second World War: stable or falling rates until the mid-1950s, very sharp increases throughout the 1960s and 1970s, and more fluctuating, though still rising, patterns during the 1980s and 1990s. In relation to population, Sweden, West Germany and England and Wales have generally exhibited the highest levels of recorded crime, while, at the other extreme, Switzerland has always appeared from its official statistics to experience so little crime that a distinguished American academic was moved to write a book to try to explain the phenomenon (Clinard 1978). Clinard attributed it to the country's tight social cohesion and tradition of citizen participation rather than reliance on a central welfare state, its conservative values, the absence of large cities, and the lack of a strong, separate youth culture. However, Balvig (1987) has cast doubt on Clinard's inferences, observing that Denmark, which has traditionally liberal values, a large-scale centralised welfare system, a large city, and a flourishing youth culture, also has an exceptionally low crime rate.

There are always serious doubts about the comparability of crime figures between countries, owing to differences in definitions and in reporting and recording practices. For this reason, the publication in 1990 of the first international crime victimisation survey (van Dijk *et al.* 1990) – in which random samples of households were contacted by telephone to ask whether they had recently been victims of specified criminal offences – marked an important step forward in the field of comparative criminology. The first survey was conducted during 1988 in 11 European countries, as well as the USA, Canada and Australia; subsequent surveys have included the larger countries of the developed and underdeveloped world (van Dijk and Mayhew 1993; Mayhew and van Dijk 1997). Such research is not without serious methodological problems (not least, major variations in response rates), but it provides an extremely valuable alternative to official statistics.

Results from the victimisation surveys differ according to whether we take percentage victimised – which conceals repeat victimisation – or crime rates per 100 persons. Thus, the US, which is third highest among industrialised nations in crimes per capita, is seventh in terms of the proportion of the population victimised in 1995. Although The Netherlands and England and Wales have twice the number of crimes per capita as they have percentage victimised, the *ranking* of European countries remains unchanged: The Netherlands emerges as the most 'criminal' environment, followed closely by England and Wales, Switzerland, Scotland, France, Sweden, Finland, Austria, and with Northern Ireland the most law-abiding country. These findings certainly conflict with our *images* of countries, for example of Switzerland being peaceful: the convergence of Switzerland and Sweden also prima facie falsifies Clinard's proposition about the effects of citizen participation and a weak central welfare state in reducing crime.

Rather than jumping to general conclusions based solely on the aggregate totals of 'crime', it is important to examine carefully the component parts of each set of figures and to interpret them in the light of knowledge about particular conditions within the various countries. To take a simple example, Holland's relatively high crime rate is largely accounted for by the exceptional numbers of bicycle thefts which, not unexpectedly, occur in a country where cycling is an important part of the culture. (The same, incidentally, can be said of Oxford and Cambridge!) Looking at specific types of crime, risks of theft of cars and thefts from cars were easily the highest in England and Wales, where 'joyriding' may be especially prevalent. Meanwhile, Mayhew and White (1997) observe that car recovery rates have fallen markedly in Austria, Switzerland and The Netherlands: this suggests professional theft, supporting suspicions that stolen cars are increasingly distributed to former communist countries of central and eastern Europe. In burglary, too, England and Wales top the industrial nation tables, followed by The Netherlands, France, Scotland, Northern Ireland, Switzerland, Sweden, Austria, and Finland (with Austria and Finland having only a fifth of the English rate). England and Wales also top the 'contact crime' (i.e.

Table 9.1   **Homicide rates in Europe**

City	Homicide rates per 100 000 in selected European cities				
	1990	*1991*	*1992*	*1993*	*1994*
London	2.5	2.5	2.4	2.2	2.3
Belfast	5.7	18.5	14.0	14.0	10.2
Edinburgh	2.7	1.8	2.1	2.5	2.0
Dublin	1.1	1.2	2.1	0.8	1.3
Amsterdam	8.2	3.7	7.1	6.9	8.4
Berlin	–	2.7	3.2	4.4	3.9
Brussels	–	3.4	3.5	3.1	3.7
Lisbon	–	4.0	4.8	4.5	5.6
Rome	2.9	2.1	1.6	1.5	1.6
Stockholm	3.7	3.4	3.8	5.4	–

(We are grateful to Gordon Barclay of the Home Office Research and Statistics Directorate for supplying the data on which this section is based.)

violence) table, with Sweden, Finland, Scotland, Switzerland, France, The Netherlands, Austria and Northern Ireland following. Indeed, the indications from successive surveys are that England and Wales have experienced the most significant rise in crime in Europe, across the whole spectrum of offences.

At the lower end of the violent crime table in 1988 and 1991 were Switzerland, Italy and (lowest of all) Japan, illustrating that:

1 one can have a low crime rate and various styles of capitalism, from highly individualistic to corporatist; and
2 in the case of Switzerland, one can have very low rates of violence at the same time as commonly available guns for the 'citizen army' (Killias 1993), showing the importance of culture as well as opportunity factors in the aetiology of violence. (Switzerland, it is worth noting, also has a low homicide rate, though not a low suicide rate.)

Naturally, victimisation surveys cannot measure homicide rates and here we are reliant on statistics generated by the police and courts. While again not without their problems, such figures are probably more reliable in this area of crime than in many others. Table 9.1 shows per capita homicide rates (including murder, manslaughter and infanticide, but excluding attempts) for a number of European capitals. Note the stability of homicide rates, except for Stockholm (caused by changes in recording practice) and Belfast (where changes in homicide rates reflect the ebb and flow of political violence). The exceptionally high rate in Amsterdam (which, with London, had by far the highest raw totals of homicides) is almost certainly linked to its extra, though far from unique, problems of violence arising out of competition in the drugs trade. Otherwise, there is modest but intriguing variation within Europe which is hard to explain by religious, ethnic or other demographic criteria.

Cross-border crime

In contrast to the wealth of data collected about criminal offences, reported or not reported to the police, in every European country, there is almost no hard information available about cross-border crime for gain in Europe. Because police forces and national governments define their responsibilities for the production of statistics in terms of crimes occurring within their own jurisdictions, and because victimisation surveys exclude both consensual crimes and frauds against organisations (the main victims of cross-border criminals) and do not specify the origins of offenders, no data are collated routinely. Nor are there many specific research studies which demonstrate with any accuracy the proportion of all offences which possess a cross-border dimension.

There are individual forms of crime which constitute exceptions to this dearth of knowledge. These include frauds against the funds of the EU, estimated at ECU 60 billion (around £50 billion); software piracy, estimated in Western Europe at ECU 1.3–4.8 billion in 1994 (Deloitte and Touche 1997); and cross-border credit card fraud which, for example, accounts for a quarter of the cost of UK plastic card fraud (£25 million in 1996) and an even higher proportion of French plastic fraud (Levi and Pithouse 1998). They include also terrorism cases, and – because the scope of customs agencies, and hence their statistics, is restricted to importation – drug trafficking. Nevertheless, despite the enormous effort put into the tracking of drugs – most notably by the vast network of American agents – this is an unknown and possibly fluctuating proportion of the total amount smuggled. Although a certain amount of retrospective analysis can be done on the origins of drugs seized on the streets, it is generally true that the data on trafficking are less a reflection of underlying trading patterns than of where detection resources are put: clearly, for example, if relatively few White people are searched at the borders or within them, Whites will be under-represented among the population of officially defined drug-traffickers. Meanwhile, for burglary, robbery, vice, white-collar crime, and even frauds against the European Community, cross-border crimes simply merge into the general statistics of recorded crime.

The fact that inter-state crimes cannot be counted and tabulated in the same way as intra-state crimes does not mean that nothing can be said about these phenomena. On the contrary, a number of pioneering writers are beginning to piece together information from interviews with offenders, from police and customs sources, and from specialist agencies set up to control serious cross-border offending. Let us look briefly at some of their findings.

Types of enterprise crime

In discussing serious cross-border offending, much of which takes place under the guise of legitimate business transactions, we use the term 'enterprise crime' because the conventional division into 'white-collar' and 'organised' crime (e.g. Mack and Kerner 1975) is no longer appropriate, if it ever was. The term 'white-collar crime' may mislead the reader into assuming that business crime is committed only by members of the social élite. Conversely, 'organised crime' conjures up images of unambiguously criminal groups, composed of gangland figures whose practices routinely include the use of violence, extortion and the corruption of officials: this, too, may not be typical.

We are not denying that many company fraudsters never commit any other type of crime, or that most drugs dealers, let alone other criminals, have no sophisticated business networks. But the realm of serious cross-border business crime is the place where the activities of 'professional criminals' and 'criminal professionals' increasingly intersect (e.g. van Duyne 1991, 1993a, 1993b, 1996; Ruggiero 1996.) Groups involved in large-scale drug-smuggling include ostensibly legitimate business people who also help to evade value-added tax, commit subsidies frauds against the European Community, dump toxic waste across or within borders, and evade excise duties on imported or exported goods such as tobacco (from Ireland to England via Holland) or alcohol. Again, armed robbers may operate to a limited extent in other countries, but for them, the main cross-border connection arises should they decide to move their money off-shore (Levi 1991, 1993; van Duyne 1991, 1996) and/or flee abroad. Are any of the above groups white-collar criminals sometimes and organised criminals at other times? Such a demarcation has no point, for the crucial empirical question is what range of activities they embark on and what affects that range of choices.

As a result of their banking secrecy rules, some European countries – Austria, Liechtenstein, Luxembourg and Switzerland – have a well-deserved global reputation for laundering the proceeds of crime (and of conduct that may later be viewed as crime on the fall of a Third World government, as happened in Haiti, the Philippines and Zaire). But it should be remembered that for persons outside Britain, the UK is an offshore financial centre, and we too offer many services for foreign criminals. We devote special attention to money-laundering later. Looking at other crimes, the main ones with a cross-border component are smuggling (of legal and illegal goods), fraud, and drug-trafficking. These can be illustrated with a few concrete examples.

Securities fraud

In the UK, the Financial Services Act 1986 made it illegal to make an unsolicited call to someone who has not requested financial services.

Moreover, all people selling investments must be licensed by a state-authorised body, a Self-Regulatory Organisation. However, during the mid-and late 1980s, groups of fraudsters – mainly Canadians – set up in Amsterdam and 'cold-called' people in Britain with 'wonderful' investment opportunities that later proved valueless. When the Dutch tightened up their law enforcement, the fraudsters moved to Belgium, as well as to the Dutch Antilles, the Caribbean and Gibraltar, whose systems are legitimated in the eyes of prospective victims by their connection to the British and Dutch colonial powers.

The above frauds are termed 'boiler room operations', and all they need is a respectable country and a good telephone system. Likewise, company directors, accountants, surveyors and bankers with inside information about a company's prospects can arrange, using overseas corporations, to purchase or sell that company's shares: the crime of insider dealing. Like many other kinds of major business, significant forms of criminal enterprise – price-fixing cartels, for example, or securities frauds – can be carried out within one country as well as internationally. However, using an overseas base (European or not) gives the perpetrators a major advantage in that effective mutual assistance between investigators from different countries is necessary to convict them: this poses many problems in Britain, with its cross-border investigation budgets losing ground within 'devolved policing', and where the absence of a continental-style penal code makes international collaboration relatively unfamiliar and difficult, officers having to operate through the judicial system rather than police-to-police, as is normal in the UK. Most detected major securities frauds – for example, those investigated by the UK Serious Fraud Office and the Department of Trade and Industry – have an overseas element, whether in their perpetration or in the laundering of proceeds: but a specific 'European connection' has no particular rationale.

European Union fraud

At the simplest, firms are paid subsidies for the production of vast quantities of wine, olives or other products that in reality do not exist. They can produce forms stamped by local officials (who are bribed) testifying to the cultivation of the vineyards or olive groves, but despite the advent of 'spy-satellite' technology, checks are modest. In other, more complex cases, export subsidies are obtained on meat which is claimed to be produced for non-EU countries – whereas, in fact, it is either not produced at all, or is produced for home consumption (see, more generally, Passas and Nelken 1993.) There is a vast amount of fraud, not only against the agricultural funds but also against the development funds of the EU: for example, organised criminals in the Italian Mezzogiorno simply take money for projects that they do not build, or at best construct with poor-quality materials. Such frauds are not inherently linked to the European Union: in principle, they can be committed just as easily against domestic governments. However, the EU is a particularly attractive target because of the peculiar nature of its regulatory structure, and the fact that individual states which may not be harmed by fraud against the EU (and indeed, may have to reimburse the EU for any fraud they detect) have sole charge over prosecuting it: in the jargon of crime prevention, neither the EU nor the member state is a 'capable guardian'.

Value-added tax fraud

Here, pending VAT harmonisation within the EU, advantage is taken of differential VAT rates in European countries. Some good examples exist of trade between Northern Ireland and the Republic, but a typical European situation is described by van Duyne (1991) in relation to a Belgian/Dutch team:

Depending on the availability of forged customs stamps and the possibility of profitable disposal in Belgium, there was either a real export or only a transfer of invoices. The profits were realised by evading 25 per cent VAT plus 8 per cent luxury tax on the Belgian side, and 20 per cent VAT on the Dutch side ... The same shipments were sometimes used a number of times before they were sold in the open market at a knock-down price ... Holland [company] 1 imports and sells to Holland 2, charging 20 per cent VAT. Holland 2 exports (for the same price or at a loss) and reclaims the VAT from the taxman, because VAT is remitted on exports. Holland 1 does not pay the VAT it charged Holland 2. Holland 2 has sold to Belgium 1 and the same game is played, selling to Belgium 2, which exports the same batch back to Holland 1. Holland 1 and Belgium 1 are front companies designed to go bankrupt. In some cases the last act of the dying firm consisted of an ordinary long-firm [bankruptcy] fraud.

Modes of organisation

While quite a lot is known about the modes of operation described above, the haphazard development of criminological research in different parts of Europe has meant that knowledge about the modes of organisation of crime remains very patchy. There has always been a tendency to contrast North European forms of criminal organisation with the 'crime corporation'-like structures supposedly existing in North America and South Italy. For example, Mack and Kerner (1975) seemed to be obsessed with distancing North European crime from American organised crime, implying that if crime is not 'syndicated' (and supported by widespread police corruption), it cannot be 'organised'. However, more recent work suggests that crime, even in the US and certainly in Europe, could more aptly be described as 'disorganised' (Reuter 1983; Ruggiero and South 1995, 1997; van Duyne 1996). The situation is not far removed from the summary of Kelly (1986) over a decade ago, reviewing articles on organised crime in a number of countries:

In England there are no criminal syndicates of the size and scope of those in the United States. The reasons for this are mainly economic. Great Britain's legislators and law enforcement officials have recognized the public demand for certain goods and services (gambling and drugs) in a highly administered manner which has taken the market away from criminal organizations that would have developed to fill the gap. Criminals ... tend to work in small groups but, nonetheless, maintain extensive networks of contacts through which they can procure wider services ... [Sicilian] Mafiosi are not a residue of a state of lawlessness; they are not bandits or outlaws; Mafia groups are not outside the mainstream of social life living on its margins; rather they belong to, and often occupy, prominent positions in a reliable, protective and success-ful chain of patron-client relationships ... Mafiosi resemble local party bosses operating the urban political machines which for votes and support return favors and provide a range of services that the large municipal and state governments are incapable of performing.

From this juxtaposition, we can see the contrasts even within Europe in the forms of criminal organisation. In Italy, the weakness of the central state and peculiar historical characteristics have shaped the form of organised crime there, though even in Sicily, 'the' Mafia really takes the form of networks of alliances rather than a line-management national criminal organisation (Arlacchi 1986; Hess 1986; Walston 1986; Gam-betta 1994). In Italy, as in many parts of the United States (Chambliss 1978), organised crime groups were linked heavily into the local and national political networks, frequently combining with right-wing pol-itical groups: however, this has broken down since the collapse of com-munism removed the necessity for the West, especially the US, to tolerate and even support the corrupt links between the organised crime groups and the major political parties in Italy. This in turn enabled some Italian magistrates to do something about the vast corruption in Italian busi-ness and politics (Nelken and Levi 1996). We would add that issues such as the spread of ethnic groups – for example, Albanians, Chinese, Nigerians, Russians and Turks – within Europe and elsewhere is an important feature facilitating social networks within which criminals can trust each other.

Perhaps a more fruitful way of looking at modes of criminal organ-isation is that adopted by McIntosh (1975), who distinguished them in terms of the technological and policing barriers the particular crime con-fronts. In short, as policing and prevention strategies improve, organisa-tion shifts from routinised craft groups – e.g. pickpockets, and even safecrackers – to looser, perhaps even one-off, alliances between project criminals. A further move in the game may be to extend operations across borders. As Levi (1981) points out, since the sixteenth century, bank-ruptcy ('long firm') fraudsters in particular have found cross-border crime attractive because it creates problems of legal jurisdiction, in-vestigative cost, and practical interest by police, prosecutors and even creditors themselves. European Union harmonisation does not itself make any difference to this, except in providing new pretexts or 'storylines' for fraudsters to use to get credit or investment, and in as much as it changes the structures of control: for example, reducing customs paper-work makes VAT evasion easier. (Customs officers inform us that VAT evasion, as well as smuggling of persons and goods, has become a bigger problem since 1992, when formal customs controls were greatly reduced.)

Until recently, comparisons between organised crime in America and western Europe did not actually look at cross-border crime, and even their comments about criminal organisation intra-nationally for different European countries were patchy. The growth of interest in and concern about 'organised crime' has stimulated more research, but it has seldom been incremental (see, for a sceptical review, van Duyne 1996). The lack of a research base on patterns of criminal relationships in most European countries – including, regrettably, the UK – means that we have little information about how domestic criminals meet and decide what to do, let alone how (and to what effect, or lack of effect) 'Eurocriminals' meet. Major offenders do not advertise their services in the media, and apart from common holidays in Spain, marinas and casinos, such contacts – mediated no doubt by language difficulties – may often be tentative. Most plausible is the notion that Eurocriminals are either crime entrepreneurs who already exploit international trade for the purposes of fraud and/or smuggling, or money-launderers who put their clients in touch with each other (see Dorn, Murji and South 1992; Ruggiero 1996; Hobbs 1997).

The above comments remain substantially in the realm of specu-lation, and a great deal of research remains to be done. But it must be reiterated that, however important the activities of a few such major criminals, in most European countries almost all crime remains local in character, and is not highly organised in the sense of being conducted under the aegis of a crime syndicate. This does not mean that there are not small-scale 'syndicates' to be found, even involving systematic corruption of police and public officials, in areas such as smuggling, toxic waste-dumping, fraud, and narcotics distribution. In a sense, ex-cept where it is officially tolerated – as cannabis is in The Netherlands – 'service crime' almost requires such corrupt liaisons, for vice has to advertise in order for potential clients to know of its availability. But we ought to be careful in asserting that 'there is organised crime' in country X when all we mean is that some tiny proportion of criminal activity is run by a syndicate. Ruggiero and South (1997) usefully characterise the late-modern city in Europe as a bazaar, a special sort of market-place in which relationships entail incessant bargaining, trade and manoeuvre and in which licit and illicit economies (including the drug economy) interweave. But some bargainers have very unequal financial and physical power to coerce consent, and charismatic, as well as institutional, factors such as the organisation and integrity of crim-inal justice agencies may determine the modes of organisation of crime for gain.

Crime control and criminal justice policy

Variation and convergence

Perceptions of the seriousness or otherwise of various types of crime differ considerably between European countries, as do ideas about appropriate kinds and levels of punishment. A good example is drunk driving, an offence about which, despite a gradual hardening of public opinion, British attitudes have always been somewhat ambivalent. In Scandinavian countries, by contrast, and especially in Sweden, this has long been regarded as a very serious offence, often resulting in imprisonment and producing social stigma comparable to conviction as a thief. Another example is drug use and small-scale dealing in drugs. While the British and the Germans tend to see such activities essentially as 'crime problems', the Dutch perceive them to a large extent as a health or education problem, to be met by policies based on harm reduction and normalisation. These include efforts to demythologise drug-taking, to present it to the public as a normal social problem, to discourage its glamorous image among the young, and to avoid driving the drug culture underground through police harassment and stigmatisation. City councils readily fund services such as syringe exchange and drop-in centres for addicts (Mol 1991): an approach that has spread to many other European cities, for example in Britain, Germany and Switzerland, as the HIV and hepatitis-B threats have enhanced the public health risks that flow from purist moralism. And, against official American-dominated policy, Amsterdam has experimented with the de-penalisation of the consumption of cannabis: it is openly sold in small quantities in hundreds of coffee shops, the sales being technically illegal, but rarely interfered with by the police. These policies reflect a traditionally liberal attitude towards crime (other than serious violent or sexual offences) peculiar to The Netherlands, which – though frequently under threat, especially in recent years – has been reflected over the past two decades in distinctive sentencing policies and progressive experimentation in crime prevention, prison management and other areas of the criminal justice field. The Amsterdam example, especially, illustrates the further general point that, while there are pressures towards conformity, there is still room for radically different thinking to be translated into action at a local level, and particularly at the level of local government in large cities. Even in Germany, where the national government fosters an unambiguously repressive approach to drugs problems, the level of police tolerance towards small-scale dealing and use varies widely between individual cities.

There are other notable variations across Europe in, *inter alia*, crime-prevention strategies, sentencing practice, levels of assistance to victims, attitudes to prison reform, and satisfaction with and confidence in the police. The latter, for example, is low in Poland, Norway, Italy,

Czechoslovakia, and Spain and – paradoxically, in the light of the crime rates – relatively high in the UK and Sweden; it has also fallen significantly during the 1990s in France, Finland and, above all, The Netherlands (van Dijk and Mayhew 1993; Mayhew and van Dijk 1997). On the other hand, the differences seem in many cases to be narrowing, even in areas without high priority, as a result of increasing discussion and collaboration – for example, through meetings arranged by the Council of Europe and the United Nations (Council of Europe 1985; United Nations 1990). Within individual countries, too, there are currently signs of convergence. Crime policy has traditionally been a matter of ideological difference between political parties with, broadly speaking, conservatives favouring 'hard line', deterrent or retributive strategies, and socialists favouring strategies aimed at changing the social conditions thought to generate crime. Yet there seems to be an increasing convergence towards an essentially 'tough' or punitive stance – albeit with political shading on the lines of what the British Labour Prime Minister Tony Blair memorably termed 'tough on crime; tough on the causes of crime'. Similar trends have been noted in Italy, The Netherlands and Germany, in particular, all of which have moved away to some extent from traditionally liberal policies over the last few years.

Even so, quite wide differences still exist in the use of imprisonment. Van Dijk (1991) provided some interesting figures comparing governments' relative expenditure on different parts of the crime control system. He calculated that, in the mid-1980s, England and Wales were spending almost three times as much (per 100 000 inhabitants) on prisons as France and considerably more than West Germany, but spending less than either on police officers. Indeed, the ratio of expenditure on police to expenditure on prisons varied between 13:1 in France to under 3:1 in Sweden. Sweden's low ratio is explained mainly by its commitment to maintaining good conditions in prisons – it has also been a leader in the field of prisoners' rights. (A detailed comparative account of approaches to prisoners' rights in France, Germany and the UK can be found in Vagg 1991.) On the other hand, a similarly high rate of spending on prisons in England and Wales (the police/prisons ratio being 4.5:1) reflects something quite different: one of the highest incarceration rates in Europe, combined with the legacy of a stock of ageing penal institutions in a poor state of repair and exceptionally expensive to staff.

The years 1993–97 saw an exceptionally rapid rise in the use of imprisonment in England and Wales. In the first edition of this book, we quoted incarceration rates for most European countries in 1989. England and Wales then stood at the top of the list in terms of prisoners per 100 000 population, with a rate (96) around twice those of countries such as The Netherlands (44), Italy (54) and Sweden (57) and well above those of France (80), Spain (80) and Germany (83). While several of these other countries, especially The Netherlands and Italy, have since seen significant rises in their incarceration rates, England and

Wales (after a brief fall in the early 1990s), has continued to reach new record levels. In 1997, its prison population passed 60 000, a rate of over 120 per 100 000 population. British judges have traditionally resorted to sentences of imprisonment more readily, and for longer terms, than their counterparts in mainland Europe. They have been particularly harsh in dealing with young adult offenders, for example, the proportion of prisoners under the age of 21 being twice that found in France or Spain. This situation is difficult to alter, partly because of their selection from a narrow social and professional background, and partly because of their jealous guarding of their constitutional independence, which has made them resistant to government attempts to introduce judicial training or to constrain their discretion (Devlin 1976; Ashworth 1995). When combined, as in the last three years of John Major's Conservative government, with a strong and persistent message from the Home Secretary that 'prison works' and clear encouragement to sentencers to use it more, this tough judicial tradition produced rapid and dramatic pressure on the already overcrowded prison system. Judges' attidues also reflect the greater punitiveness of the general public in the UK, nearly half of whom are ready to imprison a recidivist burglar, compared with The Netherlands (31.2 per cent), Sweden (22.1 per cent), and especially France (10.7 per cent), Austria (9.8 per cent) and Switzerland (9.4 per cent). There is, however, no direct correlation between the rank order of preferred imprisonment for burglars and the burglary rates (Mayhew and van Dijk 1997).

Another important difference in emphasis noted by van Dijk (1990) is between countries with a high and a low commitment to crime-prevention programmes. Sweden and Denmark, who led the field in this respect, have had National Crime Prevention Councils for more than 20 years, encouraging and evaluating local projects, stimulating research and collating and disseminating ideas and information (Jensen 1988). In the 1980s, too, France set up Prevention Councils at local, regional and national level, and the government funded an array of projects, involving a wide range of agencies, aimed especially at young people (King 1988).

The Dutch government, too, while deciding against such a council, has tended to put an exceptionally large proportion of its resources into crime-prevention projects: in the mid-1980s it was spending nearly 3 per cent of its total crime-related budget on such projects, compared with only 1 per cent in England and Wales. This reflects its consistent policy, since the early 1970s, of seeking alternative crime-control strategies to that of incarcerating offenders: the Dutch were well in advance of other countries in taking seriously research findings which suggested that prison is ineffective as a deterrent or rehabilitative measure and, in contrast to Britain (and despite some toughening of public and judicial attitudes in Holland over the past few years), their judges have generally been persuaded to use custody only in the last resort.

In Britain, crime prevention has remained less institutionalised, but private agencies such as Crime Concern have received considerable government support, while research sponsored by the Home Office Crime Prevention Unit is receiving a higher profile than in the past. These developments, together with clear efforts in several countries to enhance the profile of crime prevention, once moved a former head of the Home Office Research and Planning Unit (Tuck 1988) to speak, in somewhat grandiose fashion, of a Europe-wide move away from the 'carceral' society towards 'a preventive, community-based approach to crime control'. Such optimism was very short-lived, and the carceral society remains very much alive and kicking. Nevertheless, there is no doubt that significant advances have been made in crime prevention, most dramatically in the rapid spread in Britain of video camera surveillance of streets, buildings and car parks (Norris, Armstrong and Moran 1998). This has been slower to take off in continental Europe, where concerns about privacy tend to be more widely voiced (and where there is greater awareness of the protections contained in the European Convention on Human Rights), but if other countries follow Britain's lead, it may eventually have a very strong impact on thinking about crime right across Europe.

In addition to increased interest in, and imitation of, other countries' policies, harmonisation continues to be encouraged in a more formal way by the promulgation of Conventions, Recommendations and Resolutions by the Council of Europe. These are not binding on member countries, and many are 'watered down' when implemented. Nevertheless, they have clearly had some influence on domestic policies in a number of crime-related areas. A good example is policies towards victims of crime, where two important Resolutions and a Convention have helped to stimulate advances in compensation, welfare support and victims' rights in several countries where there was previously virtually no provision (Waller 1988; Maguire and Shapland 1997).

Finally, mention must be made of the influence of the European Court of Human Rights, which, though so far limited to fairly narrow areas, has been of great importance in these areas, as its decisions are binding on national governments. In the field of prisoners' rights, for example, several key decisions have compelled the UK government to amend its policies. These include findings in the early 1980s that denying prisoners access to solicitors and censoring prison mail constituted breaches of the European Convention on Human Rights (Fawcett 1985): as a result, new Standing Orders were introduced and a substantially different set of attitudes has grown up towards communications between prisoners and the outside world. More recently, the Court found that parole decisions on the release of certain categories of 'lifer' should not be taken by government ministers, and the UK government agreed to cede full powers in this regard to the independent Parole Board. Several other legislative changes have been made by the British government in anticipation of losing cases in the European Court. Recently, much attention has been focused on cases involving covert methods of crime investigation, such as 'bugging' and other forms of intrusive surveillance (Maguire and John 1996). The announcement of the new Labour government in 1997 that the Convention is to be incorporated directly into UK legislation, is likely to stimulate more legislation in such areas.

Cross-border crime control

We turn now to the important question of the regulation of cross-border crime within Europe. We must first ask here what is special about Europe? The answer is that, with the exception of crime issues that are specifically affected by the organisation and laws of the European Union – notably the establishment of Europol – there is nothing special about Europe. Interpol (see below) is not restricted by its borders, and even the Council of Europe has links outside Europe. With the disintegration of Comecon and the transition of all former communist countries to market economies, the boundaries of Europe are once again problematical. In some important respects, Britain's common law tradition sets it apart from the other European nations which operate on strictly defined Penal Codes, and this – plus insular political attitudes which distrust all harmonisation as the 'thin end of the wedge' towards the acceptance of 'inferior' foreign justice – means that (subject to any changes arising from the Labour government of 1997) Britain finds greater difficulty in cooperating in the criminal justice sphere than do any other western European countries, members of the EU or not.

Police cooperation: the 'drugs war' and the legitimation of new tactics

The history of cooperation between European police forces can be traced back to the early nineteenth century, when it was concerned almost exclusively with political control. It continued mainly at an informal and secret level until 1923, when Interpol was created – albeit as a worldwide, not exclusively European agency. Interpol's first objective was to facilitate the exchange of intelligence, although over the years attempts have been made to expand its role into more direct investigative assistance to national police forces.

Interpol has never developed into the powerful and effective resource for cross-border policing that some of its leading members envisaged (Anderson 1989; Fijnaut 1991, 1993). This is partly because of rivalry and lack of trust and cooperation between police forces in different countries, and partly because of its own internal politics and unwieldy bureaucracy, however streamlined by managerialism and the threat of competition from Europol. However, probably more important has been formal limitations on its activities, combined with overlaps with other international agencies. Where the control of 'subversion', for example, is concerned, its role has always been limited by Article 3 of its constitution, which prohibits 'interference with political or military matters', and Interpol has consequently played second fiddle since the Second World War to the secret intelligence services which mushroomed to meet the 'Communist threat'.

Potentially a far more important overlap has been created by the recently constituted organisation, Europol, based in The Hague. Europol is a descendant of the now defunct Trevi group, which was set up by EC ministers in 1976 as an intergovernmental committee to facilitate cooperation to control a marked increase in terrorism (especially in West Germany and Italy), but then expanded its role to include other forms of international crime including drugs and arms-smuggling and armed robbery. (In doing so, it trespassed on areas squarely within Interpol's original terms of reference. Somewhat ironically, the formation of Trevi was aided originally by the reluctance of Interpol to trespass beyond its own brief, seeing terrorism as excluded by Article 3.) After finding its feet in a limited role as the 'European Drugs Unit', the creation of Europol proper was authorised by the signing of the Europol Convention in 1995. The Convention is now (1997) in the lengthy process of ratification by each member state (the UK was the first to sign). When the formalities are completed, Europol will expand far beyond its initial role of facilitating international intelligence exchange. It will be permitted to store and analyse intelligence on large numbers of individuals, and will play a more central part (albeit still in an advisory capacity, and in investigations which remain under the control of national police forces) in the planning and coordination of international investigations. Moreover, its brief has already been extended from drug-trafficking and money-laundering to cover clandestine illegal immigrant networks, the import/export of stolen vehicles, and trafficking in nuclear and radioactive waste, and arguments are already being put forward to expand the list further. Such developments are seen by some as the thin end of the wedge leading inexorably towards the creation of a European police force. Moreover, despite apparently tight lines of accountability and currently strict application of data-protection laws, there are fears that Europol will eventually become a powerful body beyond effective external scrutiny and control. An added fear is that this process will be speeded by increasing involvement with the secret services, which (thanks to the 'peace dividend') have in several countries including Britain taken over intelligence-gathering roles in relation to types of crime which are normally police territory (see, for example, Nodia 1996).

Interpol's basic intelligence-sharing role has also been superseded to some extent by more direct forms of bilateral or multilateral cooperation between police forces, as in agreements allowing 'hot pursuit' across borders (Anderson *et al.* 1995) and in high-level political and judicial, as well as police, planning of joint operations, such as the control of Dutch and English football fans in Italy in 1990. Moreover, increased international police cooperation has led to the creation of strong informal networks of contacts, through which information can be passed directly, avoiding the controls which apply to intelligence exchange through Europol and other formal channels. These so-called 'grey channels' are potentially a serious obstacle to attempts to protect privacy and regulate the use of personal data (Anderson *et al.* 1995).

Perhaps the greatest push towards coordinated policy and operations – including the generation of legal changes and even changes in national policing traditions – has come from the 'war against drugs'. Ever since the elevation of this issue by the Nixon administration to a matter of global importance, the driving force has come from the USA and, while we are here concerned with the European dimension, this can be properly understood only in the wider context of US foreign policy (Block 1991; Levi 1991; Nadelmann 1993).

The influence of the worldwide efforts of the US Drugs Enforcement Agency (DEA) to coordinate the fight against drug-traffickers (initially from South America, but latterly also from the Middle and Far East) has been felt by all European governments. One consequence has been a massive increase in the gathering and exchange of information about people suspected of involvement in the drugs trade. For example, the UK has set up its own centralised intelligence system (the National Criminal Intelligence Service), which in turn feeds into an increasingly sophisticated – and now centralised – European drugs-intelligence network. Direct bilateral exchanges of information, as well as through Interpol and Europol, are rapidly becoming routine. A second, increasingly controversial, consequence of the American-led push against drug-trafficking has been the employment – and gradual acceptance – of various forms of covert policing, now commonplace in the USA (Marx 1988), but traditionally alien in many European countries. These include wire-tapping, bugging, and the use of other sophisticated listening and recording devices, as well as deceptions by undercover agents such as 'bust-buy' and 'sting' operations. Some countries initially encouraged their police, customs and other enforcement agencies to expand their range of tactics in these directions, accepting the argument that sophisticated criminals can only be caught by sophisticated methods. Where the tactics were illegal, special legislation was sometimes introduced to legitimise them. However, as lawyers and civil rights activists have begun to challenge their propriety and legality, and a number of associated scandals have emerged, there has been something of a counter-trend to place clear limits on their use. For instance, in 1990 Belgium specified (albeit in unpublished government directives) that undercover policing can be used only in relation to offences of a certain level of seriousness and only when the goals cannot be achieved through other methods (Outrive and Cappelle 1995). Sweden, among others, has defined certain forms of sting operation as entrapment (Tollborg 1995) and even Britain has passed laws to regulate bugging (John and Maguire 1998). But perhaps the biggest legal backlash will come from the major scandal in The Netherlands, in which police malpractice and corruption in relation to large, unauthorised 'controlled deliveries' of drugs led to the widely publicised Van Traa inquiry (Inzake Opsporing 1996).

However, even if (as is doubtful in such secret areas) controls of this kind are effective curbs on over-enthusiasm by national police forces, under the Schengen agreement it has become increasingly easy for police forces and other agencies to operate in foreign countries, where they are not subject to the same regulation.

Money-laundering

Another area in which there is a strong trend towards harmonisation concerns the movement of money between countries, especially where this constitutes the 'laundering' of funds accumulated through crime. The regulation of international securities trading, like that of drugs-trafficking, tends to be conducted on a global basis, driven once again by US interests and passions for extra-territorial control. Even so, some – frequently overlapping – crime-control initiatives have emerged out of specifically European bodies, principally the Council of Europe and the EU. The fact that it had no constitutional competence in criminal matter did not prevent the Community from taking action in this area in the 1980s and early 1990s. Its responsibility for ensuring harmonisation and free trade in the economic sphere gave it a lever to regulate financial institutions in respect of insider trading, money-laundering, anti-competitive practices, and – ironically least cogent in enforcement – frauds against the Community funds.

Criminal law matters are normally an issue reserved to member governments individually: they are not within the legal competence – in the technical rather than efficiency sense – of the Community as a whole. However, in the interests of developing a single European market in financial matters, the UK and other EC countries agreed some time ago to treat attempts to combat money-laundering as being within the competence of the Community. The preamble to the Council Directive on Prevention of Use of the Financial System for the Purpose of Money Laundering of 31 May 1991 sought to justify this competence by noting, *inter alia*, that:

When credit and financial institutions are used to launder proceeds from criminal activities ... the soundness and stability of the institution concerned and confidence in the financial system as a whole could be seriously jeopardised, thereby losing the trust of the public.

It is no longer possible for a member state of the EU to refuse a licence to a bank which has been given a licence in another member state. The costs of financial supervision in the money-laundering arena are very high and if some countries act vigorously while others do not, this will distort competition between the member states. Consequently, some countries would enjoy unfair advantages over others: because laundering money gives banks extra profits, it is to the financial and social detriment of the country suffering from the crime whose proceeds are being laundered. In the same way that the importance of 'crime prevention' can be used to justify almost any action by the police in interfering with the rights of citizens, this involvement in regulating money-laundering, together with the development of anti-drug initiatives described above, could become the 'thin end of the wedge' for Community interference in domestic criminal justice issues. This is because most major crime involves putting money into financial institutions at some stage (see, further, Levi 1991). Potentially, the ambit of money-laundering rules is very wide: Article 1 of the European Community Directive defines it – if 'define' is the appropriate word – *inter alia*, as the intentional

conversion or transfer of property, knowing that such property is derived from criminal activity or from an act of participation in such activity, for the purpose of concealing or disguising the illicit origin of the property or of assisting any person who is involved in the commission of such activity to evade the legal consequences of his action.

Except in so far as it will always include the proceeds of drug-trafficking, the definition of what criminal activities are to be covered by the Directive remains unresolved, though under pressure not only from the EU but also from the Financial Action Task Force established under P8 (the eight most powerful countries), most countries have criminalised the laundering of the proceeds from all crimes (possibly excepting tax evasion), not just drugs-trafficking. So what formerly was a largely private sector matter has become a matter of public interest which is regulated by the criminal law. The Council of Europe Convention provides that bank secrecy should not, at national level, present an obstacle to the carrying out of investigations, provisional measures and forfeitures in relation to the proceeds of crime. There are several provisions to enhance mutual legal assistance in the seizing, freezing and confiscation of the proceeds of crime in Europe. The moral and political pressure is so great that it is hard for countries to resist agreement. How the formal rules work out in practice is another question. It should be noted, however, that if a regulatory 'level playing field' is to exist at a substantive rather than merely at a formal, symbolic level, more attention will have to be given by regulators to the issue of compliance and the undermining effects of competitive under-enforcement of rules. This indeed is the rationale given by the European Commission for their intervention in money-laundering. However, international bodies are normally rather poor at evaluating rigorously the implementation of what they do.

Concluding remarks: harmonisation and the problems of regulation

It is not easy to predict the future level of harmonisation of responses to crime within Europe. On the one hand, many aspects of the systems designed to combat crime bear witness to their piecemeal growth over the centuries, with major variations within countries, let alone between them. Policing *de facto* remains primarily a local rather than national responsibility; sentencing is characterised by considerable individual discretion; the philosophy of imprisonment and attitudes to prisoners' rights vary widely across Europe; and traditional strategic approaches to the prevention and control of individual forms of deviant behaviour show some striking contrasts – none more so than those concerned with soft drugs (compare The Netherlands with tough-minded France and Sweden). More fundamentally, we can contrast the adversarial basis of the British system of criminal law with the inquisitorial systems found in most of the continent (though Italy has shifted towards the adversarial system). The role of prosecutors in investigations has always been marginal in England and Wales compared with other countries, including Scotland – a situation obtaining even after the introduction of the independent Crown Prosecution Service in the mid-1980s. Priorities and strategies are still determined largely by the police.

On the other hand, while certain parts of the criminal justice system cling firmly to their own tradition, and though crime control is not formally in the province of the European Commission but is dealt with by the Council of Ministers under the Third Pillar of Maastricht, the pressures towards homogeneity are clearly to be seen. These pressures may take the form of 'Third Pillar' joint actions, such as the establishment of Europol, or the Schengen agreement; resolutions or recommendations from the Council of Europe, or, occasionally, opinions from the European Commission on Human Rights. Even prior to the Maastricht Treaty, Europe-wide policies in relation to serious cross-border crime were smuggled in through convenient back doors, as with the money-laundering initiatives described earlier, or through bilateral or multilateral agreements such as the Schengen agreement, or through the creation of Europol's predecessors such as Trevi.

Tensions between the desire for greater cross-border crime control and individual states' insistence on independence in crime policy matters, can lead to complex disputes. A good example is the conflict over the idea of a supra-national police force. In June 1991, the then British Prime Minister called for 'much greater collaboration between Europe's police forces to contain the flow of immigrants' and proposed a study of new procedures for cross-border policing, to be submitted to the European Council in 1992 (*Guardian*, 29 June 1991). However, he opposed a paper delivered at the same time by the German Chancellor, who proposed a European federal police force on the lines of the FBI.

Police collaboration, Mr Major argued, should be 'intergovernmental, not supranational' (op. cit.). This debate was linked to Britain's persistent reluctance to sign the Schengen agreement, under which border controls on movements of EU nationals are waived. It was hinted that if a 'strong perimeter fence' against both legal and illegal immigration could be established, the UK might be willing to change its opposition to Schengen, but this did not materialise. Equally, despite its popularity with some Conservatives, an alliance of right and left libertarians and the lack of enthusiasm by senior police appear to have 'killed off' the proposed UK Identity Card.

To conclude, a fundamental point of concern about many of the developments in cross-border policing and crime control discussed in this article, is that they have occurred quickly, without much public debate, and the resulting operations have been (to some extent necessarily) shrouded in secrecy. Legal and other forms of local control over actions of police, customs and other enforcement agencies have been eroded, the justification being the seriousness and the international dimension of the problems. There has been little serious discussion about what forms of behaviour actually merit drastic responses: if football hooliganism, for example, warrants massive surveillance, restrictions of movement, summary deportations, and so on, what other kinds of deviance may be subjected to such measures in the future? Or can closer surveillance of ethnic minorities be justified by the need to control illegal immigration? Above all, little thought has been given to effective international mechanisms of accountability to prevent abuses by the authorities – especially by supranational bodies. Some protection is given by the European Convention on Human Rights – the European Court has, for example, pronounced on the subject of the acceptable limits of telephone tapping – but even after the Labour government incorporates the European Convention into domestic legislation, *ex post facto* review in the courts may not be the best way of organising safeguards in the rapidly changing circumstances of international crime control.

References

Anderson, M. (1989) *Policing the World*, Oxford: Oxford University Press.

Anderson, M., den Boer, M., Cullen, P., Gilmore, W., Raab, C. and Walker, N. (1995) *Policing the European Union: Theory, Law and Practice*, Oxford: Clarendon Press.

Arlacchi, P. (1986) *Mafia Business: The Mafia Ethic and the Spirit of Capitalism*, London: Verso.

Armstrong, G. and Hobbs, D. (1995) 'The professional foul. Covert policing in Britain: the case of soccer', in C. Fijnaut and G. Marx (eds) *Undercover: Police Surveillance in Comparative Perspective*, London: Kluwer International.

Ashworth, A. (1995) *Sentencing and Criminal Justice*, 2nd edn, London: Butterworth.

Balvig, F. (1987) *The Snow White Image*, Oxford: Oxford University Press.

Block, A. (ed.) (1991) *Crime, Law and Social Change: Special Issue on The Politics of Cocaine*, Vol. 16, No. 1, July 1991.

Brants, C. and Field, S. (1995) *Participative Rights and Proactive Policing: Convergence and Drift in European Criminal Process*, Deventer, Netherlands: Kluwer.

Brants, C. and Field, S. (1997) 'Le recherche proactive et la gestion du risque', *Deviance et Société*, 21(4).

Chambliss, W. (1978) *On the Take: From Petty Crooks to Presidents*, Indiana: Indiana University Press.

Clinard, M. (1978) *Cities With Little Crime*, Cambridge: Cambridge University Press.

Council of Europe (1985) *Research on Victimisation, Collected Studies in Criminological Research*, Vol. XXIII, Strasbourg: European Committee on Crime Problems.

Deloitte and Touche (1997) *Fraud without Frontiers: an Executive Summary*, London: Deloitte & Touche.

Devlin, Lord (1976) *The Judge*, Oxford: Oxford University Press.

Dijk, J. van (1991) 'More than a matter of security: trends in crime prevention in Europe', in F. Heidensohn and M. Farrell (eds) *Crime in Europe*, London: Routledge.

Dijk, J. van and Mayhew, P. (1993) 'Criminal victimisation in the industrialised world: key findings of the 1989 and 1992 International Crime Surveys', in A. del Frate, U. Zvekic and J. van Dijk (eds) (1990) *Understanding Crime: Experiences of Crime and Crime Control*, Rome: UNICRI, UN.

Dorr, N., Murji, K. and South, N. (1992) *Traffickers*, London: Routledge.

Downes, D. (1988) *Contrasts in Tolerance*, Oxford: Oxford University Press.

Duyne, P. van (1991) 'Organised crime and business crime enterprises in The Netherlands', *Crime, Law and Social Change*, 19: 103–42.

Duyne, P. van (1993a) 'Implications of cross-border crime risks in an open Europe', *Crime, Law and Social Change*, 20: 99–111.

Duyne, P. van (1993b) 'Organized crime markets in a turbulent Europe', *European Journal on Criminal Policy and Research*, 3: 10–31.

Duyne, P. van (1996) 'The phantom and threat of organised crime', *Crime, Law and Social Change*, 24(4): 341–77.

Fawcett, J. (1985) 'Applications of the European Convention on Human Rights', in M. Maguire, J. Vagg and R. Morgan (eds) *Accountability and Prisons: Opening Up a Closed World*, London: Tavistock.

Fijnaut, C. (1991) 'Police co-operation within Western Europe', in F. Heidensohn, and M. Farrell (eds) *Crime in Europe*, London: Routledge.

Fijnaut, C. (ed.) (1993) *The Internationalization of Police Cooperation in Western Europe*, Deventer and Boston: Gouda Quint, Kluwer.

Fijnaut, C. and Marx, G. (eds) (1995) *Undercover Policing: an International Perspective*, Amsterdam: Kluwer.

Gambetta, D. (1994) *The Sicilian Mafia*, Cambridge, Mass.: Harvard University Press.

Gilmore, W. (1995) *Dirty Money*, Strasbourg: Council of Europe Press.

Graham, J. (1990) 'Decarceration in the Federal Republic of Germany: how practitioners are succeeding where policy-makers have failed', *British Journal of Criminology*, 30(2) Spring: 150–70.

Heidensohn, F. and Farrell, M. (1991) *Crime in Europe*, London: Routledge.

Hess, H. (1986) 'The traditional Sicilian mafia: organised crime and repressive crime', in R. Kelly (ed.) *Organised Crime: A Global Perspective*, New Jersey: Rowman & Littlefield.

Hobbs, D. (1997) 'Organised and professional crime', in M. Maguire, D. Morgan and R. Reiner (eds) *The Oxford Handbook of Criminology*, 2nd edn, Oxford: Oxford University Press.

Hood, R. (ed.) (1989) *Crime and Criminal Policy in Europe: Proceedings of a European Colloquium*, Oxford: Oxford University Centre for Criminological Research.

Inzake Opsporing (1996) *Enquetecommissie Opsporingsmethoden*, Bijl. Hand. TK 1995–6, 24072.

Jensen, L. (1988) 'Crime prevention in Denmark', in *Home Office Research Bulletin: Special European Edition*, London: Home Office.

John, T. and Maguire, M. (1998) 'Police surveillance and its regulation in England and Wales', in S. Field and C. Pelser (eds) *Invading the Private*, Aldershot: Ashgate.

Kelly, R. (ed.) (1986) *Organised Crime: A Global Perspective*, New Jersey: Rowman & Littlefield.

Killias, M. (1993) 'Gun ownership, suicide and homicide: an international perspective', in A. del Frate, U. Zvekic and J. van Dijk (eds) *Understanding Crime: Experiences of Crime and Crime Control*, Rome: UNICRI, UN.

King, M. (1988) 'Crime Prevention in France', in *Home Office Research Bulletin: Special European Edition*, London: Home Office.

Levi, M. (1981) *The Phantom Capitalists: The Organisation and Control of Long Firm Fraud*, London: Heinemann.

Levi, M. (1991) 'Pecunia non olet: Cleansing the money-launderers from the Temple', *Crime, Law and Social Change*, 16: 217–302.

Levi, M. (1993) 'The extent of cross-border crime in Europe: the view from Britain', *European Journal on Criminal Policy and Research*, 1(3): 57–76.

Levi, M. (1997) 'Evaluating the new policing: attacking the money trail of organised crime', *Australian and New Zealand Journal of Criminology*, March: 1–25.

Levi, M. and Pithouse, A. (1998) *Victims of White-Collar Crime: the Media and Social Construction of Business Fraud*, Oxford: Clarendon Press.

Mack, J. and Kerner, H-J. (1975) *The Crime Industry*, Farnborough: Saxon House.

Maguire, M. (1982) *Burglary in a Dwelling: The Offence, The Offender and The Victim*, London: Heinemann.

Maguire, M. and John, T. (1996) 'Covert and deceptive policing in England and Wales: issues in regulation and practice', *European Journal of Crime, Criminal Law and Criminal Justice*, 1994: 316–34.

Maguire, M. and Shapland, J. (1997) 'The "Victims' Movement" in Europe', in R. Davis, A. Lurigio and W. Skogan (eds) *Victims of Crime*, Newbury Park: Sage.

Marx, G. (1988) *Undercover: Police Surveillance in America*, Berkeley: University of California Press.

Mawby, R. (1979) *Policing the City*, Aldershot: Gower.

Mayhew, P. and van Dijk, J. (1997) *Criminal Victimisation in Eleven Industrialised Countries*, The Hague: Dutch Ministry of Justice.

Mayhew, P. and White, P. (1997) *The 1996 International Crime Victimisation Survey*, Research Findings No. 57, London: Home Office.

McIntosh, M. (1975) *The Organisation of Crime*, London: Macmillan.

Mol, R. (1991) 'The liberal image of the Dutch drug policy', *The International Journal on Drug Policy*, 2(5): 16–20.

Nadelmann, E. (1993) *Cops Across Borders*, Philadelphia: University of Pennsylvania State Press.

Nelken, D. and Levi, M. (1996) 'The corruption of politics and the politics of corruption: an overview', Special Issue of *Journal of Law and Society on The Corruption of Politics and the Politics of Corruption*.

Nodia, G. (1996) 'The evolution of cross-border policing in Europe', *Current Politics and Economics of Europe*, 5(2/3): 107–28.

Norris, C., Armstrong, G. and Moran, J. (eds) (1998) *Surveillance, CCTV and Social Contract*, Aldershot: Ashgate.

Outrive, L. and Cappelle, J. (1995) 'Twenty years of undercover policing in Belgium: the regulation of a risky police practice', in C. Fijnaut and G. Marx (eds) *Undercover Policing: Surveillance in Comparative Perspective*, Dordrecht: Kluwer.

Passas, N. and Nelken, D. (1993) 'The thin line between legitimate and illegitimate enterprises: subsidy frauds in the European Community', *Crime, Law and Social Change*, 19(3): 223–44.

Reuter, P. (1983) *Disorganised Crime: The Economics of the Visible Hand*, Cambridge, Mass.: MIT Press.

Ruggiero, V. (1996) *Organised and Corporate Crime in Europe*, Aldershot: Dartmouth.

Ruggiero, V. and South, N. (1995) *Eurodrugs: Drug Use, Marketing and Trafficking in Europe*, London: UCL Press.

Ruggiero, V. and South, N. (1997) 'The late-modern city as a bazaar: drug markets, illegal enterprise and the "barricades"', *British Journal of Sociology*, 48(1): 51–70.

Taylor, I. (1992) 'The international drug trade and money-laundering: border controls and other issues', *European Sociological Review*, 8(2): 168–82.

Tollborg, D. (1995) 'Covert policing in Sweden: the Swedish Secret Service', in C. Fijnaut and G. Marx (eds) *Undercover Policing: an International Perspective*, Amsterdam: Kluwer.

Tuck, M. (1988) 'Crime prevention: a shift in concept', in *Home Office Research Bulletin: Special European Edition*, London: Home Office.

United Nations (1990) *Crime Prevention and Criminal Justice Newsletter: Special Issue on the Eighth UN Congress on the Prevention of Crime and the Treatment of Offenders*, Vienna: United Nations Office.

Vagg, J. (1991) 'A touch of discipline: accountability and discipline in prison systems in Western Europe', in F. Heidensohn and M. Farrell (eds) *Crime in Europe*, London: Routledge.

Waller, I. (1988) 'International standards, national trail blazing, and the next steps', in M. Maguire and J. Pointing (eds) *Victims of Crime: A New Deal?*, Milton Keynes: Open University Press.

Walston, J. (1986) 'See Naples and die: organised crime in Campania', in R. Kelly (ed.) *Organised Crime: A Global Perspective*, New Jersey: Rowman & Littlefield.

Williams, J. (1989) *Hooligans Abroad*, London: Routledge.

CHAPTER 10

From AIDS to Alzheimer's: policy and politics in setting new health agendas

BRIDGET TOWERS

This is an interesting time for sociologists to be studying the changes that are being wrought in the design and operation of health-care services in Europe. Assumptions about core concepts of 'health', 'illness', 'disease', 'medicine', 'care' and 'therapeusis' are being challenged, not just in the academic domain but also in the public forums of the media, the legislatures, political parties, trade unions and professional associations. Health issues are now high on the agendas of economists and accountants as they try to construct new measurements and forecasts for regulating the demand and supply of a major item of public spending. Health care is now a growing specialism within management as the organisational parameters of medical goods and services have become widened and bureaucratised. Political scientists and policy analysts are using questions of health-care decision-making to monitor and evaluate changes in power relationships between the central state and local organisations. Feminists have centred a large part of their critique of patriarchy on scientific medicine's appropriation of their bodies, their selves and their knowledge. Even within the community of professional sociologists we can note the rapid expansion of 'medical sociology' as a legitimate and funded field of expertise.

In such a context perhaps one of the most useful contributions a sociological perspective can make is to do what we have always been best at and most unpopular for: namely, to stand back and study the process of the construction of the 'object'. In this case we can chart the making of a new 'discourse community' around health. In a rather obvious way it is about looking at who is sitting around what table, where, using what kinds of language and knowledge claims when something called a 'health issue' is on the agenda for discussion.

There is no shortage of detailed descriptive material on the present changes and developments in health-care policy in Europe, and it is not such a hard task to assemble charts and tables of comparative epidemiological data, per capita health-spending, ratios of health-sector funding, medical manpower or even consultation and referral rates. The OECD reports, *Measuring Health Care, 1960–83* (1985) and *Financing and Delivering Health Care* (1987), together with the WHO report on the European Region's health situation, *Evaluation of the Strategy for Health for All by the Year 2000* (1986) provide comprehensive databases for such an exercise. The purpose, however, of this chapter is to explore critically only some of these developments and to see if a specifically sociological mode of analysis can yield any further understandings.

Health for all

Probably the most accessible starting point for considering the current trends and developments in health-care policy in Europe is the World Health Assembly's global strategy of *Health for All by the Year 2000*. The strategy was built out of the Alma-Ata declaration of 1977 which located 'primary health care' as the bedrock of all future health-care planning. The strategic task was to ensure that by the year 2000 'all the people in all the countries should have at least such a level of health that they are capable of working productively and of participating actively in the social life of the community in which they live'.

The main objectives of the strategy were to promote healthy lifestyles, to prevent preventable conditions, and to enable rehabilitation of those whose health has been impaired (Ashton 1990). In the language of WHO-speak, these millenarial objectives were clarified into the 'health goals' of health prevention and health promotion, and further focused by the European Regional Office into 38 'targets' accepted by all member states to be achieved by the year 2000.[1] These targets cover a wide range of conditions and activities, specifying particular levels of reduction in mortality rates from heart disease, lung and cervical cancer, infant and maternal mortality, and road-traffic accidents; also included are reductions in lifestyle risk factors such as alcohol and tobacco consumption. However, the major emphasis within the targets is the reorientation of medical care towards health promotion, prevention and primary health care and its bearing on the need for community participation and intersectoral cooperation. Health-care planners distinguish between primary, secondary and tertiary models of medical care provision, in terms of emphasis on specialist hospital, general hospital, and outpatient- or community-based treatment services.

There is a significant difference between the medical concept of 'primary *medical* care', which is individualistic in terms of the patient/ practitioner treatment-specific base, and 'primary *health* care', which is a social concept involving a wide range of health providers in addition to medical personnel and focused on whole communities and their general health status (Ashton 1990; The OECD reports, *Reform of Health Care Systems. A Review of 17 OECD Countries* (1994) and *New Directions in Health Care Policy* (1995).

While it has to be acknowledged that global policy objectives often command only lip-service application in collaborating countries, and that there are wide variations in the enthusiasm, manner, form and comprehensiveness with which they are implemented at the national level, nevertheless it is clear that there has been a radical shift in the direction of health-care planning. Up until the mid-1970s it had been assumed that the best model to be pursued was a specialist/hospital-based medical service and that the task of governments was to focus on increasing access and utilisation.

In trying to account for this change it is tempting to have recourse to arguments of economic determinism (*Health for All Monitoring Report* 1993/4 (1994)). By the early 1970s health-care costs were presenting major problems for all European countries, regardless of the structure of their health services or methods of financing them, and in the context of what was called the 'fiscal crisis', redirecting spending from other public sectors was not an option that was believed to be available. Additionally, it was clear that the technological developments in treatment methods entailed a massive increase in future costs, together with a changed demographic profile that indicated a new heavy demand for medical care from the elderly. While it is correct to say that the economic conditions provided the basic operational constraints, these were mediated by political and ideological factors which led to the selection of particular policy choices and the rejection of others.

Early responses to this concern over predicted increasing expenditure were focused on policies of cost containment which involved, among other things, restrictions on the training and supply of medical manpower, limiting the purchasing power of providers of health care and restricting capital expenditure on high technology. This type of policy was still rooted in the model of equating good health care with the consumption of medical goods and services. The shift away from this way of thinking was influenced partly by the opposition of the medical profession to any attack on their autonomy and their resistance to implementing policy, and also partly by the recognition that cost containment was an inadequate basis for long-term planning in so far as it was purely reactive. In the multinational context of pharmaceutical companies and medical technology, price controls at the national level were inoperable, and so a major component of the increasing expenditure remained uncontrollable.

There is a paradox here, in that traditional accounts of historical changes in health policy have attributed the central role to developments in medical knowledge; that is, that the history of medical care can be seen as therapeutically led. This interpretation is no longer seen as adequate (Wright and Treacher 1982). And yet it appears that it was the new medical knowledge and practices which posed the financial problems even before the recession deepened.

The challenge to the legitimacy of this therapeutic optimism was already under way in the late 1960s from a variety of academic studies on psychiatry, public health and chronic disability which questioned both the efficacy of medically based care and also its monopoly of the knowledge field. Taking a broad historical sweep, Thomas McKeown argued persuasively that improvements in health status could not be attributed to curative medicine and that personal behavioural and environmental changes were the key to past and future advances in health (McKeown 1976). These ideas were taken up and endorsed in Canada in the Lalonde Report *A New Perspective on the Health of Canadians* (1974); probably the first modern community diagnosis, it stressed the primacy of preventive health care at the national level. It set an agenda for a new era of health policy in Canada and had a direct influence on the formulation of the WHO strategy.

The Lalonde Report was a powerful weapon for governments in their confrontation with medical establishments. As Jane Lewis has argued, it implied that 'if expansion of the health care system could not have much impact on mortality and morbidity, then neither could curtailing its growth' (Lewis 1987). Indeed, the very likelihood that a relatively small increase in expenditure on the public-health sector would result in a saving on total health-care costs made it a compelling option for European countries similarly placed with demands from high medical-care spenders.

Health-care systems

Although it is possible to identify this broad consensus of policy shift, we need to be aware of the differences between countries not only in terms of their health-care spending but also of where 'health' is situated in their wider social policy traditions and welfare systems. In Europe we find a diversity of patterns of origins and forms of health-care systems, and earlier forms established before the Second World War have sometimes remained in central European countries as a legacy of an infrastructure despite changes in their geopolitical boundaries and ideologies (Hellberg 1987).

There have been a number of attempts to categorise the European systems of health care, most of them drawing on existing developmental and political classifications (Pyle 1979; Maxwell 1980; Roemer and Roemer 1981), and while they do generate clarity out of diversity, we should be mindful of the dangers in constructing rigid typologies and categories which iron out the overlaps and ambiguities that are so often the very substance of a system that is in a state of change. For instance, Pyle's (1979) five-fold classification of types of health-care systems – (1) free enterprise; (2) welfare state; (3) socialist; (4) transitional; (5) underdeveloped – fails to allow for the changing direction towards internal markets and privatisation within welfare state and socialist types.

Another approach is to construct a matrix of economic and political systems, which has been done by Roemer (1977). This identifies the importance of the degree of centralisation of decision-making in the political apparatus of the state, and how within welfare states we can identify a spectrum from centralised to provincial to localised district structures. This allows us to make comparisons between the Scandinavian countries and Britain, which share the general characterisation of a welfare-state model of health care; it also allows for a more detailed consideration of the differences between the various eastern European socialist systems.

Babson (1972) focuses specifically on the degree of centralised control of health services as a critical factor for comparison within Europe. He makes a four-fold classification: (1) the Scandinavian systems (Denmark, Finland, Norway and Sweden), typified by high levels of local autonomy; (2) the eastern European systems (USSR, Poland, Hungary and East Germany), which have a high level of centralised control and ownership; (3) the central European systems (Austria, Germany and Switzerland), which have provincial and regional decentralisation; and (4) the Latin–Benelux countries (Italy, Belgium, France and The Netherlands), which have great diversity of controls and ownership within different sectors.

There is a considerable difference, however, between a country which has historically built up a pattern of health care based on a conscious policy of decentralisation and democratic decision-making, and countries such as Greece, Portugal and Spain where an historical legacy of inaction or political conflict has led to separatism or neglect of rural health services. Unless we take into account the methods of financing health care, it is easy to assume that decentralisation is a 'good thing' in that it allows for a more sensitive response to local 'need'. Decentralisation of decision-making may be simply the political rhetoric which justifies reductions in central government funding; and placing the responsibility for revenue-raising as well as budgetary management at the local level can lead to a decline in health-care provision, as has been painfully found to be the case recently in Poland, Hungary and the USSR.

Another axis for comparing health-care systems in Europe is their method of financing. All countries have some level of central exchequer funding of health care, but there are variations in where, when, to whom and for what these moneys are actually paid. Broadly, we can distinguish between countries which finance their health services mainly out of collective taxation (the United Kingdom, eastern Europe); those which are based on state-run health-insurance funds (Germany, Sweden, Norway, Denmark, Belgium); those based on a combination of private and state-run insurance (Ireland, France, Switzerland); and those based wholly on private insurance schemes (Greece, Austria, The Netherlands). In all countries there is some state regulatory control of insurance.

There is a wide literature on the complexities and mechanisms of health-care financing. A non-technical rehearsal of the debates is to be found in Binns and Firth (1988) and in Appleby (1993).

It is the method of financing which has been traditionally identified as a critical factor in explaining inequities in access and utilisation of medical care. However, while studies in Switzerland would appear to confirm that insurance-based schemes result in health inequalities among poor and disadvantaged groups (Egger, Minder and Smith 1990), the evidence from the United Kingdom would suggest that the same pattern results even when a national health service operates (Townsend and Whitehead 1988; Benzeval, Judge and Whitehead 1995). More complex models of explanation and redress (Phillips and Joseph 1984) are now being sought to deal with what is perceived as a major failure of the health-care system in The Netherlands to reach urban minority groups (WHO 1986). It is now recognised that the dynamics of individual health practitioner/patient consultations are mediated by a broad context of discriminatory attitudes and practices running through a wide spectrum of social institutions and not just limited to a cash nexus (Klein 1989; Defever 1990).

Much has been written about a new convergence of patterns of health and welfare provision, and whereas there are clearly discernible trends in the main economic determinants, there is wide diversity in the realised practice. Nobody constructing policy, unless they are an ideologial zealot or scenario-constructing academic, can start from Year Zero. We ignore to our peril, or convenience, 'schemes on the ground' (SOGs), which are constructed and realised out of the messy business of trying to reconcile new programmes with past practices, existing buildings and real people who have to turn up for work on Day 1 of 'the new policy' with their everyday routines still intact.

Participant observer studies can be an important counterweight to some of the grandiose WHO reports given by member states on their radical restructuring of health care. A practitioner on an observation visit to the Soviet Union gives this account of the Moscow Accident and Emergency Service: 'Paramedics we accompanied on urban ambulance runs were rationed two to three reusable hypodermic needles and one syringe, necessitating mixing of medications before infusing. This practice is apparently common, judging from wall charts of miscible medications we saw on hospital walls' (Schultz and Rafferty 1990).

This is something that organisational analysts and health managers have begun to give attention to in their newly claimed knowledge field of the 'management of change'. But there is a considerable difference between the potentially controllable interests and concerns of health-care organisations and the worlds of service users. In Britain we are familiar with the length of time it took, sometimes generations, before service users stopped seeing the Poor Law ethic as implicit in their engagement with any public health and welfare service. So we should be mindful when we appraise a change in health policy and philosophy as to what its perceived implications are for service users. Not only is there often an information gap on what the changes are, but they may also be perceived purely in terms of the financial bite of increased insurance contributions and higher additional charges of goods and services. In Poland an attempt to build a direct line of communication with service users is found in a requirement that all local sector managers hold weekly complaints surgeries.

Cultural contexts

The material so far has been concerned with structures and policies, but medicine is also a culturally based ideology and practice, and despite its claims for a 'scientific' knowledge status it involves values and beliefs. How that involvement of culture with medicine can be theoretically explained and empirically validated is best approached by considering health-care systems as cultural systems (Fabrega 1973). Like other cultural systems, it is a symbolic system built out of meanings, values and behavioural norms. Being ill in a foreign country can make us acutely aware that there is no neutral, 'transcendent', scientific medical care. We know that the experience of sickness often leads to a need for security, familiarity and stability for recovery to take place.

In her comparative study of the influence of culture on medical practice in France, Germany and England, Lynn Payer (1989) attributes differences in the style, methods and forms of diagnosis and treatment to differences in national cultural epistemologies. She argues that French medicine is characterised by Cartesian thought and is reflected in the specific cultural concept of the 'terrain'; German medicine, by the influence of Romanticism and the concepts of synthesis and *Gestalt*; while English medicine is seen as rooted in empiricism and parsimony. Her evidence is illustrative and often anecdotal, but her approach provides an interpretative framework for variations in such things as surgical practice, radiography, diagnostic tests and prescribing practices. A particularly interesting link is made with these different intellectual traditions and doctors' responses to treatment evaluation based on preference for experimental (Germany), theoretical (France) or controlled trial (England) research methods. We might hypothesise that the failure to make a definition of 'brain death' in Denmark is similarly rooted in a national philosophical tradition.

Arthur Kleinman (1986) succinctly captures the comprehensiveness of this relationship between culture and medicine:

The health care system articulates illness as a cultural idiom, linking beliefs about disease causation, the experience of symptoms, specific patterns of illness behaviour, decisions concerning treatment alternatives, actual therapeutic practices and evaluations of treatment outcomes. Thus it establishes systematic relationships between these components.

It is therefore not surprising that when health-promotion programmes target particular health-risk lifestyles, they reflect the different cultural values given to 'health' and 'risk'. This can be seen in the comparison between the alcohol campaigns of France, The Netherlands and the

Soviet Union. France launched a health-based campaign focused on alcohol-related disease. The Netherlands focused on the social costs of fractured lives and emphasised social and collective responsibility; while the Soviet Union went for a straight link between alcohol and social disorganisation in terms of crime and lost production (Ivanets and Lukomskaya 1990).

Preventive policies

Health promotion is an important part of the package of the new primary health care; it is linked to a philosophy which stresses 'individual responsibility' for one's own health. Many countries have directly embodied this philosophy in their prologues to their health-policy statements. The Danish statement clearly asserts, 'in the years to come, health policy will aim, *inter alia*, at increasing recognition by individuals of their responsibility for their own health' (WHO 1986). In the 1984 legislation on patients' rights in The Netherlands, the relationship between the rights of patients and the individual's responsibility for their own health was fundamental. There is a long history of health education in Europe, going back to the mobilising role of the American-led League of Red Cross Societies and the Rockefeller Mission to Europe during the First World War and in the early 1920s, when it changed from being part of the package of tuberculosis-control measures to a more general, healthy lifestyle promotion. It was always an area of political sensitivity, and the American dominance of both styles and materials led to cultural misunderstandings, particularly in France (Towers 1987). Similar conflicts are to be found in the present AIDS campaigns, although this time there is less American dominance of both finance and materials.

Health promotion is an interesting area of health policy despite its low status in medical hierarchies of legitimacy. It commands support, albeit sometimes sceptical, from all countries, as it is both a cheap form of health care and has a high profile of visibility. It serves perhaps the primary function of promoting the state's own commitment to health without necessarily entailing any follow-up expenditure. There is the additional attraction that it is an activity which can be jointly funded by other public-service departments and voluntary bodies. However, in Scandinavia there is an increasing scepticism of its efficacy, and in Finland and Sweden there is a move towards more formal methods of evaluating large-scale education campaigns.

In efforts to bypass even the expense of health promotion, some countries have simply introduced statutory controls to limit health-risk behaviours. Most of the eastern European countries as well as Italy, Norway and Finland have imposed total bans on all forms of cigarette promotion. Alcohol consumption can be similarly more cheaply controlled by statutory regulation of the supply or through tough fiscal measures. Drug dependency is also increasingly being tackled by focusing on the supply and penalising providers, a policy which does not incur health-care costs of users, and effectively sheds this area of concern from the health domain. This is a marked change from the mid-1970s, when the treatment and rehabilitation of drug-related offenders was claimed as a health province.

There is a long tradition of coercive public-health powers in Europe rooted in the medical policing of infectious diseases (Towers 1980). Compulsory notification, isolation and treatment were the favoured measures in most countries' response to venereal disease and tuberculosis. At the Health Committee of the League of Nations during the inter-war years the case for compulsory powers was vigorously advanced, and many of the same arguments have been revitalised in formulating new public-health policies for AIDS.

Another element in the new health policies is the expansion of health-screening as a tool of preventive medicine. Again this is a health-care development which, although it can be expensive to mount, commands a high public visibility and appears to offer a service, but if there is no treatment follow-through then it similarly does not commit the state to further expenditure. The type of technology involved and its operating costs, the possibility of clinic and non-medical site location, have the advantage of taking a health-care service away from more expensive hospital- and doctor-based services (Reisler 1978). From a case-finding function of screening, which had its origins in the early mass radiographic screening for tuberculosis, there has been an expansion of the programme towards 'multiphasic' screening. In one comprehensive examination, a range of tests are now administered which not only identify communicable disease but also incipient chronic disease. It is claimed that this is the most cost-effective way of delivering preventive health care, since it saves the expense of separate campaigns, reduces administrative costs, saves both public and physician time and is adaptable for new tests. However, critics have demonstrated that the value of screening procedures vary greatly and that screening is only valuable as part of a larger health programme of follow-up diagnosis and therapy (Reisler 1978).

At a certain point, multiphasic screening has become a parallel development to the battery tests which a number of countries find their doctors using on a routine basis. In Germany there is evidence that patient expectations of a consultation are that it should involve 'testing' and an element of laboratory science in order to legitimise the practitioner's own diagnostic skill (Payer 1989). Such tests inevitably throw up results that justify some medical intervention even though the condition may be pre-symptomatic and have a natural history of self-termination. It is a good example of the uncontrolled escalation of health-care demand that is generated by unrestricted medical practitioners operating even at the primary level of care.

The introduction of HIV antibody testing has led to an additional demand for laboratory services, and a strengthening of the bargaining power of the public-health and laboratory sectors for a greater share of resources.

Health surveillance

The HIV epidemic has also effected an increase in manpower and services for epidemiological data collection and analysis. In France this has provided the foundation for a new set of organisations. These 22 regional health 'observatories' were designed to make use of new information science, employing statisticians and epidemiologists to construct databanks for health surveillance and forecasting, and eventually to operate a system of automatically processed individual health records.

Portugal, having had to make a very late start on constructing a national framework of health care, has decided to make information technology and epidemiology key features in a system-planned health service, and has invested heavily in linked computer systems.

These two examples illustrate an interesting change taking place within a knowledge field. There is a shift from the knowledge domain of traditional medical statistics as an aid to evaluating treatment outcomes to a broader social science domain of long-term forecasting of health demands based on complex matrices. The level and type of statistical techniques and modelling that are being developed and marketed through packages, means that this new 'knowledge object' is increasingly becoming a major influence on health-care planning. It shares a communicative language with the planners and lies outside the professional monopoly on 'medical knowledge'. It has to be stressed, however, that where there is a coincidence of doubtful diagnostic practice, inappropriate statistical reasoning and an international climate in which data production is a necessary membership card for participation and credibility, then it may happen that the new epidemiology will resemble the Ten Year Plans of Stalin (Miles 1979). There is a hierarchy of credibility of epidemiological data at the unofficial level of international health policy, and there is a rigorous scepticism in most countries of their own data claims. However, the WHO statistics are still used as evidential material and often uncritically appended to the more rigorous economic reports of the OECD.

Medical practitioners

Medical monopolies have also been challenged and threatened by the political dynamics of decentralisation policies. More regional or local autonomy has meant in effect more managerial and bureaucratic control over health-care decision-making at levels which they had traditionally seen as their clinical monopoly. Previously they had more direct political influence on central government policy through professional state advisory bodies, or by direct roles within ministerial departments. However, as governments began to make economic policies of cutting public spending and targeting specifically the high costs of seemingly unregulated medical-care demands, so the vulnerability of their traditional power base in tertiary and secondary health-care systems became apparent. The new policy shift towards a lower-cost primary system to be managed and implemented locally became enthusiastically taken up and defended by these local authorities who were eager to manage their own restricted budgets. The primacy placed on efficiency and the critical role of local health managers in implementing cost-effective services has threatened the power and authority of the medical profession. Doctors have been further weakened by the political culture within which local health policy is made. They have reacted to this by defending their traditional institutional base (the hospital) through populist appeals and not infrequently by direct political action (Johnson, Larkin and Saks 1995).

The situation of the doctors in Spain is interesting in this light (Rodriguez 1995). The political role of the medical profession had a high profile in the opposition to the first socialist government and culminated in strike action in 1987. Under Franco the doctors had a monopoly of health care, but at the political price of being state-employed salaried officials. With the socialist government they found themselves lacking their political power and undercut by new emphasis on regional and local decision-making, stressing primary care. While the transition to the new system required their cooperation, they were still state employees and the old Fascist controls still existed, their traditional if illusory claim of freedom of action was called into question and they resorted to populist appeals and strikes.

Sweden is an instance where doctors have retained their political power and inhibited any real change in the reallocation of health-care resources. Here their base has been through tight control of the family practitioner and specialist services (Calltorp 1990; Anell 1995). It would appear that where the family practitioner is used as the basic unit in primary-care organisation, then doctors are able to tie their specialist referrals into a network of mutual support for a private market which keeps the core hospital-based services well-funded.

Radical change

The effects of the fundamental economic restructuring and political changes in the Soviet Union and eastern Europe have inevitably had major implications for the organisation of health care. The overall impression that can be gained from the new reporting and availability of information is that the effects of economic recession have borne particularly heavily on the health-care services. At the same time there was evidence of the existence of a separate system of medical care available only to privileged or élite groups. There appears to be a breakdown in the provision and distribution of supplies and the development of a black market, which is tacitly endorsed by the authorities.

In the former Soviet Union the evidence suggests that the basic infrastructure of health care has been in chronic danger of collapse under the pressure of non-funding and shortages of basic supplies, while new market-oriented policies have been subject to lengthy debate and haphazard implementation. It has been aptly characterised as a 'high-wire balancing act of encouraging private delivery with public financing in order to maintain the reality of a right to health' (Mckeehan 1995). The issue appears to be that as the Soviet Union moved towards autonomy for the republics, so the financial and administrative responsibility for health care was decentralised. The problem was that without any start-up funding and the sudden withdrawal of central financing support, the first response to the financial crisis was to move away from the Leninist tradition of centrally planned and fiscally financed health care available to all, and to move towards an insurance-based service with supplementary charges and fees. The effect of this rapid change-over was to reinforce the *ad hoc* private markets for specialist services and to create separate occupationally specific insurance and health-care schemes; the result was a picture of gross inefficiencies and inequities (WHO 1994).

The shift away from centrally planned and funded health care towards local autonomy is also to be found in Poland and Hungary. Poland has had a longer period in which the restructuring of its political and economic system has been under way and, like Czechoslovakia, inherited from the prewar period an established system of institutionally based medical manpower which has continued to be focused on the large and capital cities, with the result that geographical inequities are pronounced. In Czechoslovakia, the government introduced graduated insurance contributions and also allowed the development of a private market in insurance. Recognising the problems associated with stimulating a private health sector, strict controls on maximum insurance payments and fixed service pricing on treatment services were introduced (Heitlinger 1995).

Yugoslavia had historically developed a strong political infrastructure of decentralised planning; regional and local autonomy was an integral part of the Tito ideology attempting to reconcile a mosaic of nationalisms. This has now clearly failed. During the past few years armed conflict in the former Yugoslavia killed more than 150 000 people, wounded hundreds of thousands and displaced close to 4 million (WHO 1994). The effects of the war and conflict have also caused the deterioration of the social enviroment with a potentially long-lasting negative impact on people's health and well-being. The newly independent republics of Bosnia, Herzogovinia, Croatia and the Federal Republic of Yugoslavia

(Serbia and Montenegro) present a picture of basic health-care systems still in place but with very great variations in quality and chronic shortages of supplies (Istenic 1995).

In eastern Germany, unification meant the virtual abandonment of its socialist model of health care. However, organisational change was only gradually implemented following a wide-ranging package of healthcare reforms covering the whole of Germany in 1993. In an attempt to forestall professional carpetbagging there was an initial prohibition on any West German doctor practising in the East. The Federal Republic had made its intentions clear from the begining that it would not take up the financial responsibilities for a health-care system based on state-financed health insurance and state-employed health practitioners. A rather deprecating account of the old GDR heath-care system up to the time of the reunification suggests it brought as its dowry 'badly paid and demoralised health care professionals, inefficient and poorly equipped hospitals; and a population whose health status was markedly worse than the poorest countries of Western Europe' (Rowland 1991). The future of the big multipurpose health centres, the 'Polikliniken', which were the jewel in the crown of the GDR system, had initially looked parlous but now appears to be more positive as they become regarded as highly innovative, as well as cost-saving, models of health delivery in the new Germany (Moran 1994).

Both systems had problems in trying to contain and reduce healthcare costs, although there was a fundamental difference in their healthcare models. The East German model had a large medical manpower base which was state-salaried. In West Germany, however, the power of the medical establishment has led to a large manpower base that was in a secure position in so far as it was not state-salaried; costs were covered by both the private and state insurance funds, which led to unrestricted pricing and escalating demand.

Southern Europe

A different set of problems faces countries like Portugal and Greece, which experienced their political revolutions in the 1970s and 1980s and have commenced major economic and industrial development plans. These states have only recently begun to create state-funded health and welfare services, and are concerned to integrate themselves into the European market with all its implications for harmonised social policy. In these countries medical manpower has been relatively uncontrolled, and capital city-based hospitals have retained specialist monopolies which led to gross imbalances in rural and regional provision.

The state's priority has been to build a framework of environmental and public health and to target the primary problems of illness and disease. Inevitably, this means that there are large gaps in service provision, particularly in the fields of mental health and chronic illness. Perhaps the opportunities are greatest for these countries in that they have not as yet revealed the high degree of modern chronic illness and have the chance to create health-care systems which are not hospital-intensive. However, forecasters look to the reductions in infant mortality and increasing life expectancy and anticipate that the future epidemiological profile will converge to the European norm.

The epidemiological picture

We have looked at the politics and organisation of health care, and now it is appropriate to consider the reported patterns of illness and disease in Europe. Since the 1990s the political transformations have rendered what constitutes the European region more heterogenous with very significant variations in the pattern of health indicators. It is therefore very difficult to make assessments of the health status and trends of the European region as a whole. In order to deal with this problem, comparative epidemiological data is usually constructed on the basis of two and sometimes three 'European groupings': (i) The European Union and Nordic Countries; (ii) Countries of Central and Eastern Europe (CCEE); and (iii) the 15 newly independent states (NIS) of the former Soviet Union.

Life expectancy at birth is commonly used as a summary indicator of the mortality patterns in each of the European populations and looking at this data a clear general picture of a widening East/West gap in health is apparent (Figure 10.1). The average life expectancy is about six-and-a-half years lower in central and eastern Europe than in western Europe. In seeking to explain this gap we need to know which diseases

*Figure 10.1   **Trends in life expectancy at birth***

Source: WHO (1994) *Health in Europe*

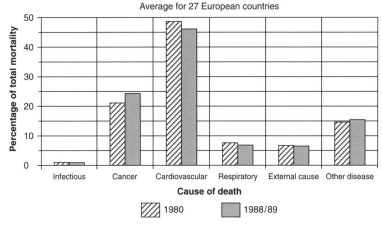

Figure 10.2 **Changes in causes of mortality**

Source: WHO (1994) *Health in Europe*

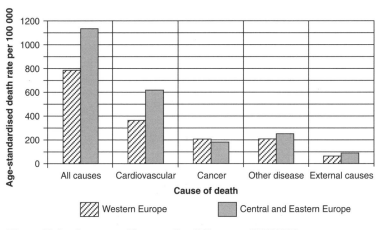

Figure 10.3 **Cause-specific mortality differences 1988/1989**

Source: WHO (1994) *Health in Europe*

contribute most in terms of surplus mortality. There is only space here to look at a few of the more prominent features of the picture, which Wilkinson explores in greater analytical and theoretical depth (Wilkinson 1996). Perhaps the most striking factor is that despite the prevailing media panics and concerns about communicable diseases and deaths from external causes, the predominant pattern of mortality and morbidity is from circulatory diseases and malignant neoplasms (cancers); (see Figures 10.2 and 10.3) in other words, the diseases of developed industrial societies. Cardiovascular diseases (CVD) are the leading cause of death in Europe, they are the cause of a half of all deaths and one-third

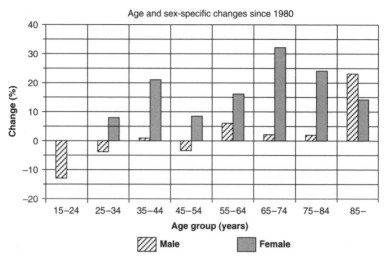

*Figure 10.4   **Lung cancer mortality in Europe***

Source: WHO (1994) *Health in Europe*

of all permanent disabilities; and it is the CVD which account for a very large, and rising, proportion of health-care costs across Europe. Premature mortality from CVD is twice as high in central and eastern European countries as in western Europe.

Cancer comes second in the main cause of mortality, accounting for 20 per cent of all deaths in Europe, and it is showing a slow but steady increasing trend. Lung cancer is the main component of this and although other sites of cancer have a gradually reducing mortality, the increase in lung cancer mortality for both men and women more than wipes out any favourable trends (Figure 10.4). Breast cancer is the leading cause of cancer deaths among women and is increasing in most European countries; the highest mortality rates are to be found in western Europe. Cervical cancer shows a more positive picture of a reducing trend, albeit far more pronounced in western Europe and particularly those countries with the highest GDP; and it is still the case that mortality rates from cervical cancer in the central and eastern European countries is three times that of the average of those countries in the European Union. Although this is the overall pattern, there are considerable variations within each country. We find that in Poland, Norway, Greece and Italy lung cancer rates are rising, and in Spain, cervical cancer is rising; that in eastern Europe there is an increase in cerebrovascular disease (strokes), while this may be also accompanied by a decrease in ischaemic heart disease. Lifestyle and diet are identified as contributory factors in these diseases, and it is clear that countries with high rates of tobacco consumption appear to have higher lung cancer rates. Denmark is particularly interesting in this context since it appears that the unusually low and falling position of Denmark in the life-expectancy league tables can be attributed to high excess lung cancer mortality among women. But it is advisable to be cautious about such causal explanations, and careful of such gross patterns, particularly when there are likely to be additional factors such as industrial pollution and occupation-related bronchial diseases. The development of anti-smoking campaigns in order to reduce both the mortality rates and the costs of chronic respiratory disorders is a feature of most European societies.

There is evidence that there is a social-class gradient in all these rates. Circulatory diseases also need to be seen in a context of an ageing population; so while we find that in Greece the rates are lower, this is unlikely to be due to the same factors that we find in Norway. Austria is a good example of an ageing population, predominantly rural but with urban clusters. Here the circulatory disease rates are particularly high, and it is perhaps useful to compare Austria with Finland where, hitherto, high rates have been brought down apparently as a result of health-promotion campaigns.

Infant mortality rates are used as a crude indicator of the level of development of a country, and we find that all European societies show reductions in the last ten years (see Table 10.1). The IMR clearly demonstrates the East/West health gap in Europe as can be seen in the pattern of variations. The lowest levels of between 6–7 per 1000 live births in the Nordic countries, the highest in Albania (33.8) Romania (23.3) and former Yugoslavia (18.4) and Bulgaria (15.9). Since two-thirds of this mortality is neonatal (i.e. occurs during the first 28 days after birth), explanations have tended to be focused on the availability of hospital-based maternity services. However, it is likely to be a more complex combination of factors, as countries with some of the highest rates of home births are accompanied by the lowest IMR rates, such as The Netherlands and Denmark.

Maternal mortality rates also reflect East/West differences but with less extremes. The WHO target for the European region was set at less than 15 per 100 000 live births and while the EU and Nordic countries have rates of between 3 to 8, many eastern and central European countries have rates of between 15 to 19.

The steady and sustained improvement in maternal mortality across Europe during the last 20 years cannot be attributed solely to improvements in obstetrics and hospital-based birth management; it is likely to be also linked to improvements in general standards of living, particularly nutritional levels, longer birth intervals and the availability of contraception. In some of the eastern European countries the use of abortion as a method of contraception results in very high figures for abortion-related maternal mortality. The most notable example is Romania, which in 1988 had a maternal mortality rate of 156, a figure which seems to have been due in large part to illegal abortions, a consequence of the legislation against abortion. The recent repeal of this legislation has seen maternal

Table 10.1   **Basic socioeconomic indicators and infant mortality for selected European countries**

Country	GDP PPP$_a$ per head (1991)	Total health expenditure % of GDP (1991)	Infant mortality per 1000 live births (1992)
Albania	3500	4	33.8
Austria	17 690	8.5	7.5
Belgium	17 510	8.1	8.5
Bosnia Herzegovina			18.4
Bulgaria	4813	5.4	15.9
Croatia			11.6
Czech Republic			9.9
Denmark	17 880	7	6.5
Finland	16 130	8.9	5.2
France	18 430	9.1	7.3
Germany	19 770	9.1	7.0
Greece	7680	4.8	9.0
Hungary	6080	6	14.1
Ireland	11 430	8	7.6
Italy	17 040	8.3	8.6
Luxembourg	20 800	6.6	7.2
Netherlands	16 820	8.7	7.1
Norway	17 170	8.4	7.0
Poland	4500	5.1	14.4
Portugal	9450	6.2	9.3
Romania	3500	3.9	23.3
Slovakia			11.3
Slovenia			8.9
Spain	12 670	6.5	7.6
Sweden	17 490	8.8	5.8
Switzerland	21 780	8	6.4
United Kingdom	16 340	6.6	6.6

a PPP = Purchasing Power Parity

Source: WHO (1994) *Health in Europe*

mortality fall by two-thirds. Also, it is the case that some countries like France and Greece invest highly in infant and maternal care, especially where there is a history of a declining population; this in turn can influence the whole skew of medical services towards issues of fertility as opposed to regulating and controlling the availability of reproductive technologies.

There is a general tendency towards the expansion of non-hospital-based maternity-care units. In some countries this is a specific feature of the development of private market 'nursing homes', whereas in others it is an extension of the clinic principle. A parallel feature is the widely different pattern of midwifery. In some countries there has been a dramatic decline in the number of midwives. Where this is not accompanied by a decline in the overall number of nurses it seems likely to be part of the trend towards hospital-based births; in other countries, it may be associated with the surplus of doctors and the use of doctors for home births; in yet others the traditional demarcation of district nurse and specialist midwife may not have developed; and some countries (such as Portugal) are specifically training a paramedical nurse who is also qualified to deliver.

How can we account for changes in the policy and control of childbirth? In part it may be as a result of pressure from the women's movement, which is concerned about the medicalisation of childbirth (as has been the case in Germany and the United Kingdom); or it may be due to the overall rationalisation and concentration of health services in the one hospital/clinic; or again it may be due to the specialisms within medicine wishing to retain control of this clearly ongoing demand for health care (Teijlingen and van der Hulst 1995). Another factor could be to do with the changing expectations about perinatal mortality: this is clearly true where developed systems have invested in special baby units or even high-technology paediatric care.

Immunisation programmes show a fairly consistent pattern; where they are tied to infant care support, or the education system, some countries operate a policy of compulsory vaccination. Even the less economically strong countries have high rates of vaccination, possibly because of the WHO support for these basic health measures and the subsidised cost of vaccines. It is interesting therefore that the lowest rates of vaccination are in those countries like The Netherlands and the United Kingdom where parents may be exercising discretionary judgements about 'risk' in view of possible side-effects. Some countries are persisting with BCG vaccination against tuberculosis. This is a good example of the heritage of past practice, for the efficacy of this method of tuberculosis control was always inconclusive, but very early on some countries adopted this measure and tied it to the school health service and it now appears to be a residual part of the vaccination battery. There has been growing concern about increases in tuberculosis morbidity and possible new more virulent strains which are drug resistant. Whereas the rates of notification had been consistently declining in the 1980s, in the last decade this trend has been reversed in a number of western European countries, particularly Austria, Denmark, Switzerland, Ireland, Italy and The Netherlands. In the context of renewed concern about infectious diseases, environmental health policies may be the preferred route to provide a more powerful impact on tuberculosis, which is classically a disease occuring during periods of economic transition and depressed immunological status (Bhatti, Law and Morris 1995).

AIDS and HIV infection are the most topical disease that concerns both inter-country and domestic health policy. Because of the designation of AIDS as a global epidemic, the WHO has established special

Figure 10.5a   **Distribution of AIDS cases in Europe**

Source: WHO (1994) *Health in Europe*

Figure 10.5b   **Annual new cases of AIDS in Europe**

Source: WHO (1994) *Health in Europe*

AIDS monitoring centres which produce detailed and voluminous epidemiological updates. The annual incidence of AIDS cases is now showing signs of slowing down, but there has been a steady increase in the proportion of cases transmitted by injecting drug use and heterosexual contact (see Figures 10.5a and b). It is not possible in this overview to deal with the complexities of this disease and the politics of its epidemiological mapping which have been recently well documented (Blaxter 1991; Berridge 1996).

One new disease that is responsible for a high consumption of healthcare resources is Alzheimer's disease. There is some question about the degree of overlap with other dementing conditions, and there are still considerable problems about its diagnostic reliability, except *post mortem*. We should therefore be reserved about the existing epidemiological data, which estimates a prevalence of between 2.5 and 5.6 per cent of the population over 65. Where health-care resources are specifically linked to diagnostically related groups and carry a price ceiling for insurance, then there may be an incentive in diagnosing a disease-specific category, rather than the open-ended general dementias. However, it does seem to be the case that many European societies are faced with an increase in the amount of resources they will need to find to cover this condition. Since it is a chronic degenerative condition and in the advanced stages needs a high level of care, the emphasis in most countries is to develop community-support services for home nursing for as long as possible. However, there is increasing concern that the burden of care is extreme, and the secondary carers' health-care costs are gradually becoming recognised. There is a convergence of research towards the development of drugs that will either delay its progress or the possible connection between its genetic base and other environmental factors.

Mental illness, despite its low profile in terms of health-care resource allocation, is now widely regarded in most countries as particularly problematic. Its rising incidence in central and eastern Europe needs to be seen in the context of the psychosocial impact of a period of unusually rapid and extensive political and economic change (Wilkinson 1996). Historically, mental health accounted for a large share of most countries' stocks of hospital beds. However, since the mid-1980s there has been a substantial decline in the number of beds for psychiatric care; in Denmark and Finland they have declined by a half, by a third in Sweden and by one-fifth in Britain. Across Europe the pattern of care varies enormously from minimal treatment or incarceration in asylums (Greece) to an almost total outpatient community psychiatric service (Italy) (Ramon 1996). In many respects countries which had not developed the mental hospital pattern of institutional care are better placed than those who are having to shift towards decarceration policies. Again the costs of 'community care' can be passed on to families and a significant saving is made through what is now characterised as 'informal care'. Ireland is another country which is making a priority of developing community psychiatric services. At the other extreme, Germany and France have well-developed psychotherapeutic services within the insurance-based health services.

Where there is a private market for psychiatric services then there is likely to be an increased status for the medical specialism, a climate of research, and work opportunities that are treatment-based. This contrasts with eastern Europe where for a long time psychiatry was associated with state policies of social control and the morale and status of psychiatrists was low, even to the extent where they were somewhat regarded as international pariahs. There is an increasing pressure on psychiatrists to reconcile treatment concerns with the legal rights of patients in western Europe, and the concomitant development of forensic psychiatry has become a new focus for those concerned with civil liberties, particularly in the context of the European Court of Human Rights.

This is a field which touches on changes within jurisprudential thinking that have occurred because of harmonisation; it is a development that has implications for an increasing range of medically controlled technologies which had hitherto not been subject to legal scrutiny. It is an example of both the medicalisation of law and the legalisation of medicine (Wynne 1989). Once we see medical issues in a broader frame than their familiar sectoral neighbours, we are not shocked to find that the issue of the regulation of cadaveric organs for transplant surgery is a question of 'trade' of commodity items, and that the present arrangements between countries are dangerously vulnerable to abuse (Defever 1990).

Environmental health

It would be absurd to talk about health and medicine without considering the relationship of health care to environmental health. We have seen that in some countries this is at the basic level of introducing access to main sewage and water supplies; in others it is at the level of monitoring and regulating atmospheric pollution. Throughout Europe there is a recognition that all aspects of economic and industrial development should also be considered in terms of their impact on the health of the population. But this may well be more honoured in proclamation than in action; and although Chernobyl was a devastating example of the international health dangers caused by one country's nuclear capability, there has been a reluctance to link issues such as the transportation of hazardous materials, the regulation of chemical plants, the development of genetic engineering to main-stream health policy until after a catastrophe has occurred (WHO 1996). This is well indicated in the secondary position in which health claims and concerns are treated in the context of food and agricultural policy, where national self-interest of the agro-business communities is pursued with little consideration of the impact that it might have on health status and well-being.

Conclusions

What conclusions can be drawn from this overview? In many ways it is a paradoxical time of contrary trends in medicine and health care in Europe. On the one hand, there is the move away from secondary health care and the emphasis on primary health care, and the attempt to move away from doctor-based medicine to see the overlap with other sectors of welfare work, to move away from single ministry planning and control. On the other hand, the developments within medicine itself indicate an increasing move towards higher and more expensive technology and more expensive treatments. The state and the insurance companies are locked into a conflict with the medical professionals, whom they see as equating health care with medical care, who defend their clinical judgement regardless of the costs involved; and yet as new therapies and interventions become available, then the impetus within the medical profession is to adopt them as part of their mandate to practise according to the possibilities within their grasp, and with that goes the patient's expectation that the doctor–patient relationship is based on the clinical contract which stresses the primacy of the 'health need', not the adjudication of the health-care budget. Governments respond to their constituents in terms of rationing public spending in order to secure the economic strength of the country. They can reconcile this policy with the demands for greater decentralisation of government and diversity of service, by pushing the responsibility for health finance and management down to the local or regional level, or outwards to private insurance companies, while still retaining a central overview by fixing budget limits and subventions and price regulation. In this context doctors become potentially vulnerable and their control over health policy is weakened. In response they make populist appeals under the traditional banner of representing the 'health' interests of the people. However, it is clear that what is happening is that 'health' and 'medicine' are no longer the monopoly of doctors. The fight is about resources and also about legitimacy and the right to identify and control the process of demand.

Note

1 The 38 targets of the European Region of the World Health Association are as follows:

1 By the year 2000, the actual differences in health status between countries and between groups within countries should be reduced by at least 25 per cent, by improving the level of health disadvantaged nations and groups.

2 By the year 2000, people should have the basic opportunity to develop and use their health potential to live socially and economically fulfilling lives.

3 By the year 2000, disabled persons should have the physical, social and economic opportunities that allow at least for a socially and economically fulfilling and mentally creative life.

4 By the year 2000, the average number of years that people live free from major disease and disability should be increased by at least 10 per cent.

5 By the year 2000, there should be no indigenous measles, poliomyelitis, neonatal tetanus, congenital rubella, diphtheria, congenital syphilis or indigenous malaria in the Region.

6 By the year 2000, lifes expectancy at birth in the Region should be at least 75 years.

7 By the year 2000, infant mortality in the Region should be less than 20 per 1000 live births.

8 By the year 2000, maternal mortality in the Region should be less than 15 per 100 000 live births.

9 By the year 2000, mortality in the Region from disease of the circulatory system in people under 65 should be reduced by at least 15 per cent.

10 By the year 2000, mortality in the Region from cancer in people under 65 should be reduced by at least 15 per cent.

11 By the year 2000, deaths from accidents in the Region should be reduced by at least 15 per cent through an intensified effort to reduce traffic, home and occupational accidents.

12 By the year 2000, the current rising trends in suicides and attempted suicides in the Region should be reversed.

13 By 1990, national policies in all Member States should ensure that legislative, administrative and economic mechanisms provide broad intersectoral support and resources for the promotion of healthy lifestyles and ensure effective participation of the people at all levels of such policy-making.

14 By 1990, all Member States should have specific programmes which enhance the major roles of the family and other social groups in developing and supporting healthy lifestyles.

15 By 1990, educational programmes in all Member States should enhance the knowledge, motivation and skills of people to acquire and maintain health.

16 By 1995, in all Member States, there should be significant increases in positive health behaviour, such as balanced nutrition, nonsmoking, appropriate physical activity and good stress management.

17 By 1995, in all Member States, there should be significant decreases in health-damaging behaviour, such as overuse of alcohol and pharmaceutical products; use of illicit drugs and dangerous chemical substances; and dangerous driving and violent social behaviour.

18 By 1990, Member States should have multisectoral policies that effectively protect the environment from health hazards, ensure community awareness and involvement, and support international efforts to curb such hazards affecting more than one country.

19 By 1990, all Member States should have adequate machinery for the monitoring, assessment and control of environmental hazards which pose a threat to human health, including potentially toxic chemicals, radiation, harmful consumer goods and biological agents.

20 By 1990, all people of the Region should have adequate supplies of safe drinking-water, and by the year 1995 pollution of rivers, lakes and seas should no longer pose a threat to human health.

21 By 1995, all people of the Region should be effectively protected against recognized health risks from air pollution.

22 By 1990, all Member States should have significantly reduced health risks from food contamination and implemented measures to protect consumers from harmful additives.

23 By 1995, all Member States should have eliminated major known health risks associated with the disposal of hazardous wastes.

24 By the year 2000, all people of the Region should have a better opportunity of living in houses and settlements which provide a healthy and safe environment.

25 By 1995, people of the Region should be effectively protected against work-related health risks.

26 By 1990, all Member States, through effective community representation, should have developed health care systems that are based on primary health care and supported by secondary and tertiary care as outlined at the Alma-Ata Conference.

27 By 1990, in all Member States, the infrastructures of the delivery systems should be organized so that resources are distributed according to need, and that services ensure physical and economic accessibility and cultural acceptability to the population.

28 By 1990, the primary health care system of all Member States should provide a wide range of health-promotive, curative, rehabilitative and supportive services to meet the basic health needs of the population and give special attention to high-risk, vulnerable and underserved individuals and groups.

29 By 1990, in all Member States, primary health care systems should be based on cooperation and teamwork between health care personnel, individuals, families and community groups.

30 By 1990, all Member States should have mechanisms by which the services provided by all sectors relating to health are coordinated at the community level in a primary health care system.

31 By 1990, all Member States should have built effective mechanisms for ensuring quality of patient care within their health care systems.

32 Before 1990, all Member States should have formulated research strategies to stimulate investigations which improve the application and expansion of knowledge needed to support their health for all developments.

33 Before 1990, all Member States should ensure that their health policies and strategies are in line with health for all principles and that their legislation and regulations make their implementation effective in all sectors of society.

34 Before 1990, Member States should have managerial processes for health development geared to the attainment of health for all, actively involving communities and all sectors relevant to health and, accordingly, ensuring preferential allocation of resources to health development priorities.

35 Before 1990, Member States should have health information systems capable of supporting their national strategies for health for all.

36 Before 1990, in all Member States, the planning, training and use of health personnel should be in accordance with health for all policies, with emphasis on the primary health care approach.

37 Before 1990, in all Member States, education should provide personnel in sectors related to health with adequate information on the country's health for all policies and programmes and their practical application to their own sectors.

38 Before 1990, all Member States should have established a formal mechanism for the systematic assessment of the appropriate use of health technologies and of their effectiveness, efficiency, safety and acceptability, as well as reflecting national health policies and economic restraints.

(*Evaluation of the Strategy for Health for All by the Year 2000*, WHO Copenhagen 1986)

References

Anell, Anders (1995) 'Implementing planned markets in health services: the Swedish case', in R. Saltman and C. von Otter *Implementing Planned Markets in Health Care*, Buckingham: Open University: 209–27.

Appleby, J. (1993) *Financing Health Care in the 1990s*, Buckingham: Open University.

Ashton, J. (1990) 'Public health and primary care: towards a common agenda', *Public Health*, 104: 387–98.

Babson, J. H. (1972) *Health Care Delivery Systems: a Multinational Survey*, London: Pitman.

Benzeval, M., Judge, K. and Whitehead, M. (1995) *Tackling Inequalities in Health*, London: King's Fund.

Berridge, V. (1996) *Aids in the UK. The Making of a Policy 1981–94*. Oxford: Oxford University Press.

Bhatti, N., Law, K. and Morris, J. K. *et al.* (1995) 'Increasing incidence of TB in England and Wales: a study of likely causes', *British Medical Journal*, 310: 967–70.

Binns, T. B. and Firth, M. (1988) *Health Care Provision under Financial Constraint*, London: Royal Society of Medicine.

Blaxter, M. (1991) *AIDS: Worldwide Policies and Problems*, London:

Calltorp, J. (1990) 'Physician manpower politics in Sweden', *Health Policy*, 15: 105–18.

Defever, M. (1990) 'The politics of organ transplantation in Europe: issues and problems', *Health Policy*, 16: 95–103.

Egger, M., Minder, C. and Smith, D. (1990) 'Health inequalities and migrant workers in Switzerland', *Lancet*, 29 Sept.: 816.

Fabrega, H. (1973) *Health and Social Behaviour*, Cambridge, Ma: MIT Press.

Heitlinger, A. (1995) 'Post-communist reform and the health professions: medicine and nursing in the Czech republic', in T. Johnson, G. Larkin and M. Saks (eds) *Health Professions and the State in Europe*, London: Routledge, pp. 213–18.

Hellberg, H. (1987) 'Health for all and primary health care in Europe', *Public Health*, 101: 151–7.

Istenic, M. C. (1995) 'Slovenia', in N. Johnson (ed.) (1995) *Private Markets in Health and Welfare*, Oxford: Berg.

Ivanets, N. and Lukomskaya, M. (1990) 'The USSR's new alcohol policy', *World Health Forum*, 11: 246–51.

Johnson, T., Larkin, G. and Saks, M. (eds) (1995) *Health Professions and the State in Europe*, London: Routledge.

Klein, R. (1989) *Infertility*, London: Pandora.

Kleinman, A. (1986) 'Concepts and a model for the comparison of medical systems as cultural systems', in C. Currer and M. Stacey (eds) *Concepts of Health, Illness and Disease*, Oxford: Berg.

Lalonde, M. (1974) *A New Perspective on the Health of Canadians: a Working Document*, Ottawa: Ministry of National Health and Welfare.

Lewis, J. (1987) 'What has become of public health? Past patterns and future prospects in England, Ontario and Quebec', *Public Health*, 101: 357–68.

Mckeehan, I. (1995) 'Planning of national primary health care and prevention programmes. The First Health Insurance Law of Russia 1991–1993', in E.

Gallagher and K. Subedi (eds) *Global Perspectives on Health Care*, New Jersey: Prentice Hall.

McKeown, T. (1976) *The Modern Rise of Population*, London: Arnold.

Maxwell, R. (1980) *International Comparisons of Health Needs and Services*, London: King's Fund.

Miles, I. (1979) 'The development of forecasting towards a history of the future', in T. Whiston (ed.) *The Uses and Abuses of Forecasting*, London: Macmillan, pp. 5–42.

Moran, M. (1994) 'Health care policy', in J. Clasen and R. Freeman (eds) *Social Policy in Germany*, New York: Harvester Wheatsheaf, pp. 83–102.

OECD (1985) *Measuring Health Care, 1960–83*, Paris.

OECD (1987) *Financing and Delivering Health Care*, Paris.

OECD (1994) *The Reform of Health Care Systems: A Review of 7 OECD Countries*, Health Policy Series No. 5. Paris: OECD.

OECD (1995) *New Directions in Health Care Policy*, Health Policy Series No. 7, Paris: OECD.

Payer, I. (1989) *Medicine and Culture*, London: Gollancz.

Phillips, D. and Joseph, A. (1984) *Accessibility and Utilization*, New York: Harper & Row.

Pyle, G. F. (1979) *Applied Medical Geography*, New York: Wiley.

Ramon, S. (1996) *Mental Health in Europe: Ends, Beginings and Rediscoveries*, London: Macmillan.

Reisler, S. J. (1978) 'The emergence of the concept of screening for disease', *Millbank Memorial Quarterly*, 56(4): 403–25.

Rodriguez, J. (1995) 'The politics of the Spanish medical profession: democratization and the construction of the national health system', in T. Johnson, G. Larkin and M. Saks (eds) *Health Professions and the State in Europe*, London: Routledge, pp. 141–62.

Roemer, M. (1977) *Systems of Health Care*, New York: Springer.

Roemer, M. and Roemer, R. (1981) *Health Care Systems and Comparative Manpower Politics*, New York: Marcel Dekker.

Rowland, D. (1991) 'Health status in East European countries', *Health Affairs*, 10(3): 203–15.

Schultz, D. and Rafferty, M. (1990) 'Soviet health care and Perestroika', *American Journal of Public Health*, 80(2): 193–6.

Teijlingen, E. and van der Hulst L. (1995) 'Midwifery in The Netherlands: more than a semi-profession', in T. Johnson, G. Larkin and M. Saks (eds) *Health Professions and the State in Europe*, London: Routledge, pp. 178–87.

Towers, B. A. (1980) 'Health education policy 1916–1926: venereal disease and the prophylaxis dilemma', *Medical History*, 24: 70–87.

Towers, B. A. (1987) 'The politics of tuberculosis in Western Europe 1914–40', Unpublished MS, London University.

Townsend, P. and Whitehead, M. (1988) *Inequalities in Health*, London: Penguin.

WHO (1994) *Health in Europe. The Health for All Monitoring Report*, Copenhagen: WHO.

WHO (1996a) *The Implementation of the Global Strategy for Health for All*, 2nd Evaluation, 8th report, Vol. 5, (European Region), Copenhagen: WHO.

WHO (1996b) 'The health consequences of Chernobyl', *WHO Statistical Reports*, Vol. 49, No. 1, Copenhagen: WHO.

Wilkinson, R. (1996) 'How can secular improvements in life expectancy be explained?', in D. Blane, E. Brunner and R. Wilkinson (eds) *Health and Social Organisation*, London: Routledge.

Wright, P. and Treacher, A. (1982) *The Problem of Medical Knowledge*, Edinburgh: Edinburgh University Press.

Wynne, B. (1989) 'Establishing the rules of laws: constructing expert authority', in R. Smith and B. Wynne (eds) *Expert Evidence*, London: Routledge.

CHAPTER 11

God and Caesar: religion in a rapidly changing Europe

GRACE DAVIE

This chapter falls into three sections. The first examines in some detail the broad outlines of religious life in western Europe. In other words, it concentrates on what Europe has in common, not least its shared religious heritage. The second section adopts a rather different focus. It looks at the way in which such common patterns as can be established have been differently refracted across a variety of European countries. A whole range of factors comes into play in this section, the differing combinations of which account for the religious diversities of western Europe rather than its unity. One theme of this chapter – balancing unity against diversity (across time as well as space) – begins to emerge as the two sections are drawn together. The third section not only introduces a second theme; it also adopts a more explicitly theoretical framework. More particularly, it aims to set the religious data presented in the first two sections within a theoretical discussion of modernity. In so doing it shifts the principal focus away from the secularisation debate and introduces theoretical approaches developed initially among French sociologists of religion.

It is necessary to make one further (rather extended) point at the outset. This chapter, like the others in this book, will deal with western Europe rather than a wider definition of the continent. It is, however, important to remember that the relatively recent division between east and west (communist and non-communist) Europe pales into insignificance compared with the split between Roman Catholicism and Orthodoxy that divided the continent a millennium ago. Indeed the terms 'east' and 'central' Europe have significance in this respect, for east Europe (Romania, Bulgaria and most of European Russia) belongs to the Orthodox tradition, whereas the central European countries (Poland, the Czech Republic, Slovakia, Hungary and what was East Germany) developed within western Catholicism. The position of the Baltic states is equally revealing. Roman Catholic Lithuania and Poland are closely linked historically; in contrast, Latvia and Estonia belong essentially to northern (Lutheran) Europe.

We would do well to remember these distinctions in our discussions about the future of Europe. The countries which shared the experience of postwar communist domination represent very different religious traditions (Walters 1988). These traditions are likely to have contemporary significance. Countries that belonged – and continue to belong – to western rather than Orthodox Christianity may well find it easier to realise their political and economic aspirations. Despite their real economic difficulties, their aim is to re-establish Western traditions; they are not learning something totally new.[1]

The vicissitudes in the Balkans in the early 1990s exemplify – albeit rather differently – the same point. The postwar entity known as Yugoslavia combined within one country not only contrasting Christian traditions but also a sizeable Muslim presence. For a relatively short space of time (two generations, perhaps) the country held together under the personal authority of President Tito. As that authority – and the creed that underpinned it – collapsed, it is hardly surprising that Yugoslavia's pseudo-unity began to fall apart. Ethnic nationalisms, bolstered by religious differences, interacted with a multiplicity of factors (linguistic, historical and economic) to create an explosive situation. At the same time, the presence of sizeable ethnic minorities within the borders of each state rendered the dissolution of the country as problematic as its retention. Long-term stability remains elusive.

In more ways than one, Europe reaches its limits in the Balkans; the essentially European patterns that will emerge in the following section start to disintegrate at the margins of the continent.

The European framework

What, then, do the countries of western Europe have in common from a religious point of view? There are several ways of looking at this question.

First, the historical perspective. O'Connell (1991) (among others) identifies three formative factors or themes that come together in the creation and recreation of the unity that we call Europe: these are Judaeo-Christian monotheism, Greek rationalism and Roman organisation. These factors shift and evolve over time, but their combinations can be seen forming and reforming a way of life that we have come to recognise as European. The religious strand within such combinations is self-evident.

It is, however, equally important to grasp from the outset the historical complexity of European identity. O'Connell approaches this question by introducing a series of interlocking and overlapping blocs which exist within the European whole. There are seven of these: the western islands, western Europe, central Europe, the Nordic/Baltic countries, the Mediterranean group, the former Ottoman territories and the Slav peoples. Not all of these will concern us in this chapter, but the 'building bloc' approach underlies a crucial aspect of modern as well as historical Europe:

If I have taken this building bloc approach, it is to make clear, on the one hand, how closely knit Europe comes out of its history and how important it may be to make a future unity, and to suggest on the other hand, how complex Europe is and, in consequence, how varied might future unity mosaics prove to be. (O'Connell 1991: 9)

There is nothing deterministic about the future shape of Europe: several approaches are possible; so, too, are several outcomes.

For the time being, however, we need to stress one point in particular: the shared religious heritage of western Europe as one of the crucial factors in the continent's development – and, possibly, in its future – and the influence of this heritage on a whole range of cultural values. Other very different sources reinforce this conclusion. One of these, the European Values System Study Group (EVSSG),[2] provides a principal source of data for this chapter. In contrast with O'Connell's primarily historical approach, the European Values Study exemplifies – for better or worse – sophisticated social science methodology.[3] Using careful sampling techniques, the EVSSG aims at an accurate mapping of social and moral values across Europe. It has generated very considerable data and will continue to do so. It is essential that we pay close, and at the same time critical, attention to its findings.

Two underlying themes run through the EVSSG study. The first concerns the substance of contemporary European values and asks, in particular, to what extent they are homogeneous; the second takes a more dynamic approach, asking to what extent such values are changing. Both themes involve, inevitably, a religious element. The first, for example, leads very quickly to questions about the origin of shared value systems: 'If values in Western Europe are to any extent shared, if people from different countries share similar social perceptions on their world, how had any such joint cultural experience been created?' (Harding, Phillips, with Fogarty 1986: 29). As the European Values Study indicates, the answer lies in deep-rooted cultural experiences which derive from pervasive social influences which have been part of our culture for generations, if not centuries. A shared religious heritage is one such influence.

Both in historical and geographical terms, religions – or more specifically, the Christian religion – provides an example of an agency which through the promulgation of a universal and exclusive faith sought to create a commonality of values and beliefs across Europe, and elsewhere. A shared religious heritage based on Christian values, therefore, may be seen as one formative cultural influence at the heart of and giving substance to 'European' civilisation. (Ibid.)

So much is unproblematic and confirms O'Connell's historical conclusions. On the other hand, as soon as the idea of value change is introduced, the situation becomes more contentious. A series of unavoidable questions immediately present themselves. How far is the primacy given to the role of religion in the creation of values still appropriate? Has this role not been undermined by the process known as secularisation? Can we really maintain in the 1990s that religion remains a central element of our value system? The influence of religion is becoming, surely, increasingly peripheral within contemporary European society. Or is it?

It will be these questions that preoccupy us in the final section of this chapter. In the meantime it is important to indicate the principal findings of the 1981 and 1990 EVSSG surveys for a variety of religious indicators. (For a fuller picture of these data – essential for any detailed work – see Stoetzel 1983; Harding, Phillips, with Fogarty 1986; Barker, Halman and Vloet 1992; Ester, Halman and de Moor 1994, together with the analyses for each European country involved in the survey.)

There are, broadly speaking, five religious indicators within the data: denominational allegiance, reported church attendance, attitudes towards the church, indicators of religious belief and some measurement of subjective religious disposition. These variables have considerable potential: they can be correlated with one another and with a wide range of socio-demographic data. In this respect the survey shows commendable awareness of the complexity of religious phenomena and the need to bear in mind more than one dimension within an individual's (or indeed a nation's) religious life.

However, what emerges in practice with respect to these multiple indicators is a clustering of two types of variable: on the one hand, those concerned with feelings, experience and the more numinous religious beliefs; on the other, those which measure religious orthodoxy, ritual participation and institutional attachment. It is, moreover, the latter (the more orthodox indicators of religious attachment) which display, most obviously, an undeniable degree of secularisation throughout western Europe. In contrast, the former (the less institutional indicators) indicate a considerable persistence in some aspects of religious life.

In particular, some form of 'religious disposition' and acceptance of the moral concepts of Christianity continues to be widespread among large numbers of Europeans, even among a proportion for whom the orthodox institution of the Church has no place. (Harding, Phillips, with Fogarty 1986: 70)

The essentials of this contrasting information are presented in Tables 11.1, 11.2 and 11.3, reproduced from the EVSSG data. These tables can be used in two ways: either to indicate the overall picture of the continent or to exemplify some of the national differences to which we refer in the second section of this chapter.

First, though, the trends common to the continent as a whole. We should start, perhaps, by echoing one conclusion of the European Values Study itself: that is, to treat with considerable caution statements about the secularisation process – particularly unqualified ones – either within Europe or anywhere else. For the data are complex, contradictory even, and clear-cut conclusions become correspondingly difficult (Harding, Phillips, with Fogarty 1986: 31–4). Bearing this in mind – together with the clustering of the variables that we have already mentioned – it seems to me more accurate to suggest that west Europeans remain,

Table 11.1 *National variations in denominational affiliation and reported church attendance (%)*

Country	Predominant denomination	Denominational affiliation				Church attendance			
		Catholic	Protestant	None	Others and no answers	Weekly or more often	Monthly	Never	'Score'[1]
$N =$		7071	3214	1607	1940	3073	1456	4267	
Eire	Catholic	95	3	0	2	82	6	4	9.8
Italy	Catholic	93	0	6	1	36	16	21	4.6
Spain	Catholic	90	0	9	1	41	12	25	5.2
Belgium	Catholic	72	2	15	10	30	8	34	3.6
France	Catholic	71	2	26[2]		12	6	57	1.6
Denmark	Protestant	1	92	1	6	3	9	43	0.9
Britain	Protestant	11	74	9	5	14	9	46	2.0
N. Ireland	Protestant	24	66	0	9	52	15	11	6.7
W. Germany	Protestant	41	48	9	1	21	16	20	3.0
Holland	Mixed	32	26	36	6	27	13	41	3.5
West European average	Mixed	57	28	12	2	32	13	30	3.2

All Catholics ($N = 7071$) — 37, 14, 22, 4.6

All Protestants[3] ($N = 3214$) — 9, 12, 35, 1.5

All non-affiliated ($N = 1607$) — 1, 1, 87, 0.2

Notes:
1 Weighted average across all church attendance categories
2 Two categories coded together
3 Excluding Nonconformists ($N = 239$)

Source: Harding *et al.* (1986: 36–7)

Table 11.2 Traditional beliefs, with trend comparisons

% Believing in	Europe		France				Great Britain				Holland				W. Germany			Eire		N. Ireland		Belgium		Spain		Denmark		Italy	
	1981	1990	1947	1968	1981	1990	1947	1968	1981	1990	1947	1968	1981	1990	1968	1981	1990	1981	1990	1981	1990	1981	1990	1981	1990	1981	1990	1981	1990
God	73	70	66	73	62	57	84	77	76	71	80	79	65	61	81	72	63	95	96	91	95	77	63	87	81	58	64	84	83
A soul	58	61			46	50			59	64			59	63		61	62	82	85	80	86	52	52	64	60	33	47	63	67
Sin	57	57			42	40			69	68			49	43		59	55	85	84	91	89	44	41	58	57	29	24	63	66
Life after death[1]	43	43	59	35	35	38	49	38	45	44	38	50	42	39	41	39	38	76	78	72	70	37	37	55	42	26	34	47	54
Heaven	40	41		39	27	30		54	57	53		54	39	34	43	31	31	83	85	81	86	33	30	50	48	17	10	41	45
The devil	25	25		17	17	19		21	30	30		29	21	17	25	18	15	57	53	66	72	20	18	33	28	12	8	30	35
Hell	23	23		22	15	16		23	27	25		28	15	14	25	14	13	54	50	65	68	18	15	34	27	8	19	31	36
Reincarnation	21	21		23	22	24		18	27	24		10	10	15	25	19	19	26	19	18	30	13	13	25	20	11	17	21	22
A personal God	32	38			26	20			31	32			34	29		28	24	73	67	70	66	39	29	55	50	24	–	26	66
Some sort of spirit or life force	36	33			26	32			39	41			29	41		40	43	16	24	18	20	24	20	23	27	24	–	50	22
Don't really know what to think	16	15			22	24			19	15			17	15		17	17	6	7	8	12	15	29	12	13	22	–	11	6
Don't think there is any sort of spirit, God or life force	11	10			19	16			9	10			12	14		13	11	2	1	1	2	8	14	6	7	21	–	6	5

Note:
1 The question in the 1947 survey was worded, 'Do you believe in the immortality of the soul?' Trend data from J. Stoetzel (1983) *Les Valeurs du Temps Present* (Paris: Presses Universitaires de France), p. 115.

Source: Adapted from Harding *et al.* (1986: 46–7). Additional information from 1990 EVSSG Study

Table 11.3 **Percentages of people not belonging to a religion and never attending church, national differences by age group**

	Europe	France	Great Britain	N. Ireland	Eire	Holland	Belgium	Spain	Denmark	W. Germany	Italy
Percentage not belonging to a religion											
Age											
18–24	18	38	14	5	2	47	24	15	6	9	9
25–34	20	45	10	7	2	45	16	19	9	15	12
55–64	7	16	4	5	1	26	13	5	4	8	4
Percentage saying that they never attend church											
Age											
18–24	43	63	59	20	5	44	41	39	53	31	26
25–34	45	72	54	16	7	52	38	39	52	28	31
55–64	29	50	36	5	5	30	34	16	36	22	19

Source: Harding *et al.* (1986: 42)

by and large, unchurched populations rather than simply secular. For a marked falling-off in religious attendance (especially in the Protestant north) has not resulted, yet, in a parallel abdication of religious belief. In short, many Europeans have ceased to belong to their religious institutions in any meaningful sense, but they have not abandoned, so far, many of their deep-seated religious motivations.[4]

Two short parentheses are important in this connection. The first may seem obvious, but the situation of believing without belonging (if such we may call it) should not be taken for granted. This relatively widespread – though fluctuating – characteristic within European religion in the late twentieth century should not merely be assumed; it must be examined, probed and questioned. The second point illustrates this need for questioning. It introduces two contrasting situations where believing without belonging is not the norm. Indeed, in east Europe prior to 1989, the two variables were (in some places at least) reversed, for the non-believer quite consciously used Mass attendance as one way of expressing disapproval of an unpopular regime. The second, very different, contrast comes from the United States. Here religious attendance has maintained itself at levels far higher than those that prevail in most of Europe; around 50 per cent of the American population both believe and belong.[5] Once again the situation should not be taken for granted; it must be examined, sociologically as well as theologically.

If we return now to the west European data and begin to probe more deeply, we find further evidence of consistency in the shapes or profiles of religiosity which obtain across a wide variety of European countries. One very clear illustration of such profiling can be found in patterns of religious belief, about which Harding, Phillips, with Fogarty (1986: 47) make the following observation:

Varying levels of belief in each country are similar to those seen on other indicators. Interestingly, irrespective of level of belief, the rank order among items is almost identical across Europe. The one exception to a consistent pattern, paradoxically, is the higher ranking given by English speaking countries to heaven than to life after death.

This kind of consistency is persuasive, the more so in that it is not easily predictable.

Correlations between religious indices and socioeconomic variables confirm the existence of socioreligious patterning across national boundaries. For throughout west Europe, it is clear that religious factors correlate – to varying degrees – with indices of occupation, gender and age (social class as such is more problematic). The correlation with age is particularly striking, and raises once again the future shape of European religion (see note 4). Indeed, it prompts the most searching question of the study: are we, in west Europe, experiencing a permanent generational shift with respect to religious behaviour, rather than a manifestation of the normal lifecycle? The EVSSG findings seem to indicate that this might be so:

> The survey data are consistent with the hypothesis that there has been a degree of secularisation in Western Europe. Markedly lower church attendance, institutional attachment, and adherence to traditional beliefs is found in younger compared with older respondents, and data from other sources support the notion that these are not lifecycle differences. (1986: 69–70)

If this really is the case, the future shape of European religion may be very different indeed. The data from the 1990 restudy reinforce this point.

So much for the similarities across west Europe. What about the differences? The first, and most obvious, of these lies between the notably more religious – and Catholic – countries of southern Europe and the less religious countries of the Protestant north. This variation holds across almost every indicator; indeed, they are interrelated. Levels of practice, for example, are markedly higher in Italy, Spain, Belgium and Ireland (closer in its religious life to continental Europe than to Britain) than they are elsewhere. Not surprisingly, one effect of regular Mass attendance is a corresponding strength in the traditional orthodoxies through most of Catholic Europe.[6]

There are, however, exceptions to this rule, and at this point it is necessary to anticipate the discussion in the second part of this chapter. For France displays a very different profile from the other Catholic countries, a contrast that cannot be explained without reference to the particular history of the country in question. The distinctiveness of France's religious history will form one focus of the second section. Other exceptions to a European pattern, or patterns, should be looked at in a similar light; notably, the countries which do not conform to the believing-without-belonging framework. Conspicuous here are the two Irelands. Once again, the particular and problematic nature of Irish history accounts for this; for religion has – regrettably – become entangled with questions of Irish identity on both sides of the border. The high levels of religious practice as well as belief in both the Republic and Northern Ireland are both cause and consequence of this situation. In the Republic especially, the statistics of religious practice remain very high indeed.

Before such particularities are explored in detail, one further variation within the overall framework is important. In France, Belgium, The Netherlands and, possibly, Britain (more especially England) there is a higher-than-average incidence of no religion, or at least no denominational affiliation. Indeed, Stoetzel (1983: 89–91) – in the French version of the 1981 EVSSG analysis – distinguishes four European types in terms of religious affiliation rather than three:[7] the Catholic countries (Spain, Italy and Eire); the predominantly Protestant countries (Denmark, Great Britain and Northern Ireland); the mixed variety (West Germany); and what he calls a 'région laïque': that is, France, Belgium, The Netherlands and, possibly, England, where those who recognise no religious label form a sizeable section of the population. In many ways this analysis is more satisfying than groupings suggested elsewhere in the European Values material (see note 7), where countries which have very different religious profiles find themselves grouped together.

In anticipating the following section, we have already indicated one of the severest limitations within the EVSSG data. There is no way of telling from the data why a particular country should be similar to or different from its neighbours. Apparently similar statistical profiles can mask profound differences, a point that we explore in some detail with reference to France and Britain. Before doing so, a second drawback must also be mentioned. The EVSSG sample sizes for each country are too small to give any meaningful data about religious minorities. It would, however, be grossly misleading to present an image of Europe at the end of the twentieth century without any reference to these increasingly important sections of the European population.

The first of these minorities, the Jews, has been present in Europe for centuries; a presence, moreover, that has been inextricably bound up with the tragedies of recent European history. Nor can it be said, regrettably, that anti-Semitism is a thing of the past. It continues to rear an ugly head from time to time right across Europe, itself an accurate indicator of wider insecurities. Estimations of numbers are always difficult, but there are, currently, around 1 million Jews in west Europe, the largest communities being the French (500 000–600 000) and the British (300 000). French Judaism has been transformed in the postwar period by the immigration of considerable numbers of Sephardim from North Africa.[8]

Former colonial connections also account for other non-Christian immigrations into Europe. The Islamic communities are, probably, the most significant in this respect, though Britain also houses considerable numbers of Sikhs and Hindus. Islam is, however, the largest other-faith population in Europe, conservative estimates suggesting a figure of 6 million.[9] Muslims make up approximately 3 per cent of most west European populations (Clarke 1988; Nielsen 1992; Lewis and Schnapper 1994). More specifically, the links between France and North Africa account for the very sizeable French Muslim community (2–3 million). Britain's equivalent comes from the Indian subcontinent (1.2 million). Germany, on the other hand, has absorbed large numbers of migrant workers from the fringes of south-east Europe, and from Turkey in particular. The fate of these migrants in the face of growing numbers of east Europeans looking for work within the new Germany remains to be seen.

Whatever the outcome of this particular situation, however, one fact remains increasingly clear: the Islamic presence in Europe is here to stay. It follows that Europeans can no longer distance themselves from the debates of the Muslim world. Whether they like it or not, the issues are present on their own doorstep. Admitting that this is the case is not easy for many Europeans, for the Islamic factor undoubtedly challenges the assumptions of European life, both past and present. Peaceful coexistence between Islam and Judaeo-Christian Europe cannot – and never could be – taken for granted.[10] Nor can Muslims accept unequivocally the live-and-let-live religious attitudes assumed by the majority of contemporary Europeans. This, surely, remains the problem at the heart of the Salman Rushdie controversy.

One further source of diversity remains: the presence of new religious movements in all European societies. The significance of such movements remains a controversial issue. There can be no doubt that new religious movements attract considerable media attention (often negative in tone); the numbers involved, however, are relatively small. Be that as it may, such movements fulfil an important function for the sociologist of religion. Inadvertently, they have become barometers of the changes taking place in contemporary society (Beckford 1985, 1986). New religious movements 'represent an "extreme situation" which, precisely because it is extreme, throws into sharp relief many of the assumptions hidden behind legal, cultural, and social structures' (1985: 11).

We can use this perspective to examine one of the most urgent questions facing Europe at the present time: the need to create and to sustain a truly tolerant and pluralist society, both in Europe as a whole, and in its constituent nations – a society, that is, which goes well beyond an individualised live-and-let-live philosophy; a society able to accommodate 'that unusual phenomenon' in contemporary Europe, the person (of whatever faith) who takes religion seriously (*The Times*: 6 February 1989). By examining the divergent attitudes displayed towards new religious movements in different European countries, we can learn a great deal about underlying attitudes. After all, tolerance of religious differences in contemporary Europe must mean tolerance of all religious differences, not just the ones we happen to approve of. If a country 'fails' in its tolerance of new religious movements, it is unlikely, or at least very much less likely, to succeed with respect to other religious minorities.

Unity and diversity

The third chapter of David Martin's *A General Theory of Secularization* (1978) focuses on the tensions between religion and nationhood within the European situation. It starts from the following premise:

Europe is a unity by virtue of having possessed one Caesar and one God, i.e. by virtue of Rome. It is a diversity by virtue of the existence of nations. The patterns of European religions derive from the tension and the partnership between Caesar and God, and from the relationship between religion and the search for national integrity and identity. (1978: 100)

The second section of this chapter examines these relationships with particular reference to France and to Britain.[11]

It also suggests that recent shifts in perspective – shifts that derive both from the implementation of the Single European Act and from the revolutions in east Europe – need to be taken into account in an up-to-date assessment of the tensions or partnerships between Caesar and God in contemporary Europe. Will there, for example, be more room for regional or subcultural identity if national profiles in west Europe diminish, relatively speaking? Conversely, will the re-emergence of nationalisms all over east Europe alter the patterns established – or rather, imposed – in the postwar period? The religious factor, suppressed along with so much else under communism, is a crucial element in these unpredictable events.

But, first, Britain and France.[12] If we look at statistics for believing and belonging in France we find, superficially at least, a pattern rather similar to that in Britain. Around 80 per cent of the French call them-selves Roman Catholics, whereas regular weekly attendance at Mass is as low as 13 per cent. A further 7 per cent attend Mass once or twice a month (Hervieu-Léger 1986).[13] The figures for Britain are not dissimilar (Brierley 1991; Brierley and Wraight 1995), though the denominational mix is, clearly, quite different. Only 14 per cent of the British popula-tion attend church with any regularity, and even fewer in England, but nominal allegiances (especially to the national churches in England and Scotland) remain moderately high.

Such statistics must, however, be carefully interpreted. Why is it, for example, that almost all the indices of secularity are higher in France than in Britain? (Despite the apparent Catholicism of the French, the EVSSG data tell us that less than 60 per cent of the French now say that they believe in God.) Why, if we look at another set of comparisons, do British Roman Catholics not only practise with greater enthusiasm than French ones, but behave quite differently from a political point of view? Conversely, the French Protestant minority, though tiny, has been dis-proportionately influential in many aspects of French life.[14] It has, more-over, voted to the Left traditionally, quite unlike its counterpart in Northern Ireland. These differences can only be explained sociologically; that is, by taking into account a whole series of interrelated contextual variables (economic, social and political) that derive from a particular national or regional context.

This is the essence of Martin's thesis: that broad social processes – among them the secularisation process – must always be considered in relation to particular historical situations. What, then, are the key con-textual variables that have operated so decisively on either side of the Channel?

The greater prominence of secularity in France derives from a reli-gious history quite different from that in Britain. Despite our persistent quarrels about various forms of Christianity, Britain has never experienced a major religious split that corresponded with a political divide. In contrast, the French were for generations politically divided about religious questions rather than anything else. The animosity of the early years of the Third Republic culminated in the separation of church and state and the establishment of an emphatically secular public-school system. The residual bitterness of these quarrels can still be felt; it accounts for the higher profile of anti-religion as well as non-religion in France. It also accounts for the persistence of political allegiances along religious lines right through the first half of the twentieth century.

In Britain, a considerably greater degree of pluralism was established at an earlier stage (its Roman Catholic and Nonconformist minorities are substantial). The existence of such minorities permitted a certain amount of choice between different flavours of Christianity, a choice quite unlike the French obligation to accept Catholicism or nothing at all. This is one reason, a major one, why the 'feel' of British religious life remains qualitatively different from the French, a contrast which persists despite a marked decline in institutional religion on both sides of the Channel.

Two parallel episodes exemplify these differences. The first, the controversy surrounding the publication of Salman Rushdie's *The Satanic Verses*, was, initially, a British affair. Very quickly, however, the episode escalated to the point where it attracted considerable international attention. The French critique reflects very clearly French preoccupations about religious matters.

For a start, the divisions in France were far more clear-cut than those in England. Cardinal Decourtray (the then President of the French Bishops' Conference) called *The Satanic Verses* 'an offence against religious faith', and lost no time in drawing the comparison with Martin Scorsese's film, *The Last Temptation of Christ*. President Mitterand responded in similar vein: 'All dogmas which through violence, violate the freedom of the human spirit and the right to self-expression represent, in my eyes, absolute evil.' The controversy was, it seems, gradually translated into French terms; in other words it became 'part of France's hallowed battle between Christian and Freethinkers' (*Independent* 23 February 1989 and 10 February 1990; see also Appignanesi and Maitland 1989). In Britain the response was far more pragmatic, a question of both/and rather than either/or. Much of the debate concerned the law against blasphemy. The Archbishop of Canterbury called for a strengthening of this law to cover religions other than Christianity (*Independent* 22 February 1989); others insisted that we should abolish laws concerning something as outmoded as blasphemy altogether. The French, understandably, were mystified by the domestic implications of these exchanges.

A second episode, or rather pair of episodes, confirms these impressions. Not long after the Rushdie controversy became headline news, two or three Muslim girls began to attract attention – on either side of the Channel – by wearing the traditional Muslim scarf (or *foulard*, to use the French term) within school. So much for the similarities. The differences arise in the reactions of each country to the initial gesture. The French were offended, above all, by the wearing of a religious symbol within the public-school system: that is within the *école laïque*.[15] The British, in contrast, were unlikely to be bothered about religious symbols *per se* in state schools, for certain elements of religious life (including religious symbols) form an integral part of our educational system. Instead, we became concerned about school uniform, a peculiarly British preoccupation. Muslim scarves must be rejected because they do not conform to school uniform regulations. Mercifully, the school governors in the British case found a satisfactory a compromise: navy-blue scarves would, after all, be acceptable.

There is, however, a more serious aspect to this situation, for Britain has denominational schools that are, very largely, funded by the state – a situation unthinkable in France.[16] And if the French were preoccupied about the wearing of a religious symbol in their state schools, the British have to face the anomaly of refusing to the Muslim minority what we have allowed, and continue to allow to Anglicans, Roman Catholics and Jews. Such a policy is at best illogical, at worst discriminatory.[17]

If these, very recent, events exemplify the continuing religious (even ideological) differences between two neighbouring European countries, are there, perhaps, aspects of the present situation which do the reverse? What, to be more precise, will be the effect of greater European unity on this kind of situation? Common rulings from Strasbourg or Brussels on the rights of religious minorities might, for example, iron out some of the anomalies. On the other hand, individual nations could resist such interference, feeling that the regulation of religious minorities is a purely domestic affair. One way or another, we find ourselves returning to one of the recurrent themes in the religious life of contemporary Europe: the problematic of a truly pluralist society.

We need now to set this problematic into a broader perspective and reconsider, more generally, the relationship between God and Caesar in a rapidly changing Europe. Such an exercise will enable us to draw some of the threads in this chapter together. Setting or resetting the tensions between God and Caesar in the context of contemporary Europe requires, however, that an important theoretical assumption within this chapter be properly articulated. This can be stated quite simply. Just how far does the religious life of a country (or indeed of a continent) reflect a context rather than create one? In other words, is religion primarily a reactive rather than proactive sociological variable? In my opinion, the potential for proactivity lies at the heart of the matter.

Looking back, for example, it is clear that the religious factor played a crucial part in the forging of something that we recognise as European. At the same time, this common historical heritage has undoubtedly been moulded by a great diversity of contextual factors into a number of sub-types or national variations, some of them (not least the British case) very distinct indeed. In the 1990s, as the Single European Act becomes reality, the situation alters once again. Bearing this in mind, two lines of thought suggest themselves. First we need to ask whether the religious factor has – in the supposedly secular late twentieth century – the capacity to do anything effective at all. And second, we must examine not only the degree of independence of the religious factor, but the direction in which it might operate.

Paradoxically, the first of these questions will be kept until last: it forms the focus of the third section of this chapter. The second can be elaborated as follows. On the one hand, we need to ask what 'use' might be made of the religious factor, either by the state or by any number of interested parties. Can, for example, the religious element be pressed into service by pro-Europeans to emphasise what Europe has in common, or will it be used by their opponents to provide support for discrete and independent nations each with their own, carefully circumscribed religious sphere, possibly a national church? Either scenario is possible. The argument, can, however, be turned the other way round. For the churches (national or otherwise), religious individuals or a wide variety of religious organisations may themselves attempt to initiate – rather than reflect – shifts in public opinion. In other words, the religious factor may operate as an independent variable in bringing about a greater European consciousness, or, conversely, in resisting just such a move. A theoretically informed examination of contemporary events, bearing this framework (or these frameworks) in mind, is one of the most urgent empirical tasks of the sociology of religion in the 1990s.

The British case is particularly apposite, the more so if a Northern Irish perspective is also included.[18] For we have, then, not only a considerable denominational mix but four distinct national perspectives as well. It is, for example, hardly surprising that the Northern Irish treat Europe with considerable suspicion. They are only too well aware of Catholic majorities in Ireland, let alone in Europe, to risk much down that road. In contrast, the Scots – and to some degree the Welsh as well – have everything to gain, for greater European integration necessarily diminishes English domination. The Scots, moreover, have a national church (the Kirk), which belongs, both theologically and organisationally, to one of Europe's major spiritual traditions, Calvinism.[19] In Scotland, therefore, economic, political and religious factors are mutually reinforcing.

The English case is altogether more complicated, but two factors are, perhaps, crucial. The Church of England is exactly what that name implies; it is the national church of England and can still, at times, operate very effectively in that capacity (Davie 1990, 1993, 1994). It has also been inextricably linked to our colonial past, for missionaries followed the flag, or vice versa, for centuries. One very obvious consequence of this past has been a multiplicity of organisational links with churches overseas. But neither the essential Englishness of the domestic church nor its imperial connections are going to be much help in forming effective and creative links with Europe; they may well, in fact, be a hindrance. It remains to be seen whether the English churches have either the will or the capacity to overcome this situation.

Careful comparative work can reveal similar tensions elsewhere in Europe; the tensions between regional and national loyalties are one example. For the former may well find greater room for manoeuvre as national identities diminish, relatively speaking. There are certainly parts of Europe where the regions are claiming greater autonomy. The affirmation of Scottish and Welsh identity is mirrored elsewhere: in Catalonia and the Basque country, or in the Italian autonomous regions, to name but a few. But it is in east Europe that ethnic nationalisms are the most potent force. A detailed examination of these is beyond the scope of this chapter, but the religious factor is, clearly, of immense importance in such struggles. They should, certainly, be borne in mind in the theoretical discussion which follows.

Religion and modernity in contemporary Europe

There have been a number of references to secularisation, or to the secularisation process, in this chapter. We have seen, for example, that the authors of the European Values Study evaluate much of their religious data with this framework in mind. Their conclusions are far from clear-cut. None the less, the importance of the age factor in the EVSSG analysis suggests a crucially significant change with respect to the secularisation process; the possibility of a generational shift towards a more secular frame of reference far more deep-seated than the expected lifecycle differences. The 1990 data encourage such an interpretation.

Martin's thesis – the focus of the second section – finds its fullest expression in a book entitled *A General Theory of Secularization* (1978). The 'theory' that Martin puts forward is by no means deterministic; nor does he propose that secularisation is 'a very long-term or inevitable trend'. Rather, Martin describes a particular period (varying from two to four centuries) in which 'certain tendencies can be noted . . . with regard to the role, power and popularity of religious beliefs and institutions' (1978: 12). These tendencies are described in considerable detail. Secularisation is, however, the dominant theme; the material – subtle, perceptive and nuanced though it is – is ordered with this, rather than another, framework in mind.

In some ways, it is hardly surprising that ideas about secularisation have dominated thinking about Europe both in the sociology of religion and elsewhere (Edwards 1987), for the evidence is, in many respects, overwhelming. Something, in Owen Chadwick's phrase (Chadwick 1975), has happened to European society – to the European mind – in the last 200 years. Exactly what this was, and why it came about, remains a matter of much enquiry by students of many disciplines, but an unmistakable shift has, undoubtedly, taken place. For want of a better word, we label this shift 'secularisation'.

On the other hand, if the impetus towards secularisation is as strong as some commentators imply (not, on the whole, those so far mentioned), a very great deal of explaining remains to be done. For not everything seems to be working in this direction. Indices of religious belief, for example, have not dropped in a way that might have been predicted a generation or so ago. Nor have religious controversies ceased to catch the public's imagination; the Rushdie controversy dominated the media for weeks. And governments – far from denying the existence of the sacred – are, increasingly, faced with moral, ethical, even religious, decisions as they grapple with the consequences of scientific advance. Bioethical and environmental issues remain at the forefront of public controversy, for science, it seems, has become the creator just as much as the solver of society's problems.

Indeed, just as it seemed possible that secularisation might, all other things being equal, begin to assert itself in a big way, all the other things have ceased, increasingly, to fulfil that condition. Sociologists are left trying to readjust their frameworks. At least, they are left trying to come to terms with a great deal of conflicting evidence. Is there any way, for instance, in which we can hold together the persistence of religious belief in contemporary Europe alongside the marked decline – but not the disappearance – of religious practice? Can we find satisfactory explanations for the prevalence of Christian nominalism alongside the hardening of religious boundaries associated with the growth of evangelical (even fundamentalist) tendencies within Christianity, and with the increase in other faith communities across contemporary Europe? What about the disturbing evidence of fundamentalisms worldwide? And what about the increasing tendency for politicians and other public figures to consult the 'religious sector' about matters that they know to be beyond their competence? Diverging and conflicting data make heavy demands on sociological theorists.

One line of thinking has been to abandon the idea of an overall framework altogether; a trend which can be illustrated both within sociological theory and within the religious phenomena that such theory seeks to explain. For 'postmodern' sociology is as much subject to the relativisation process as postmodern theology or religion; both involve parallel rejections of the all-explaining, all-encompassing metanarrative. Postmodern individuals, including sociologists, must evolve whatever explanations of life – and death – that they can, from whatever is available at the time.

In many ways notions of believing without belonging (the dominant mood, perhaps, of European religion) fit quite well into this kind of framework; for the phenomenon of detached belief, of privatised religion, permits us, surely, to select at will from the religious goods on offer and mould these into personal packages that suit our particular lifestyles and subcultures. At the same time, the institutional features of religious life representing orthodoxy become less and less important as we set and reset the parameters of faith according to whim. That the so-called theological certainties are also under attack need not concern us unduly.

If we look at the evidence, however, this approach becomes increasingly hard to sustain. For the phenomenon of detached belief, though prevalent, is not the only religious phenomenon in contemporary Europe. The existence of significant other-faith communities alongside an active, sometimes demanding Christian minority, have to be taken into account. Indeed, the all-too-evident need to create in modern Europe a pluralist society capable of accommodating such elements is paramount. It requires, moreover, that differing religious creeds are treated with considerably greater seriousness than interchangeable supermarket alternatives.

Hervieu-Léger (1986, 1990; see also Davie 1992) offers a rather different approach. Her analysis suggests an open-ended concept of modernity which almost – if not completely – renders a postmodern dimension unnecessary. *Vers un nouveau christianisme* (1986) focuses on the relationship between religion and modernity in advanced western societies, a relationship which is both complex and paradoxical. The argument works at two levels: it begins by acknowledging the contradictory features within contemporary religious life (and in particular within the French situation); and it continues by relating these contradictions to the tensions within the concept of modernity itself.

Hervieu-Léger underlines the dilemma facing those who try to understand the nature of contemporary religious life. On the one hand, there is no lack of data to support the secularisation thesis: a fall in religious practice, a drop in clergy vocations (a truly dramatic one in the French Catholic church) and a crumbling of traditional morality. On the other hand, we cannot deny the evidence of religious renewal, notably the emergence of a whole range of 'warm', emotional communities both within and outside the traditional churches. The latter aspect has been further documented by Hervieu-Léger in a series of case studies (for the most part French ones) published under the title *De l'émotion en religion* (Hervieu-Léger and Champion 1990).

The 'paradox of modernity' – the second level – attempts to make sense of these contradictions by examining them in relation to strains within the concept of modernity itself. The paradox is defined in the following terms:

modernity destroys religion as a system of meaning and as a motivator of human effort, but – at the same time – modernity creates the time-space of a utopia which, through its very structure, remains attached to the religious problematic of fulfilment and salvation. (Hervieu-Léger 1986: 224)

In other words, modernity, at the same time as it destroys traditional religious forms, creates an ongoing requirement for something beyond itself. If religion – in an infinite variety of forms – provides one response to this ongoing requirement, it follows that religion as such will continue to persist despite the destructive aspects of modernity. The secularisation process is, therefore, something far more complex than the notion of religion giving way to rationality; it becomes 'a process of permanent reorganisation in the function of religion within a society which is structurally unable to fulfil the expectations that it must create in order to continue in existence' (1986: 227). Following this argument, the persistence of religion becomes an integral part of modernity rather than an antithetical or postmodern reaction to it.

This, skeletally, is the essence of Hervieu-Léger's analysis, an analysis that has emerged primarily within a French context. We need now to switch back to the European material and to examine the relevance of this argument to the principal focus of this chapter: the unity and disunity of European religion.

One area of research is, perhaps, crucial. Religious membership is, very often, most effective at a local or community level. In this way it becomes an increasingly significant way of preserving aspects of life threatened by the ever-increasing scale of modern economics, indeed of modernity itself. This facet of religious life can be found in many parts of the contemporary world. It has, none the less, particular resonance in Europe in the 1990s. For we find ourselves asking once again how the religious dimension will respond to the increasingly European stress within economic, social and even political life. Are we likely to see a corresponding homogeneity in Europe's religion, particularly in styles of belief (see Willaime 1988: 247–7)? If so, will such homogeneity extend to east European countries? Or will the religious factor take a rather different form; a form which bolsters national, regional and even local boundaries rather than European ones? In other words, will the religious life of Europe (east and/or west) reinforce the step towards wider boundaries; or will it counteract such pressures, and continue to give meaning to a more immediately accessible level of life?

We have already suggested that careful empirical work in this area as a priority for the European sociologist of religion in the 1990s. It assumes, moreover, that the sociologists involved will appreciate the continued importance of religion as a salient variable in their analysis. Despite the decline in conventional forms of religiosity, especially among the young, religion as such (following Hervieu-Léger) will continue to play a significant part in the development of modern Europe.[20] Discovering how is part of the empirical enquiry.

Notes

1 The situation is, however, far from predictable. Greece, for example, (an Orthodox country) has been a full member of the European Union for some time. Austria, in contrast, joined as late as 1995.

2 The European Values Study is a major cross-national survey of human values, first carried out in Europe in 1981 and then extended to other countries worldwide. It was designed by the European Values Systems Study group (EVSSG). Analyses of the 1981 material can be found in Harding and Phillips, with Fogarty (1986) and in Stoetzel (1983). A restudy took place in 1990. Published material from this can be found in Timms (1992), Ashford and Timms (1992), Barker, Halman and Vloet (1992) and Ester, Halman and de Moor (1994). Barker *et al.* includes a useful bibliography of the whole enterprise. A further restudy is planned for the turn of the century. The longtitudinal aspects of the study enhance the data considerably.

3 The European Values Study reveals both the advantages and limitations of survey methodology. These are discussed in the introductory sections of Harding *et al.* (1986). Particular difficulties for the religious material will be highlighted in this chapter.

4 One of the crucial questions raised by the EVSSG material concerns the future of European religion. Are we on the brink of something very different indeed: a markedly more secular twenty-first century? It is, however, very difficult to tell how the relationship between believing and belonging will develop. Nominal belief could well become the norm for the foreseeable future; on the other hand, the two variables may gradually move closer together as nominal belief turns itself into no belief at all. At the moment we can only speculate.

5 Some sociologists dispute the figures for the United States. But even if considerably lower estimates are accepted, the figures for North America are still much higher that those for west Europe (see Bruce 1996, Chapter 6, for a full discussion of this topic).

6 Protestant Europe is undoubtedly more secular. One question posed by the EVSSG data concerns the extent to which Catholic Europe will follow suit a generation or so later.

7 Halsey (1985), for example, places British attitudes in a European perspective, offering three categories: Scandinavia (Denmark, Sweden, Finland and Norway); northern Europe (Northern Ireland, Eire, West Germany, Holland, Belgium and France); and Latin Europe (Italy and Spain). The northern Europe category includes some very different religious profiles.

8 Information (including statistics) about the Jewish communities in west Europe can be found in Lerman (1989).

9 Estimates of the size of Europe's Muslim population are, inevitably, related to questions about immigration. Statistics relating to illegal immigration are particularly problematic.

10 The outstanding example of creative toleration comes from medieval Spain, where Jews, Muslims and Christians lived harmoniously for four centuries. The forcible expulsion of both Jews and Muslims from a re-Catholicised Spain in 1492 rendered the 1992 celebration of this year a very ambivalent European anniversary.

11 France and Britain have been selected as examples of the secularisation process in west Europe in view of the author's familiarity with source material. The process could, equally well, have been documented for other European nations, though up-to-date material in English is not always easy to find.

12 Detailed information on the French situation can be found in Hervieu-Léger (1986), Michel (1985) and Willaime (1996); for the British case Brierley

(1988), Brierley and Wraight (1995), Davie (1994) and Bruce (1995) are the most useful, In the main these sources support the EVSSG material though the interpretations vary considerably. Bruce, in particular, argues a very strong case for secularisation.

13 These percentages have fallen in the last ten years; less than 70 per cent of French people now declare themselves to be Catholics and only 10 per cent worship with any regularity (see the 1994 Institut CSA poll, quoted in Willaime 1996).

14 In the early years of the Reformation, the spread of Protestantism within France was considerable. Though Protestants were reduced to a minority, the subsequent tenacity of French Protestantism through centuries of persecution has coloured much of French history.

15 The words *laïcité* and *laïque* have no equivalent in English. The British have no need for such terms, given our very different religious culture.

16 This does not mean that there are no denominational schools in France; simply that they exist outside the state system of education.

17 Two Muslim schools (one in London and one in Birmingham) were awarded state funding in January 1998, the culmination of a long campaign.

18 For a more detailed discussion of the British churches in an European context, see Davie (1993).

19 The other two spiritual traditions of west Europe are Lutheranism and Catholicism. The Anglican Church, in contrast, has no roots on the European mainland.

20 Beckford (1989) offers a similar, but none the less distinct analysis of religion in advanced industrial society. He argues (1989: 170) that religion has come adrift from its former points of anchorage (among others, the institutional churches) but is no less powerful as a result. 'It remains a potent cultural resource or form which may act as the vehicle of change, challenge or conservation.' It can be 'used' in a wide variety of ways, not all of which are predictable.

References

In addition to the references that appear in the text, three useful collections have recently appeared: Gill, S., D'Costa, G. and King, U. (eds) (1994) *Religion in Europe: Contemporary Perspectives*, Kampen: Kok Pharos; Fulton, J. and Gee, P. (eds) (1994) *Religion in Contemporary Europe*, Lewiston, Queenston Lampeter: Edwin Mellen Press; and Davie, G. and Hervieu-Léger, D. (eds) (1996) *Identités religieuses en Europe*, Paris: La Découverte.

Abrams, M., Gerard, G. and Timms, N. (eds) (1985) *Values and Social Change in Britain*, London: Macmillan.

Appignanesi, L. and Maitland, S. (1989) *The Rushdie File*, London: Fourth Estate.

Ashford, S. and Timms, N. (1992) *What Europe Thinks: a Study of Western European Values*, Aldershot: Dartmouth.

Barker, D., Halman, L. and Vloet, A. (1992) *The European Values Study 1981–1990: Summary Report*, published by the Gordon Cook Foundation on behalf of the European Values Group.

Beckford, J. (1985) *Cult Controversies*, London and New York: Tavistock Publications.

Beckford, J. (ed.) (1986) *New Religious Movements and Rapid Social Change*, London: Sage/UNESCO.

Beckford, J. (1989) *Religion and Advanced Industrial Society*, London: Unwin Hyman.

Brierley, P. (1988) *UK Christian Handbook 1989/90*, London: Marc Europe.

Brierley, P. (1991) *Christian England*, London: Marc Europe.

Brierley, P. and Wraight, H. (1995) *UK Christian Handbook 1996/1997 Edition*, London: Christian Research Association.

Bruce, S. (1995) *Religion in Modern Britain*, Oxford: Oxford University Press.

Bruce, S. (1996) *Religion in the Modern World: from Cathedrals to Cults*, Oxford: Oxford University Press.

Chadwick, O. (1975) *The Secularisation of the European Mind*, Cambridge: Cambridge University Press.

Clarke, P. (1988) 'Islam in contemporary Europe', in S. Sutherland, S. Stewart, L. Houlden, P. Clarke and F. Hardy (eds) *The World's Religions*, London: Routledge.

Davie, G. (1990) 'An ordinary God: the paradox of religion in contemporary Britain', *British Journal of Sociology*, 41: 395–421.

Davie, G. (1992) 'Religion and modernity in Britain', *International Journal of Comparative Religion*, 1: 1–11.

Davie, G. (1993) 'Les Eglises britanniques et l'Europe', in G. Vincent et J. P. Willaime (eds) *Religions et transformations de l'Europe*, Strasbourg: Presses Universitaires de Strasbourg.

Davie, G. (1994) *Religion in Britain since 1945: Believing without Belonging*, Oxford: Blackwell.

Edwards, D. (1987) *The Futures of Christianity*, London: Hodder & Stoughton.

Ester, P., Halman, L. and de Moor, R. (1994) *The Individualizing Society. Value Change in Europe and North America*, Tilburg: Tilburg University Press.

Halsey, A. H. (1985) 'On methods and morals', in M. Abrams, G. Gerard and N. Timms (eds) *Values and Social Change in Britain*, London: Macmillan.

Harding, S., Phillips, D., with Fogarty, M. (1986) *Contrasting Values in Western Europe*, London: Macmillan.

Hervieu-Léger, D. (1986) *Vers un nouveau christianisme*, Paris: Cerf.

Hervieu-Léger, D. (1990) 'Religion and modernity in the French context: for a new approach to secularization', *Sociological Analysis*, 51S: 15–25.

Hervieu-Léger, D. and Champion, F. (eds) (1990) *De l'émotion en religion*, Paris: Centurion.

Lerman, A. (1989) *The Jewish Communities of the World*, London: Macmillan.

Lewis, B. and Schnapper, D. (eds) (1994) *Muslims and Europe*, London: Pinter.

Martin, D. (1978) *A General Theory of Secularization*, Oxford: Blackwell.

Michel, P. (ed.) (1985) 'Religions et société en France: problèmes politiques et sociaux', *La Documentation Française*, 518.

Nielsen, J. (1992) *Muslims and Western Europe*, Edinburgh: Edinburgh University Press.

O'Connell, J. (1991) The past and future making of Europe: the role of heritage and the directions of unity. University of Bradford: Peace Research Report, No. 26.

Rushdie, S. (1988) *The Satanic Verses*, London and New York: Viking-Penguin.

Stoetzel, J. (1983) *Les Valeurs du Temps Présent: une enquête européenne*, Paris: Presses Universitaires de France.

Timms, N. (1992) *Family and Citizenship, Values in Contemporary Britain*, Aldershot: Dartmouth.

Walters, P. (ed.) (1988) *World Christianity: Eastern Europe*, London: Marc Europe.

Willaime, J. P. (ed.) (1988) *Vers de Nouveaux Oecuménismes*, Paris: Cerf.

Willaime, J. P. (1996) 'Laïcité et religion en France', in G. Davie and D. Hervieu-Léger (eds) *Identités religieuses en Europe*, Paris: La Découverte.

CHAPTER 12

Leisure – *jeux sans frontières* or major European industry?

STAN CLARK

Leisure might be considered the climax of industrial society, the aspect of life which, for most people, makes it all worthwhile. It has, however, a protean nature. A first attempt to define leisure might be to see it in terms of non-work, yet there are activities going on in the workplace – for example, chatting during tea-breaks – which have a clearly recreational character. Leisure activities are often divided from those necessary to personal care, but eating and drinking and care of the body may also share, to a greater or lesser extent, characteristics typical of leisure activity. Going out to a restaurant for a meal or to a pub for a drink would seem to be primarily leisure activities, and visiting a hairdresser may also have a recreational component for some people. In this chapter I shall simply choose four areas of activity which are commonly regarded as leisure, which I think are important. In discussing them I hope to make clear that such activities are bound up with and influenced by other areas of people's lives: work, religion, maintenance of health, family life.

Problems in defining leisure are one reason for the considerable theoretical controversy surrounding this field. Sociologists are, however, also uncertain of how important it is. For some sociologists work, not leisure, remains the key to understanding society. Work is the precondition for life and leisure, and the generator of capital. The relationships entered into at work are said to determine social classes, which themselves influence social conflict and societal evolution. For theorists of postmodern society, however, such views belong to an obsolete paradigm. In postmodern society individuals define themselves by leisure activities and choices, creating styles and identities from the artefacts and culture of a pluralist society. There are also differences of approach among those who take leisure seriously as a social phenomenon. I make no attempt in this chapter to deal systematically with these theoretical issues, but I do hope to demonstrate that whatever our theoretical position within the sociology of leisure, the study of leisure is important as well as interesting.

· Finally, it is necessary to justify a comparative approach to the study of leisure. The case for a European framework of analysis in approaching sociological phenomena has been stated in the general introduction, and should emerge in this essay as well as in others. It is only necessary, therefore, to state here that I hope to demonstrate the continuing relevance of divisions into rural and urban, rich and poor, Catholic and anti-clerical, in the study of leisure activity, though the effect of such divisions is being modified by continuing processes of modernisation and economic integration. The study of society in a European perspective, interesting and important in itself, is necessary to gain an accurate understanding of the distinctiveness of British experience and the extent to which this distinctiveness is likely to survive.

Festivals

Two features of other western European societies when compared with that of Britain – later urbanisation and industrialisation, and the greater significance of the Catholic church – may be held responsible for an important difference in leisure patterns: namely, the greater prominence of traditional communal celebrations in the public life of the Continent. This is despite the fact that, for the most part, the close organic connection which marked the relationship between work and leisure in preindustrial Europe has disappeared, and also despite the decline in religious belief. This greater prominence of festivals is true, I believe, not just in the less urbanised and industrialised countries like Spain and Portugal, but also in highly urbanised and industrialised countries like Germany and The Netherlands.[1]

Spain and Portugal are, however, particularly interesting in this respect. One author has written about Portugal: 'With the arrival of Easter and of Spring the whole of Portugal enters into a rhythm of the festa until the first approach of autumn. A rhythm which moreover hardly slows down during the winter months' (Sanchis 1983: 15).[2]

The study from which this quotation is taken provides a detailed anthropological account of the *romarias*, popular pilgrimages which are found throughout Portugal, though they are more common in the north. The essence of the *romaria* is religious and involves a promise made to a local 'saint'. The saint in question can be a relic or an image of a saint but equally an image of Christ or the Virgin Mary. It is typical for the images to be in churches or chapels on the outskirts of towns or villages, or in the countryside beyond, and there is often a procession of pilgrims to these chapels. The pilgrims pray for aid of various kinds, and make a promise to bestow a 'gift' next year if their prayers are heard. The gift may take the form of money or agricultural produce, but it may also take such forms as proceeding to the church or going around it on one's knees, or being carried to the church in a coffin. Gifts may be repeated over many years. The main focus of the analysis is how the *romaria* has become a struggle for control between the church author-ities, who tend to see it primarily as a celebration of the saint's day, and

the strength of popular religiosity which stresses the bargain struck
between devotee and saint.

Our focus of interest, however, is the *romaria* as an occasion for
communal festivities, which may last for two or three days. A typical
element in such festivities is firework displays. Gifts may take the form
of money for fireworks, an outcome apparently not very agreeable to
the church, which prefers money for Masses or upkeep of the sanctuary.
Sometimes special cakes may be baked and sold, or there may be bullfights. Almost invariably there is music and dancing. The exact form of
festivities varies, as does the nature of the requests for aid. Some saints
are seen as particularly helpful for certain types of medical problems,
others for aiding the harvest or the fishing. What is common to all the
romarias, however, is the combination of religion and popular festivities,
a combination characteristic of leisure in preindustrial Europe, which still
survives today.

Sanchis concludes:

It would be a total mistake to imagine the romaria as an assembly of 'believers',
exclusively devoted to formal religious activities. The *romaria* is lived and experienced as a festival, that is a total event, which is constituted as a break in everyday
life, an irruption of another world. (1977: 76)

Another important type of celebration is the political festival. Rearick
has shown how the leaders of the Third Republic in France sought
to legitimise it by festivals: annual festivals, such as Bastille Day on
14 July, and exceptional festivals, such as the funeral of Victor Hugo
in 1885 (Rearick 1977). These activities took their inspiration from
the political festivals of the First Republic. Such festivals were matched
by those of the workers on 1 May and by those on the nationalist Right
celebrating Joan of Arc.

A particularly interesting example of political festivals in modern
Europe, which were consciously set up in opposition to traditional religious ones, was the *feste* of the Italian Communist Party (PCI). These
are discussed by Kertzer in his study of the PCI organisation in Albora,
a *quartiere* of Bologna (Kertzer 1980). As part of the national and local
battle for supremacy between communists and Catholics in postwar Italy
a sharp struggle took place between the two groups as to who could
mount the most attractive festivals. As each parish had its own *festa*, so
each section of the PCI developed a rival celebration. In Albora there
was no doubt about the winner. Whereas only a few hundred people
continued to participate in the church festivals, thousands attended the
sectional *feste* of the Communist Party. Such festivals lasted for three to
four days and were held outdoors. There were political speeches, but
the main activities were eating and drinking. A highlight of one of the
Albora festivals was the traditional goose-pull in which youths tried to
win a goose by pulling off its head while it was suspended above them.
Kertzer argues that the *festa* was the one time in the year when all the

community had the opportunity to come together and share common activities. The normal social barriers were broken down, men and women worked together in the kitchen, and party leaders took on the role of waiters. Political loyalty was cemented indirectly by leisure:

Alborese, who because of their lack of formal education, disinterest, timidity, or feelings of inferiority, participate in none of the specifically political activities of the Party, can and do, through the *festa* identify themselves with the PCI and are made to feel a part of it. (Kertzer 1980: 157)

It would be misleading, however, to ignore the effects of secularisation, official regulation and tourism, on the character of many traditional festivals. An article in the *Guardian* claims that in much of Spain, though to a lesser extent in Seville, Holy Week has lost a good deal of its traditional mystical value, being seen nowadays primarily as a period of family holidays.[3] Under the impact of tourism many festivals, where they have not disappeared altogether, have become to an increasing extent commercial spectacles.

Norman Lewis has related the abandonment of the festival of *Sa Cova* (the Cave) in the village where he was living in Catalonia (Lewis 1984). This festival had involved a large, particularly rich meal, and a parade through the village to the church, but it had been proceeded by a strange ceremony, perhaps a relic of some ancient fertility rite. The women and girls made a trip by boat to a nearby sea-cave, which was entered only by them, the boatmen remaining outside. One girl, who had been chosen to lead the festivities, would be lightly smacked by her mother, 'the child pretended to cry, and that was the end of the thing . . . absolutely meaningless . . . but it was far and away the most important event of the year for the people of Farol'.[4] After the abandonment of the festival the cave became a place visited by tourists, taken there by local fishermen. In the space of a few years, then, we have the transformation of the cave from the centrepiece of a preindustrial ritual to that of a postmodern spectacle.

Tourism

In the context of a European-wide study of leisure the subject of tourism is of major importance. A number of countries, such as Spain, Greece, Italy and Austria, have economies which are highly dependent on the industry, most of their visitors coming from other European countries. Tourism is indeed of great importance virtually everywhere in Europe, as more and more people each year travel away from home to subject foreign places and people to the 'tourist gaze' (Urry 1990). Travellers from Europe are also an important element in the increasing invasion of Third World countries for purposes of recreation.

Tourism is an interesting industry in that the contact between tourists and locals, whether as producers (that is, servicers of tourists) or as picturesque bystanders (objects of the tourist gaze), is an important part of the experience. Relationships should not be purely functional, at least from the standpoint of the tourist, but should involve an aesthetic or fantasy element. What can be said objectively, however, about these human contacts? It appears to have been a fairly general view in the nineteenth century that the growth of travel would lead to the breaking down of prejudice, even perhaps to the elimination of war, as increased human contacts led to a growth of understanding between nations and peoples.[5] Such a view seems implausible today. Some tourists, indeed, like many football supporters, seem to regard foreign travel as an opportunity to engage in national or quasi-tribal hostilities (Williams, Dunning and Murphy 1989). Perhaps such a view of the consequences of travel was always naïve, however. After all, Smollett in the eighteenth century suffered a good deal, according to his own account, at the hands of rapacious landlords (Smollett 1766).

The relations between tourists and locals, due perhaps to cultural, linguistic or economic differences, often seem to lend themselves to interactions which are perceived as exploitative on one side or the other. The sheer volume of tourists in many places also no doubt makes it impossible to react to them as individuals. The situation is a fertile one for negative stereotyping. Local people may appreciate the economic benefits of tourism although they bemoan the changes that result.[6] Sex-tourism seems to be the ultimate form of exploitation by tourists. Its worst manifestations probably occur in the Third World rather than in Europe (Stolle 1990).

A cynical view of the relationship between tourists and foreign cultures is too one-sided, however. Travel may indeed broaden the mind – or the appetite. English food and drink have undergone something of a transformation since the beginning of mass tourism to Europe, with a vastly increased consumption of wine and garlic. It is difficult to imagine most English people taking foreign languages seriously, yet a visit to any bookshop will reveal many language courses for sale – not just in the more usual languages, but also in Greek, Turkish and Portuguese, presumably intended for, and bought by, prospective tourists.

Let us look at material from Spain, a leading 'producer' nation.[7] Spain is above all the country of mass foreign tourism. Unlike Italy, it does not have a long history of receiving visitors from abroad. The phenomenon only took off in the 1960s and Spain now has the greater number of foreign visitors. Spanish tourism is notable for its extreme degree of regional concentration and its strongly marked seasonality. Although there is some visiting of cities in the centre of the country, this sector is still underdeveloped.

Many historic cities lack the characteristic tourist facilities which would be normal in other European countries, and many suffered from insensitive modern development from the 1960s onwards, though there are cities, such as Toledo, where tourism has been fully developed (Barke and Towner 1996). The vast mass of foreign tourists visits the coastal regions and the islands and does so during the summer. Tourism has had a massive and beneficial effect on the Spanish economy, providing much of the funds for general economic development and capital formation over the last three decades. Tourism receipts were 49 per cent of the value of exports in 1961; in 1965 this rose to 111 per cent and they still constituted 35 per cent in 1992. Thus throughout the 1960s receipts from tourism paid for a third or more of imports and in the 1990s they were still paying for over a fifth. Tourism accounted for around 9 per cent of GNP in 1992, 15 per cent in Andalusia (Robinson 1996; Sinclair and Bote Gómez 1996).

Like other industries, tourism involves disproportionate consequences for producers and consumers. Producers become dependent for their livelihood on the desires of consumers, for whom the interactions involved in tourism are of sharply limited duration. The seasonal character of tourism can have deleterious consequences for the livelihood of producers, and likewise its disruption due to political events. Apart from the economic consequences of tourism, considerable attention needs to be paid to its ecological and cultural impact. It has become a commonplace that tourism is destroying the very things that tourists want to see: ancient buildings, unspoilt nature and 'authentic' human life. It is true that not everyone is interested in such things; many people are more interested in lying on beaches and drinking in bars, but even in relation to such activities there is a danger in overloading facilities or going too far 'down-market'. Thus Spain experienced a drop in visitors at the end of the 1980s, which seems to have been related to environmental pollution and a desire to escape 'yobbish' behaviour, as well as an increase in comparative costs. In the market for old buildings and unspoilt nature the impact of tourism may not always be harmful. Tourism can preserve as well as destroy, though the preserved object may undergo more or less significant changes.

According to a Spanish author, German tourists in Spain distinguish themselves from those of other nations by their *'ecological preoccupation* . . . they want to know if the water where they intend to swim is pure or the beauty spots they plan to visit are free from contamination' (Diaz Alvarez 1989). This concern is present in a different way at the theoretical level, in German analyses of the phenomenon of tourism. Academics and publicists have become acutely aware of the real dangers to the ecological balance and cultural integrity of tourist destinations.[8] These problems may be particularly acute in the Third World but they also affect regions of Europe such as the Mediterranean and the Alps. German tourists in Spain face a dilemma; they want pure water for swimming, but their very presence may overload inadequate sewerage systems, leading to pollution. The market and the local authority

may deal with this problem in time. They are less likely to be successful in coping with the destruction of flora and fauna and peaceful,
traditional ways of life.[9]

In the face of continued market growth we cannot be too optimistic
about the long-term cultural and ecological impact of tourism in many
areas. We can only hope that the desire to maintain a lucrative industry
will call forth both market solutions and sensible planning to cope with
some of the problems posed by such a momentous physical and social
phenomenon as modern tourism (Diaz Alvarez 1989: Ch. 6). From the
standpoint of the consumer nations, the best hope would seem to be the
gradual development of *sanfter Tourismus* – gentle/soft tourism, a style
characterised by a non-exploitative, accommodating rather than arrogant
attitude towards foreign people and places (Krippendorf, Zimmer and
Glauber 1988). Tourism, however, seems here to stay, despite temporary
recessions due to economic difficulties and political factors (Lanfant 1989).

Sport

Sport is a traditional topic for writers on leisure, and another major
industry. A look at sport in a European context provides us, first, with
some interesting historical material. There is, for instance, the question
of international borrowing or influence. We may compare the development of sport in different countries, noting the similarities, differences
and influences.

This can be done quite easily for Britain and France, for we have
detailed studies of sporting developments in the two countries produced
by the same author, Richard Holt (1981, 1989). Chapter 4 of Holt's book
on France is devoted to the impact of 'English sports' (football, rugby
and athletics) at the end of the nineteenth century. The initial impetus
behind the introduction of English sports was patriotic and upper-class
in character. Following the nation's defeat in the Franco-Prussian war, a
section of the French élite began to consider that useful lessons could
be learnt from the English educational system in terms of the fostering
of desirable moral qualities such as courage, leadership and initiative.
A large element in the development of such qualities was ascribed to
the influence of sport at the public schools and universities. With the
encouragement of a few determined propagandists, of whom the best-
known was the Baron de Coubertin, a number of lycée students in Paris
began to set up sporting clubs in the early 1880s. Within a short period
these sports spread geographically, partly because of the presence of
expatriate Britons in the wine trade. It was football, however, which
became the most popular of the English sports, spreading especially to
the industrial areas of the north, and the north of Paris, as well as to
Marseille and the south-east. The sport soon lost its upper-class and

bourgeois character and became popular with workers, both as an activity, and more especially as a spectacle. Commercialism and professionalism soon followed in the period between the First and Second World Wars.

French sport, however, has its own strengths and specialities. Why did cycling become a major commercial spectacle in France, but never developed to the same extent in Britain? Holt suggests that cycling came on to the scene in France before the other major spectator sports were introduced. Initially it took the form of track races in specially built *vélodromes*, but after a while the popularity of track racing began to decline in comparison to that of the English sports. Long-distance races, however, especially the Tour de France which began in 1903, revived the popularity of cycling and made it into the premier French sporting spectacle. The great advantage of cycling was that road races cost nothing to the spectators, the costs being met by manufacturers, newspapers and advertisers. In a large country with a big rural population and comparatively few large towns, cycling proved to be a viable spectacle, where other sports made less headway due to lack of adequate demand. Commercialisation was thus integral to the sport from the beginning, and this was reflected in the cut-throat competition. Apparently there were complaints of drug-taking even before the First World War. Henri Desgrange, the organiser of the Tour de France, was an outspoken nationalist, and attempted to make the Tour a patriotic event by staging it in German-occupied Lorraine before the First World War and routing it through the battlefield areas in 1919 (Holt 1981: Ch. 5).

Politics also comes into focus, if we turn to the major international sporting spectacle of the Olympic Games. The Baron de Coubertin, mentioned above, is famous as the founder of the modern Olympic movement. The attack on Israeli athletes at the Games in Munich in 1972, the boycott of the Games in Moscow in 1980 by several nations, and athletes protesting against the Russian involvement in Afghanistan, must have made clear to everyone that international sport is intimately and inescapably bound up with politics.[10] The Olympic Games in Berlin in 1936, however, had already provided a clear example of the politicisation of sport, having been orchestrated to provide favourable propaganda for the recently installed Nazi regime (Mandell 1972; Hart-Davis 1986).

Germany provides us with another fascinating example of the politicisation of sport. The reunification of Germany in 1990 brought to an end one of the most remarkable of sporting phenomena, the creation of a sports regime in East Germany, the former GDR, which was outstandingly successful at the level of international competition. East German sports policy was avowedly political in terms of the ideological goal of demonstrating the superiority of the socialist way of life, but also in narrower diplomatic terms, for sporting contacts formed one of the means by which the GDR hoped to overcome its diplomatic isolation by western states. Having achieved this, sport remained an important element in relations with foreign states (Holzweissig 1981). Despite the GDR's avowed linkage of sport with health and physical fitness, the spectacular propaganda value of sporting success clearly won out in the sense that Olympic achievements were based not on superior sports provision for the population as a whole, but on channelling resources into the production of élite performance. Levels of general participation in sport were higher and facilities more widespread in West Germany, which in the 1970s and 1980s was far less successful in international competition, at any rate in Olympic sports.[11]

Turning to modern trends in sport, perhaps the simplest way to approach the issue is to look at a comparative account which examined trends in 15 countries, five of which are in western Europe (France, Italy, Portugal, The Netherlands and Britain) (Kamphorst and Roberts 1989). The main focus of these reports is not on international sport but on 'sport for all', on levels of popular participation. Statistics vary between countries and comparisons are therefore difficult, but trends can be ascertained. In general, there was a trend towards increased participation in sport in the 1970s and 1980s in western Europe.

Different reasons were given for these increases. For the author, Maria Carmen Belloni, writing about Italy, the reason was seen to be bound up with the modernisation of Italian society, indeed to provide an index of such modernisation. The increases in participation in France were seen as due, above all, to increased leisure time. How then are we to explain increased participation between 1979 and 1987 in The Netherlands, where the growth in free time was unequally distributed, and where free time actually decreased slightly between 1975 and 1985 for the population up to age 50?

Although increased leisure time may be linked with increased participation in sport, it seems that it cannot be the only reason. It appears that values must have changed as well as opportunities. In Italy, there was a relative shift away from the more traditional sports of hunting, fishing and football, and in the case of hunting an absolute decline. In all three countries, indeed, there was a relative trend away from traditional and team sports towards individual and unorganised sports. The British data were congruent with these results. Apparently there were insufficient data in Portugal to permit analysis of trends. Western European trends towards increased participation in sport, found also in Finland, were not true of all areas of the world.

From this study, sports participation in eastern Europe, as well as in India and Nigeria, seemed to be in decline, which perhaps reflected the growing economic problems in these areas in the 1980s. Nevertheless, even in western Europe many people appeared to take no part in sport at all. Non-participants in Italy comprised 77.8 per cent of the population in 1985. This may be thought a more significant fact than that the figure apparently dropped from 84.6 per cent three years before. It was evident that women everywhere participated less in sport than men, but also that these differences had been decreasing in recent years.

An interesting issue raised by the Dutch contribution (Kamphorst and Roberts 1989) concerns the effects of socialisation. Studies of participation in sport tend to look to aspects of an individual's present situation such as education, income or marital status to explain differences in participation. Studies in The Netherlands, however, seem to show that differences can be better explained in terms of past influences. Thus children who played soccer in childhood, and who were members of clubs at that time, were much more likely to be engaged in the game as adults than those who had had no contact with the sport as children. This may seem an unsurprising finding, but it is perhaps of important general significance for leisure studies.

Why is non-participation in sport seen as a problem by sports authorities and by some sociologists? Is such a view reasonable? Sport as a form of leisure is an ambiguous phenomenon. Like the other forms of leisure discussed in this chapter, it has been subjected to political regulation and to commercialisation. Top sport has become a major spectacle, whether watched directly or on TV, and is thus an important element in mass culture and indeed in international politics. Participant sport is in a different situation. Sport, unlike drinking, attending festivals or even tourism, is felt to be good for people, not primarily as a form of relaxation but as a means of maintaining health. This view is undoubtedly correct in general, but it results in sport being undertaken and supported for utilitarian reasons as well as for fun. This has been the case throughout the entire history of sport, which in the past was largely encouraged for military and nationalistic reasons. To regard as problematical the fact that a large proportion of the population does not engage in sport at all may be correct from a medical or public health perspective, but it makes little sense in the context of the sociology of leisure. While the promotion of 'sport for all' may be desirable, it should perhaps be recognised that sport is only one leisure option among many others. Perhaps the basic problem is that there are just too many sedentary occupations in the modern world.

Drinking and socialising

I have left this section to the last because drinking raises in a particularly clear way a number of issues which are central to the analysis of leisure and, I suspect, to its essence. In a survey into the sporting activities of Portuguese students, reported by Machado Pais, they were asked what afforded the greatest pleasure in free-time activities. The most frequent answer (60.2 per cent) was 'to be together with friends'. When asked the reasons for keeping up sports activity, only 19.6 per cent mentioned 'being together with friends' while 69.9 per cent mentioned 'to keep healthy'. Machado Pais commented that this implied that the social rewards from sport were relatively small, and hence that it was quite likely that it would always lose out as a leisure activity with many people in comparison to other activities which involved greater social rewards (Kamphorst and Roberts 1989: 261–76). I suggest that he is correct, and that sociability and the opportunities for it are among the most essential and sought-after qualities of leisure. This is not to deny that solitary leisure activities – reading, gardening, knitting, watching TV or listening to radio and records – are not important. Furthermore, these activities are not necessarily solitary: they can occur in the presence of other members of the family. The trend towards family-based leisure has been a marked one in recent years.

Nevertheless, I believe that sociability outside the family circle is of the essence of leisure and that the pursuit of it is important in both work and recreation. The booze-up after the rugby match is often as important as the game itself. *Après ski* seems as important as, or more important than, skiing to some people. Social solidarity among members of the peer group is perhaps more significant to so-called hooligans than the football. How many people choose to travel abroad as part of a tourist group not just to see the sights, or for convenience, but because of the enforced intimacy and social contact involved in a fortnight's tour? If visits to the hairdresser have a recreational component, as I suggested at the beginning of this chapter, where can this come from except from sociability, or social interaction of a particular type? If I am correct, then the rigid distinction between work and leisure made by some sociologists and thought to be characteristic of industrial society is only true up to a point.

Recreation in the sense of sociability, non-functional or non-focused social interaction, is present in the workplace as well as in the leisure centre, and forms an important part of the rewards of work. Sociability can itself become a necessary ingredient of work. Certain professions and occupations may need to develop in trainees an ability to engage in non-functional social interaction because this is sought or demanded by customers and clients. Hairdressers, shopkeepers, doctors (the bedside manner) all need to develop this skill, the exercise of which may be re- . warding or may be felt as a constraint, no doubt depending on personality.

From this standpoint, drinking has a particular interest and centrality in the study of leisure, for clearly the essence of drinking is sociability *per se*. It is thus a particularly 'pure' form of leisure activity. There are people for whom the consumption of alcohol becomes a physical need. Alcohol addiction and abuse is a serious and growing social problem, though a modest one in Britain in comparison with most of its European neighbours (Davies and Walsh 1983). The vast majority who drink alcohol and visit pubs, however, do not end up as alcoholics. Alcohol acts as a depressant, weakening inhibitions and thus facilitating social interaction, but the sociability associated with drinking as an activity does not necessarily depend on the ingestion of alcohol. In Muslim societies men drinking coffee together may do so for much the same social reasons as men in Europe gather in a pub or café. The female *Kaffeeklatsch* may also be a broad functional equivalent to the male pub group. Drinking tea provides the occasion for social interaction also (Hazan 1987). Let us concentrate, however, on the phenomenon of drinking alcohol.

There is space for only one case study: the German pub. In Germany, unlike most of southern Europe, there is a rough equivalent to the British pub (*die Kneipe*), a place essentially intended for socialising and drinking alcohol. In the past such pubs were largely seen as the preserve of workers, whereas the middle classes visited restaurants. From the late 1960s, however, pubs for students, intellectuals and the new middle classes began to appear in growing numbers. It is interesting to compare such pubs with those frequented by workers. Workers' pubs conform very largely to the traditional picture of male-dominated pub culture which is familiar from British studies.[12] This is particularly evident in those pubs near to the workplace. In the evening just after work has finished, such pubs will be invaded by workers seeking to refresh themselves and relax after the day's work. This is a world of beer, conversation and perhaps games, in an exclusively masculine atmosphere, more so than in the neighbourhood pub later in the evening, when one or two workers may bring their wives along with them (Droege and Kraemer-Badoni 1987).

Intellectuals' pubs are unlike this in a number of respects. First, the motives for going there are different. This is expressed very well in a study of pubs frequented by those in the left-wing subculture of Berlin:

An intellectual going to a pub does so only rarely with the feeling of having done a day's work ... rather as a rule he flees from demands which he thinks he hasn't fulfilled or which he is unable to fulfill ... every project seems impossible to finish. The compelling will to work necessary to finish it off permits no interruption of working time, but precisely for that reason it is more and more frequently interrupted. (Laermann 1974)

Thus those who won't arrange to go for a walk or accept an invitation because it will interrupt their work are overcome by the rigours of their task and the need for distraction, and end up spending a few hours in the pub. Another reason to visit pubs is to meet members of the opposite sex, for in this type of pub women are (almost) as numerous as men and can visit them alone, for a characteristic of such places is that they are always crowded and anyone can engage anyone else in conversation. Women are to be found in such pubs sitting alone at the bar, which is still scarcely imaginable in workers' or socially mixed pubs. Nevertheless, according to Droege and Kraemer-Badoni, women still do not like to visit pubs by themselves. Even in intellectuals' pubs the atmosphere is still dominated by male preoccupations, though in a subtle way (Droege and Kraemer-Badoni 1987: 236). In this connection it would be interesting to compare the sociology of the pub with the sociology of the party, another context in which men, women and alcohol come together. Europe, particularly France, provides us with quite a different historical model of male–female social interaction in the institution of the salon.

These accounts of pubs illustrate the familiar sociological necessity to examine a phenomenon in relation to social class and gender. They also illustrate that what appears to be the same form of leisure behaviour can have a different meaning and quality for its participants because it stands in a different relationship to work.

Perhaps the most interesting aspect of these accounts is their analysis of the nature of sociability and communication in the pub. In workers' pubs work is a main topic of conversation, along with sport, drinking, other customers and the pub itself. Telling jokes, and jokes and conversation about sex tend to be the specialities of a few people, but common with such men.[13] Politics is also discussed. In the socially and sexually mixed pubs the conversation is similar and equally varied: politics, work, sport, eating and drinking, holidays, personal relations. Sex, however, plays a subordinate role.

More significant than the topic is the nature of conversation in pubs, and the kinds of unwritten rules it seems to follow. We sometimes think of pubs as places where arguments are conducted, but the view could be put forward that pubs are places where on the whole serious arguments are avoided. According to this view arguments in pubs largely take the form of subjective assertions. Explicit arguments involving lengthy elaboration of the grounds for an opinion would destroy the social atmosphere of the pub. This atmosphere is built up of tolerance, freedom and equality, in the sense that everyone has the right to speak, and expects to speak, and to have their opinion heard and considered sympathetically. Pubs are not places where people's illusions about themselves are shattered, but where they are accepted and tolerated, if not encouraged. Despite considerable drinking, conversations in pubs rarely end in ill-will, let alone fights. On the contrary, the attraction of the pub lies in the mutual recognition, trust and warmth generated by the almosphere of sociability, but this depends paradoxically on people keeping a certain distance from one another and following the unwritten rules of pub conversation:

One may ... certainly talk at length about oneself but not become personal with others. One may not give orders to others or ask them too many questions. One may only question ironically, not categorically, their competence to express themselves about practically everything. Contradicting too strongly must be avoided for it would put in question the expected tendency towards consensus held internally by all those engaged in the conversation. (Laermann 1974: 178)

Thus sociability has its rules, which are generally observed even when inhibitions are weakened by alcohol. It is this sociability, even though it may be ephemeral, which is the attraction of pubs and which, I believe, epitomises the attraction of a wide range of leisure activities.

Despite this, visiting pubs, like sport (though in a different way), is an ambiguous leisure activity. People can become addicted to alcohol, and frequenting pubs can become expensive in terms of the time and money allocated to it. To the extent that pub-going is primarily a male phenomenon it may arouse the anxiety or hostility of wives who resent the diversion of resources from the household. Thus sociability between males may be paid for in terms of difficulties in, or destruction of, other relationships.[14]

The state has also concerned itself with drinking at various times, seeing pubs and taverns as centres of political propaganda and social disorder, and serious competitors to work (Brennan 1988). There is still official concern with drinking related to crime, especially perhaps motoring offences, and clearly it is likely to remain an activity which the state will consider it necessary to regulate.[15]

Conclusion

I trust that this chapter has given the reader some idea of the variety, and the interest, of the sociology of leisure. In conclusion I shall consider briefly the overall importance of the subject. There is a basic division in the sociology of leisure between those who lay emphasis on constraint in relation to leisure activities, and those who stress choice. For 'radical' theorists, leisure, like other aspects of life, is a field of activity structured by fundamental class, gender and ethnic inequalities. Furthermore, the activities of powerful private leisure providers, and of the state – indeed, the general ethos of capitalist society – create patterns of leisure which owe as much or more to the interests of producers as to the wishes of consumers. According to this perspective, those who stress freedom of choice and pluralism in relation to leisure are ignoring history, theory and the constraints of capitalist society, and producing for the most part naïve and unrelated empirical studies.[16] It is not my intention here to examine in detail the plausibility of such a general view of leisure.

Clearly, ethnic and gender-based inequalities are important in relation to leisure opportunities (Clark 1990). Equally, emphasis on the role of providers is necessary and valuable. Sport, tourism and drink are all major industries – tourism is well on the way to becoming the world's biggest industry – and analysis of the phenomena in terms of industrial structure and provision is indispensable to a proper understanding.

Within this general approach to leisure the value of a European focus, rather than a narrowly British one, should need little demonstration. Sport and tourism are international as well as national phenomena, and it is the international dimension which has strenghtened concern about such problems as football hooliganism and the impact of tourism, and made them into very significant public issues. Furthermore, a comparative approach to leisure provision invariably opens up the need for historical enquiry. If we wish to know why Spaniards watch bullfights and the French watch cycling, while Britons on the whole watch neither, or why the British shoot grouse and the Italians shoot songbirds, then historical explanation is required.

Leisure still remains, however, an area where people can exercise considerable freedom of choice. Sport, drink and tourism are major industries because people choose to consume their products. There is no compulsion to do so, and substantial sectors of the population in all countries choose not to consume these services, though obviously many cannot afford to do so.

It might be argued that all mature individuals have to come to terms with four areas of life: work, leisure, personal relationships and some sort of general philosophy of life or *Weltanschauung*, in the broad sense a religion.[17] Work and personal relationships obviously involve choices as well as constraints, but the choices having been made, individuals become locked into networks of commitments and obligations. Leisure and religion are not like this, or are so to a lesser extent. We might argue that the nature of modern society is to make genuinely free choice in these areas more available than at any time in the past, though the price for this has been no doubt a weakening of the bonds of community. In an interesting article on the future of research in the sociology of leisure, Dumazdier has drawn attention to the similarity between leisure and religion in the context of a 'cultural revolution of free time', and has also pointed out that they may be rivals in this search for identity. There is a field for parallel research between the sociology of religion and the sociology of leisure (Dumazdier 1990).

Such a view of leisure as choice offers a perspective for research which is surely a legitimate one. In this connection it would seem important to look at the influence of socialisation, which, as we have seen above, seems more important in some circumstances to participation in sport than present influences. This type of research could be extended to other areas of leisure. Such research would not necessarily be deterministic in its implications but could contribute to the notion of the individual as a 'productive processor of reality' (Hurrelmann 1988). This perspective on leisure also benefits from an international focus. Leisure practices are cultural forms which can be adopted, adapted and transformed, and there are significant international borrowings in this area, as we have seen.

Notes

1 See, for example, the wide range of festivals mentioned in Russ (1982).
2 See also Sanchis (1977) and Veiga de Oliveira (1984).
3 *Guardian*, 26 March 1991.
4 Lewis, (1985 Penguin edn), p. 62.

5 The Spanish writer Azorin (1912) has an interesting discussion of such ideas in relation to the development of railway travel. See 'Los ferrocarriles' in *Castilla.*
6 See Pi-Sunyer (1978); also Lewis (1985 edn), p. 180.
7 Diaz Alvarez (1989); Barke, Towner and Newton (1996).
8 See Ludwig *et al.* (1990); also Krippendorf *et al.* (1988), which contains an exhaustive bibliography on 'gentle tourism'.
9 Tourism in Africa may be playing an important role in the preservation of the more obviously spectacular 'big game'.
10 See Holt (1981: Ch. 10) and Holt (1989: Ch. 4) for illuminating discussions on the political context and implications of sport in general in France and Britain in the nineteenth and early twentieth centuries.
11 Childs (1983: 186–7); see also Knecht (1978).
12 Hey (1986), but also see note 13.
13 Droege and Kraemer-Badoni (1987: 211). There appears to be nothing equivalent to Hey's secondary account of a rural pub in Herefordshire, where 'the main topic of conversation in the pub is women's sexuality and the effective male control of it' Hey (1986: 66).
14 Hey (1986: 71). In eighteenth-century France married women could apply directly to the commissaire of police for a separation from their husbands on the ground that their dowry portion needed to be protected from the effects of their husbands' dissipation in taverns; Brennan (1988: Ch. 5).
15 Davies and Walsh (1983). Many leisure activities, including sporting events and festivals, are perceived as having a tendency to get out of control.
16 For an example of such an approach, see Clarke and Critcher (1985).
17 See Luckmann (1967) especially Chapters 5 and 6 on the relation between religion and personal identity.

References

Azorin (1976) *Castilla*, Madrid: Biblioteca Nueva. Originally published in 1912.
Barke, M. and Towner, J. (1996) 'The tourist-historic city in Spain', in M. Barke, J. Towner and M. T. Newton (eds) *Tourism in Spain: Critical Issues*, Wallingford: CAB International.
Barke, M., Towner, J. and Newton, M. T. (eds) (1996) *Tourism in Spain: Critical Issues*, Wallingford: CAB International.
Brennan, T. (1988) *Public Drinking and Popular Culture in Eighteenth Century Paris*, Princeton NJ: Princeton University Press.
Childs, D. (1983) *The GDR: Moscow's German Ally*, London: Allen & Unwin.
Clark, S. (1990) 'Shiftwork and leisure behaviour of ethnic and gender groups in the British textile industry', *Le Travail Humain*, 53(3): 227–44.
Clarke, J. and Critcher, C. (1985) *The Devil Makes Work: Leisure in Capitalist Britain*, London: Macmillan.
Davies, P. and Walsh, D. (1983) *Alcohol Problems and Alcohol Control in Europe*, London: Croom Helm.
Diaz Alvarez, J. R. (1989) *Geografia del Turismo*, Madrid: Editorial Sintesis.
Droege, F. and Kraemer-Badoni, I. (1987) *Die Kneipe: zur Soziologie einer Kulturform*, Frankfurt am Main: Suhrkamp.

Dumazdier, J. (1990) 'Pour un renouveau de la recherche en sciences sociales du loisir', *Loisir et Société*, 13(1): 63–76.

Hart-Davis, D. (1986) *Hitler's Games: the 1936 Olympics*, New York: Harper & Row.

Hazan, H. (1987) 'Holding time still with cups of tea', in M. Douglas (ed.) *Constructive Drinking: Perspectives on Drink from Anthropology*, Cambridge: Cambridge University Press.

Hey, V. (1986) *Patriarchy and Pub Culture*, London: Tavistock.

Holt, R. (1981) *Sport and Society in Modern France*, London: Macmillan.

Holt, R. (1989) *Sport and the British: a Modern History*, Oxford: Oxford University Press.

Holzweissig, G. (1981) *Diplomatie im Trainingsanzug: Sport als Politisches Instrument der DDR*, Munich: Oldenbourg.

Hurrelmann, K. (1988) *Social Structure and Personality Development: the Individual as a Productive Processor of Reality*, Cambridge: Cambridge University Press.

Kamphorst, T. J. and Roberts, K. (eds) (1989) *Trends in Sports: a Multinational Perspective*, Culemborg: Giordano Bruno.

Kertzer, K. I. (1980) *Comrades and Christians: Religion and Political Struggle in Communist Italy*, Cambridge: Cambridge University Press.

Knecht, W. (1978) *Das Medaillenkollektiv*, Berlin: Holzapfel.

Krippendorf, J., Zimmer, P. and Glauber, H. (eds) (1988) *Für einen Andern Tourismus*, Frankfurt am Main: Fischer.

Laermann, K. (1974) 'Kneipengerede: zu einigen Verkehrsformen der Berliner linken Subkultur', *Kursbuch*, 37: 172–3.

Lanfant, M-F. (1989) 'International tourism resists the crisis', in A. Olszewska and K. Roberts *Leisure and Life-style: a Comparative Analysis of Free Time*, London: Sage.

Lewis, N. (1984) *Voices of the Old Sea*, London: Hamish Hamilton.

Luckmann, T. (1967) *The Invisible Religion*, London: Macmillan.

Ludwig, K., Has, M. and Neuer, M. (Hrsg.) (1990) *Der Neue Tourismus*, Munich: Beck.

Mandell, R. D. (1972) *The Nazi Olympics*, London: Souvenir Press.

Pi-Sunyer, O. (1978) 'Through native eyes: tourists and tourism in a Catalan maritime community', in V. L. Smith (ed.) *Hosts and Guests*, Oxford: Blackwell.

Rearick, C. (1977) 'Festivals in modern France: the experience of the Third Republic', *Journal of Contemporary History*, 12: 435–60.

Robinson, M. (1996) 'Sustainable tourism for Spain: principles, prospects and problems', in M. Barke, J. Towner and M. T. Newton (eds) *Tourism in Spain: Critical Issues*, Wallingford: CAB International.

Russ, J. M. (1982) *German Festivals and Customs*, London: Oswald Wolff.

Sanchis, P. (1977) 'Les romarias portugaises', *Archives de Sciences Sociales des Religions*, 43(1): 53–76.

Sanchis, P. (1983) *Arraial: festa de um povo*, Lisbon: Publicacoes Dom Quixote.

Sinclair, M. T. and Bote Gómez, V. (1996) 'Tourism, the Spanish economy and the balance of payments', in M. Barke, J. Towner and M. T. Newton (eds) *Tourism in Spain: Critical Issues*, Wallingford: CAB.

Smollett, T. G. (1766) *Travels in France and Italy* (many modern editions).

Stolle, C. (1990) 'Sex-tourismus', in K. Ludwig, M. Has and M. Neuer (eds) *Der Neue Tourismus*, Munich: Beck.

Urry, J. (1990) *The Tourist Gaze*, London: Sage.

Veiga de Oliveira, E. (1984) *Festividades Ciclicas em Portugal*, Lisbon: Publicacoes Dom Quixote.

Williams, J., Dunning, E. and Murphy, P. (1989) *Hooligans Abroad*, London: Routledge.

INDEX